WORLD
AIRPORTS

Alan J. Wright

IAN ALLAN
Publishing

First published 1992

ISBN 0 7110 2061 2

Published by Ian Allan Ltd, Shepperton, Surrey; and printed by Ian Allan Printing Ltd at their works at Coombelands in Runnymede, England.

Front cover:
This Balair-operated McDonnell Douglas MD-83 is seen at Zurich. *Leo Marriott*

Back Cover:
An aerial view of Dusseldorf airport.
Flughafen Dusseldorf

Acknowledgements

Grateful thanks are extended to all the authorities who supplied details of their airports. Several of those contacted were reluctant to divulge some of the facilities in any detail for security reasons, a decision which is respected if not completely understood. Presumably those remaining completely silent also considered themselves likely to be at risk, or perhaps the strange request was wrongly translated. Sincere thanks are also extended to British Airways AERAD for supplying the charts used for each airport. **It must be remembered that these should NOT be used for operational purposes.**

Abbreviations

ABA	Aktiebolaget Aerotransport
ATI	Aero Transporti Italiani
BA	British Airways
CAA	Civil Aviation Authority
CSA	Ceskoslovenske Aerolinie (Czechoslovak Airlines)
CTA	Compagnie de Transport Aerien
DLT	Deutsche Luftverkehrsgesellschaft mbH
DNL	Det Norske Luftfartselskap (Norwegian Airlines)
FAA	Federal Aviation Authority
IT	Inclusive Tour
JAT	Jugoslovenski Aerotransport (Yugoslav Airlines)
KLM	Koninklijke Luchvaart Maatschappij (Royal Dutch Airlines)
LOT	Polskie Linie Lotnicze (Polish Airlines)
LTU	Lufttransport-Unternehmen
MHz	Megahertz
NFD	Nürnberger Flugdienst
RFG	Regionalflug
SAS	Scandinavian Airlines System
TAP	Transportes Aéreos Portugueses (Air Portugal)
TAT	Transport Aérien Transrégional
UTA	Union de Transports Aériens

Airport Codes

AKL _____Auckland
AMS _____Amsterdam (Schiphol)
ANC _____Anchorage
ARN _____Stockholm (Arlanda)
ATH_____Athens (Hellenikon)
ATL_____Atlanta (Hartsfield)
BWI_____Baltimore/Washington
BOS _____Boston (Logan)
BRU _____Brussels (Zaventum)
CDG_____Paris (Charles de Gaulle)
CGN _____Cologne/Bonn
CPH _____Copenhagen (Kastrup)
DCA _____Washington (National)
DEN _____Denver (Stapleton)
DFW_____Dallas/Fort Worth
DTW__Detroit Metropolitan (Wayne County)
DUB _____Dublin (Collinstown)
DUS _____Düsseldorf
EWR _____New York (Newark)
FCO __Rome (Leonardo da Vinci/Fiumicino)
FRA_____Frankfurt Main
GVA_____Geneva (Cointrin)
HEL_____Helsinki (Vantaa)
HKG _____Hong Kong (Kai Tak)
HNL _____Honolulu
IAD_____Washington (Dulles)
JFK _____New York (John F.Kennedy)
LAX_____Los Angeles
LGA_____New York (LaGuardia)
LGW_____London (Gatwick)
LHR_____London (Heathrow)
LIN _____Milan (Linate)
LUX_____Luxembourg (Findel)
MAN _____Manchester
MCO _____Orlando
MDW _____Chicago (Midway)
MEL_____Melbourne
MIA _____Miami
MXP _____Milan (Malpensa)
NCE _____Nice (Côte d'Azur)
NRT _____Tokyo (Narita)
ORD _____Chicago (O'Hare)
ORY _____Paris (Orly)
OSL _____Oslo (Fornebu)
PHL _____Philadelphia
PMI _____Palma
SEA _____Seattle (Tacoma)
SFO_____San Francisco
SIN _____Singapore (Changi)
SYD_____Sydney (Kingsford Smith)
THF_____Berlin (Templehof)
TXL _____Berlin (Tegel)
VIE _____Vienna (Schwechat)
YVR_____Vancouver
YYZ_____Toronto (Lester B.Pearson)
ZRH _____Zurich (Kloten)

Contents

Introduction

Any book dealing with the world's airports has unlimited scope but not unlimited space. This fact therefore restricted the choice of subject to a large extent, although the latter was also affected by the reluctance of some authorities to respond. Unfortunately many appeared to believe that the book would breach their security arrangements, especially those in areas prone to squabbles with neighbouring countries. In other cases language difficulties appeared to prevent a useful flow of information, even if the national tongue is English. It was also realised that since Europe is a part of the world, the majority of the entries in *abc European Airports* qualified for inclusion in this latest volume. As a result the airports covered are mainly gateways in areas more likely to be visited, rather than those in more remote and less frequented spots. For this reason it follows that the United States features prominently bearing in mind its popularity as a holiday destination and the attraction of its many busy airports. Facilities for spectators vary enormously, but generally are fairly poor these days. There are notable exceptions of course; the excellent terraces at Düsseldorf, Frankfurt and Geneva being good examples. American airports on the other hand usually have no official observation areas, but unlike the rest of the world, access to the airside of the terminals has always been possible by passing through the security checkpoint. This enables vantage points to be found along the piers for both viewing and photography through the tinted glass. Unfortunately, this facility was abruptly withdrawn at the beginning of the Gulf unrest, so that only those with boarding passes could proceed. Just what this achieved was never revealed, but it probably helped to calm the mass hysteria before it reached epidemic proportions. Subsequently, although the reason for the hasty action has long disappeared, the authorities have been slow to respond. This should therefore be borne in mind when visiting any US airport because access may be denied. Maybe one day it will be realised that by providing an enclosure at a good vantage point, casual visitors would be happy to leave terminal buildings for the exclusive use of genuine travellers. In the meantime the only alternative is to locate a suitable spot accessible to the public, always remembering that in some countries even this is viewed with alarm. Extreme caution should certainly be exercised when pointing a camera through a fence unless an interior shot of a police station is required. As in *abc British Airports* and *abc European Airports* no attempt has been made to include costs, because with exchange rate variations, devaluations, inflation and depression, accurate figures would be impossible to record. Airports at least provide a convenient opportunity to change money at a bank with the added advantage that they are often open outside normal hours. In addition the buildings also contain easily detected toilet facilities, which can prove a welcome sight after fruitless searches elsewhere. Aircraft types shown are those most likely to be operated by the airline concerned, but of course these do vary from time to time. To simplify matters the MD-80 series has been listed as DC-9 because in many instances a mixed fleet can produce either variant on a particular service.

Amsterdam (Schiphol)
Netherlands

For centuries past the Netherlands has always played a significant part in world affairs out of all proportion to its modest size. Much additional land has been reclaimed from the sea through the years, one such area being that now occupied by Schiphol. Haarlem Lake (Haalemmermeer) was a vast expanse of water which changed in shape and size at regular intervals. It covered 22,500 acres in 1250 but, as the banks were eroded by the wind driven waves, by 1544 this figure had increased to 28,900 acres. There were considerable merchant shipping movements serving the town of Haarlem while ferries criss-crossed the lake, the dimensions of the boats dependent upon the locks built at the various exits. For good measure a naval battle was fought on 26 May 1573 between the Dutch and the Spanish fleet.

During the following years the lake steadily grew, until in 1836 it was decided that something must be done to halt the shrinking countryside, particularly since both Amsterdam and Leiden came under threat after a severe storm. By 1848 all was ready to remove the water by means of three steam-powered pumping stations, a task which took four years to complete and left the bed of the lake between 10 and 15ft (3-4.65m) below sea level. Unknown at the time, it was later to provide the base for an international airport which could then claim to be at a lower altitude than any other in the world.

Before this could happen 50 years or so had to pass to await the invention of the flying machine plus a few more before the first aircraft actually landed on the site in August 1916. With World War 1 in full swing elsewhere, it was a military machine that found the grass field conveniently close to the local Fort Schiphol, a Dutch army establish-

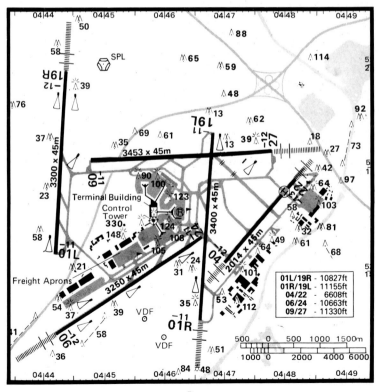

01L/19R	- 10827ft
01R/19L	- 11155ft
04/22	- 6608ft
06/24	- 10663ft
09/27	- 11330ft

500　0　　500　1000　1500m

1000　0　　2000　4000　6000

ment. Subsequently an airfield was laid out, a feature which attracted the attention of several farsighted individuals.

One of these was Anthony Fokker, a Dutch national who just prior to the outbreak of war, had built an aircraft factory at Mecklenburg, Germany. Some of the best designs were used with great success by the German air force, causing considerable problems for the allies. Following the armistice in 1918, Fokker wisely returned to his homeland with all speed accompanied by much useful liberated material and valuable expertise. Quick to appreciate the possibilities offered by civil aviation, he registered a new company in Amsterdam to embark immediately upon the design of the first of his range of airliners.

Another to recognise the potential of commercial air services was an ex-army officer named Albert Plesman. He managed to secure sufficient backing to form a new company which took the name Koninklijke Luchtvaart Maatschappij (KLM) in September 1919. Well aware of the attributes of Schiphol, not surprisingly Plesman selected the site for Amsterdam's civil terminal. By virtue of its origins, the area was completely flat, had no obstructions and embraced a more than adequate 190 acres of grass land.

International air services had been introduced by the British operator Aircraft Transport & Travel (AT&T) in August 1919 by making use of converted wartime machines. There was little alternative but to follow suit if KLM was to maintain its leading position. Still with no aircraft of its own, the company chartered the DH16 registered G-EALU from AT&T for the initial trip from Croydon to Amsterdam on 17 May 1920. Even in those days the weather was unhelpful, forcing the machine and its two pioneering passengers to cross the North Sea at an altitude of 300ft. After 2 1/4hr the DH16 became the first civil transport arrival at Schiphol, followed the next day by the new airport's inaugural departure when the same aircraft returned to the UK in equally appalling conditions.

Services gradually built up during the summer to provide links with several European cities, but on 31 October activities were suspended for the winter months as planned. The low lying field was a haven for mists and fog which in 1920 presented unacceptable dangers. During the first five months of operations, 345 passengers had passed through and 48,500lb of cargo had been handled, a creditable achievement for such a new venture.

It was 14 April 1921 before the fledgling airport stirred itself again, but in the mean-

time KLM had ordered its own aircraft from Fokker with which the company was able to restart the London service. Ground facilities had been improved during the lull and on 25 August a cafe, hotel and restaurant were opened. Throughout the 1920s the number of flights from Schiphol increased to include a variety of long distance sorties. In fact when the regular schedule to Djakarta was introduced on 12 September 1929, the 8,540 mile trip became the world's longest route.

Schiphol was of course steadily developed in sympathy with the increase in traffic. Concrete aprons were laid in front of the terminal buildings, which by the mid-1930s were far more substantial and to a modern design. The Fokker factory had also grown in size, especially after securing the European sales and manufacturing rights for the Douglas DC series. By 1938 the airport had expanded to cover 520 acres, becoming only the second in Europe to have paved runways. Scheduled services now accounted for 80 movements per day while passenger totals moved into five figures annually. Sadly this progress was destined to be abruptly halted with the advent of World War 2. Aircraft production at Schiphol in 1939 already concentrated on machines of a more aggressive nature, but their numbers were insufficient to offer anything more than token resistance when needed in 1940.

On 10 May it was Schiphol's turn to receive the full effect of the German attack. Eighteen airliners were destroyed by bombs which left Amsterdam's fine airport in a sorry state with hangars and other buildings in ruins. Nevertheless, it was not very long before the He111s of the Luftwaffe's KG4 were operating against British targets from the captured base. While a certain amount of repair work was carried out for the unwelcome visitors during the occupation, the effort was of little value. In any case the area received regular attention from Allied aircraft which added to the general destruction begun by the invaders. With the end of the dreadful period in sight, no hangars remained, all being wrecked or dismantled for transportation in pieces to less vulnerable sites. On the field Schiphol's runways were pitted with over 200 craters, effectively rendering them completely useless.

Despite this enormous problem, the Dutch workers energetically filled holes and erected temporary sheds to allow the first postwar commercial movement on 28 July 1945, the distinction going to the Swedish airline ABA. Amazingly the airport was ready for intercontinental operations on 28 November when a DC-4 resumed the five day's trek to Djakarta. Nearer home Euro-

Above:
Most of KLM's 737 fleet can be seen at Schiphol in a fairly short time. *AJW*

Below:
The vast area covered by Schiphol Central is apparent in this view. *Schiphol Airport Authority*

pean destinations were gradually reintroduced as the various terminals were made serviceable. On 21 May 1946 Schiphol became the departure point for the first scheduled postwar flight to New York, the KLM DC-4 calling at Prestwick and Gander en route. Although operational, the facilities at the Dutch airport were merely a temporary expedient until plans were agreed for its future. During the war years various schemes had been devised and these formed the basis for the reconstructed complex.

Originally the proposed layout called for six runways arranged tangentially around the centre terminal area. By the time approval was received for the project in October 1956, it was apparent that modern airliners were less concerned about wind direction than earlier types, so it was possible to reduce the total to four. At one point in the construction the main Amsterdam to The Hague road had to be rerouted to pass through two impressive tunnels under the newly laid operational area. Final completion of the main runways did not come until 1968 which then gave Schiphol the full use of two pairs of almost parallel strips plus a supplementary pair for the use of general aviation and Fokker. While all this work continued, passenger and freight traffic had been handled in the buildings reinstated after the war on the eastern perimeter. Woefully inadequate for many years, the opening of what was known as Schiphol Central in April 1967 came not a moment too soon.

This fine new structure possessed three piers equipped with airbridges, a feature not to be found on such a scale elsewhere in the world. Large as it seemed at the time, it was not long before expansion became necessary which in due course led to the erection of a fourth pier. After its opening in 1975 no further major work was needed until the mid-1980s when an extensive programme of modernisation and development began which included the complete rebuilding of C pier. A brand new freight centre was also opened to accommodate the growing amount of cargo handled by the airport. This massive programme of improvements was known as Schiphol 2000 and designed to meet the demands at the turn of the century.

Meanwhile there was every expectation that the passenger terminal's designed capacity figure of 16 million would be reached by 1989, so some form of relief was deemed necessary pending the completion of the airport's major expansion at the western end of the building. It was B pier which offered the best solution since sufficient space was available to construct an arm on its southern side. This enabled another 13 gates to be provided thereby taking the total number of airbridge-equipped stands at Schiphol to 58.

It is likely that B pier will grow a similar arm on its northern flank in the mid-1990s, but its provision is dependent upon the accuracy of the forecast figures. In the meantime, on 3 May 1990 the new section was duly declared open by HRH Prince Bernhard of the Netherlands prior to the first passengers using the facility four days later.

Although the development certainly helped loading and unloading, it was appreciated that the accommodation in the main terminal would begin to strain under the extra pressure unless some action was taken. The threat was countered by the erection of a temporary extension at the southern end of the building. This short-term structure should be adequate until the first phase of the permanent replacement is completed.

Construction work on the latter project began towards the end of 1989 and will add another 150m to the already formidable length of the existing terminal. The enterprise will be completed in stages to keep ahead of demand, with the initial section due to enter service in early 1993. By this time the fifth pier (E) will also be ready, its presence adding another seven 747-400 stands plus one for an MD80. At this point Schiphol will be able to handle up to 27 million passengers annually which the authorities are confident will be sufficient to cater for the growth until 1996. Conveniently this will coincide with the completion of the second phase of the western extension.

When the entire exercise is finished in 2003, the airport will be large enough to handle 34 million travellers per year with six piers (A to F) protruding from the large single terminal. Outline plans have been made for a seventh pier, but if this becomes necessary it will have to be remotely situated on the far side of the nearby motorway. A high-level transit system would be installed to link it with the main unit. Similarly, within the greatly enlarged building some form of people-mover will be required because of the distances involved. Currently, Schiphol's minimum connecting time is 45min, but this is in danger of becoming unrealistic without the provision of fast internal transport.

Early in the planning stages it was realised that as the piers increased in number, so it would become more difficult to monitor aircraft ground movements. A new tower was therefore commissioned so that an unobstructed view of all runways, taxiways and aprons would be possible. Construction of the 85m shaft began in April 1989 and took only 25 days to complete.

When eventually handed over to the Dutch Civil Aviation Authority, it had reached 94m in height and was ready for the installation of radar and associated electronic systems. Once its radome was in position it added another 6m 41cm to give Schiphol the distinction of possessing the world's higest control tower.

By 1991 there was an impressive total of 23 routes linking the airport with the UK, together offering some 550 flights per week to cater for the growing number of the passengers using the excellent facilities at Schiphol as a transit point. As an added bonus Holland is one of the few places left where the British are still liked, so a friendly welcome is guaranteed from a nation where most of the inhabitants can speak English.

Location and access: Situated 9.3 miles (15km) southwest of Amsterdam alongside the motorway connecting the city with The Hague and Rotterdam. Ample car parking with spectators directed to one particular area. Netherlands Railways link Schiphol directly with Amsterdam Central station in a journey time of 20min. Connections are available to a wide range of destinations. To the south the railway serves such places as Antwerp, Brussels and Rotterdam. Central Nederland Buses serve numerous districts surrounding the airport. Tickets purchased can be used on either or both forms of transport anywhere in the Netherlands.
Terminal: A large spacious building which contains a number of snack bars, restaurants, banks plus a large selection of shops. Currently four piers extend across the apron but by 1993 a fifth will have been added.
Spectator facilities: An excellent roof terrace is provided on the main terminal building from which most movements can be seen. It is also a good vantage point for photography with many of the arriving or departing aircraft taxying past. Commuter traffic is not so easily seen due to the position of the stands employed. The hours of opening are strictly observed with security staff supervising the appropriate operation at 10.00 and 18.00. Strangely the facility is usually only open in the summer between mid-May and mid-September. Excellent spots are to be found around the airport boundary particularly alongside runways 06/24 and 01L/19R. The former can be reached by taking a bus to the village of Rozenburg followed by a walk to an official car park and viewing area. Ideally private transport is preferable but at least a mobile snack bar visits this otherwise remote spot. Unlike most other airports much of the perimeter of Schiphol is marked by wide,

toad-infested ditches making the erection of 10ft-high fences unnecessary. Photography is therefore unimpeded. There is also an excellent aircraft museum located in a dome-shaped building in the centre area. Opened in 1971, the Aviodome contains about 30 airframes covering the history of aviation, particularly that relating to the The Netherlands. Unfortunately the lighting conditions within the structure do not favour the photographer, but there is a Grumman US-2N Tracker parked outside, albeit surrounded by shrubs. The museum is open daily from 10.00 to 17.00.
Operators: Scheduled services by Aer Lingus (Boeing 737), Aeroflot (Tu-134/154), Aerolineas Argentinas (Boeing 747), Air Aruba (Boeing 757), Air Exel (Brasilia), Air France (Boeing 727/737, Fellowship, Brasilia, Saab SF340, Airbus A320), Air Lanka (TriStar), Air Littoral (Brasilia, Fokker 100), Air Malta (Boeing 737), Air Portugal (Boeing 727/737), Air UK (BAe 146, Friendship, Short SD3-60), Alitalia (DC-9), Austrian Airlines (DC-9), Balkan (Tu-154, Boeing 737), Bangladesh Biman (DC-10), Birmingham European (One-Eleven), British Airways (Boeing 737/757, One-Eleven), British Midland (DC-9, Boeing 737, BAe ATP), Brymon Airways (Dash Eight), Canadian Airlines (DC-10, Boeing 767), Cathay Pacific (Boeing 747), China Airlines (Boeing 747), Continental Airlines (DC-10), Czechoslovak Airlines (Tu-134/154), Crossair (Saab SF340, BAe 146), Cyprus Airways (Airbus A320), Dan-Air (One-Eleven, BAe 146), Delta Air Lines (TriStar), Delta Air Transport (Brasilia), El Al (Boeing 747/757/767), Finnair (DC-9/10), Garuda (Boeing 747), Hamburg Airlines (Dash Eight), Iberia (Boeing 727, DC-9, Airbus A320), Icelandair (Boeing 737), Iraqi Airways (Boeing 727), Japan Air Lines (Boeing 747), JAT (Boeing 727/737, DC-9), KLM (Airbus A310, Boeing 737/747, DC-10, MD-11), KLM CityHopper (Fokker 50, Fellowship, Saab SF340), Kuwait Airways (Airbus A310), Libyan Arab (Boeing 727), Lufthansa (Airbus A320, Boeing 727/737), Luxair (Fokker 50), Malaysian Airlines (Boeing 747, DC-10), Malev (Tu-134/154, Boeing 737), Martinair Holland (DC-9, Airbus A310), NFD (Metro, ATR42), Noble Air (Boeing 727), Northwest Airlines (DC-10), Olympic Airways (Airbus A300, Boeing 727), Philippine Airlines (Boeing 747), Pakistan International (Boeing 747), Polish Airlines (Tu-134/154), Qantas (Boeing 747), Royal Air Maroc (Boeing 727/737), Royal Jordanian (Airbus A310, TriStar), Sabena (Dash Eight, Boeing 737), SAS (DC-9), Saudia (Boeing 747, TriStar), Singapore Airlines (Boeing 747), South

African Airways (Boeing 747), Suckling Airways (Dornier 228), Swissair (DC-9, Fokker 100), Tarom (One-Eleven, Tu-154), Thai International (DC-10), Transavia (Boeing 737), Trans World (Boeing 747/767), Tunis Air (Boeing 737), Turkish Airlines (Airbus A310, Boeing 727), Tyrolean Airways (Dash Eight), United Airlines (Boeing 727/767), Varig (Boeing 747, DC-10), Viasa (DC-10), Viva Air (Boeing 737), Yemenia (Boeing 727) and ZAS Airline of Egypt (DC-9).
Charter and IT operators: Adria Airways (DC-9), Air Atlantis (Boeing 737), Air Holland Regional (Boeing 757), Air Liberte (DC-9), Aviogenex (Boeing 727), Martinair (Airbus A310, DC-9/10, Boeing 747/767), Transavia (Boeing 737/757) and Transwede (DC-9).
Movements (1990): Total 200,000. Total passengers 16,500,000.
Runways: 01R/19L (11,155ft/3,400m), 01L/19R (10,827ft/3,300m), 09/27 (11,330ft/3,453m), 06/24 (10,662ft/3,250m), 04/22 (6,608ft/2,014m).
Radio frequencies: 118.1MHz, 118.9MHz (Tower), 119.05MHz (Departure), 121.8MHz (Apron), 121.975MHz (Approach).
Telephone: (020) 5172671 (Information).
Operated by: Schiphol Airport Authority.

Anchorage International, Ak USA

Anchorage International opened at its present location in 1951, but the city had been an important centre for aviation for many years before this event. Nevertheless, it was only in 1947 that it became a truly international gateway following the inauguration of a link with Tokyo by Northwest Orient. The airport was built, owned and operated by the federal government, the facilities including a primary 8,400ft (2,560m) east/west runway plus a north/south strip 5,000ft (1,524m) in length. In 1957 SAS began a pioneering service from Europe to Asia, using Anchorage as a transit stop for the DC-7 allocated for the lengthy trip from Copenhagen to Tokyo. Other airlines soon recognised the advantages offered by this route between the two continents, with the result that by 1960 seven foreign flag carriers served the airport on a regular basis. One year earlier, 25 June 1959 had marked an important milestone in the airport's history. On this date the federal government transferred ownership to the new State of Alaska which immediately gave greater independence and the opportunity for long-term planning.

It was 1960 when jet services were introduced to Anchorage with both Boeing 707s and DC-8s becoming regular visitors. The State responded by extending the main runway to its present length of 10,897ft (3,321m), while a new satellite terminal was opened in 1965. Two years later it was connected to the main building by a covered concourse as attempts were made to cope with the increasing number of travellers. Further expansion completed in 1970 involved a new parallel east/west runway which was designed to cater for the soon-to-be-introduced Boeing 747s. These facilities proved adequate for some years, but in 1980 a reconstructed north/south runway was completed to ensure that the airport remained capable of handling all demands into the next century.

A modern international terminal located some 2,000ft north of the existing building was built in 1982, this latest addition being equipped with eight gates designed to accommodate all types of aircraft in service. Meanwhile, domestic passengers had not been overlooked because a modern concourse was constructed in 1985 specifically for the use of this traffic. There has been steady growth through the subsequent years, with air cargo producing particularly impressive figures. It is now quite normal for Anchorage to handle over 90% of the freight transported between Asia and Europe and 70% of that destined for the US.

Aware of the growing deficit in available capacity at Anchorage, in the late 1980s the authorities began to plan for an orderly update of the airport's needs to 2007. It was recognised that the advent of the larger versions of the 747 would probably reduce the number of international movements, especially with the bilateral agreements for civil operations in Soviet airspace. Such a reduction could also apply to the domestic market as the smaller carriers merge with a greater concentration at the hubs. Bearing this in mind the planners specified a number of areas for improvement including high-speed taxiways from Runway 6R, expansion of the domestic terminal, a new commuter runway (14L/32R) and an additional cargo apron. The flourishing general aviation population has not been forgotten because more space has been allocated for seaplane operations. Anchorage is one of the few airports in the world with such a facility comprising of two lakes connected by a channel to create a waterfront some 11 miles in length.

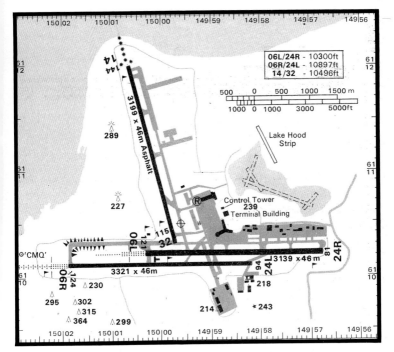

Location and access: Situated 7 miles (11km) southwest of the city to which the airport is linked by a number of bus services.

Terminals: The two-storey international terminal is remote from the domestic building, the latter possessing a concourse and satellite. A second concourse is planned for the future. Both terminals offer the usual amenities.

Spectator facilities: None specifically provided. All scheduled movements can be seen from the end of the domestic concourse, there being no vantage points in the international terminal. The proximity of hordes of floatplanes at the adjacent Lake Hood more than compensates for the lack of airliner photographs, many of which can be obtained more easily elsewhere. A considerable amount of walking is involved but the effort is well worthwhile. There are few fences and an abundance of co-operation which makes any such visit a memorable experience.

Operators: Scheduled services by Air France (Boeing 747), Alaska Airlines (Boeing 727/737), British Airways (Boeing 747), China Airlines (Boeing 747), Continental Airlines (Airbus A300), Delta Air Lines (Boeing 727/757, TriStar), Delta Express (Metro), ERA Aviation (Twin Otter, Dash Eight, Convair 580), Japan Airlines (Boeing 747), KLM (Boeing 747), Markair (Boeing 737, Dash Seven/Eight, Hercules), Northwest (Boeing 727), Peninsula Airways (Metro, Conquest), Raven Air (Cessna 207), Reeve Aleutian Airways (Boeing 727, Electra, YS-11), Sabena (DC-10), SAS (Boeing 767), Southcentral Air (Navajo), Swissair (DC-10), United Airlines (Boeing 727/737/757) and Wilburs (Cessna 401/402, Beech 99).

Movements (1990): Total 360,000 including Lake Hood. (Air transport 81,700). Total passengers 4,675,305.

Runways: 06L/24R (10,300ft/3,139m), 06R/24L (10,897ft/3,321m), 14/32 (10,496ft/3,200m). A shorter, parallel 14L/32R planned.

Radio frequencies: 118.3MHz (Tower), 118.6MHz, 119.1MHz, 123.8MHz, 126.4MHz (Departure), 121.9MHz (Ground).

Telephone: (907) 266-1400.

Operated by: Department of Transportation and Public Facilities.

11

Athens (Hellenikon)
Greece

During the last 20 years or so Greece has steadily increased in popularity with European holidaymakers with the consequence that Hellenikon has become a much busier airport. Opened in 1936, it was built on the coast with limited facilities and a fairly short strip to serve as a runway. Plans to develop the site were quickly put into effect in 1945, but five years later work was suspended until investigations had been completed into possible alternatives. Satisfied with the outcome, approval was given for the general enlargement of the airport which involved the acquisition of large areas of land to the south and east. Part of the scheme called for a new international terminal to be constructed thereby leaving the original single-storey building for the exclusive use of the national carrier, Olympic Airways.

Opened in 1969, traffic continued to grow at such a pace that the new structure had to be extended in the mid-1970s to raise its capacity as the wide-bodied types came into service. These aircraft also needed additional space for parking so the apron was increased in size to allow six 747s to be handled simultaneously. Nevertheless Hellenikon's future depended upon it expanding still further and this was limited by the shortage of suitable land. Added to this handicap were the constant complaints from members of the local population about noise and polution, so the government decided to seek once again other possible locations for a brand new Athens airport. Of the four sites studied, that at Spata-Saggani was the final choice for a complex capable of handling 15 million passengers when opened. Two parallel runways 13,000ft (3,962m) in length are envisaged, while the terminal area will contain three circular buildings each served by four triangular shaped gate-lounges. In the meantime Hellenikon continues as the main gateway to Greece, accounting for over 75% of the country's air traffic movements.

Location and access: Situated 6 miles (10km) south of Athens. The western terminal (Olympic) is served every 15min by a bus to the city centre (Avenue Syngrou 96) taking 20min for the journey. There is

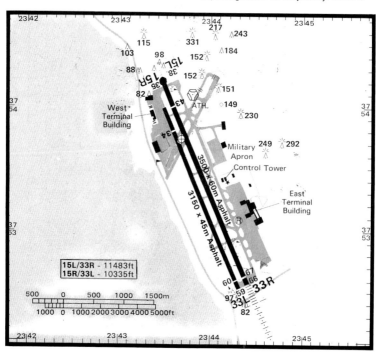

Athens can produce some interesting subjects such as this An-24RV J5-GBE. *E. Johnston*

also a Yellow Bus service between the terminal and Piraeus (Akti Tzelepi, Karaiskaki Square). This bus includes a visit to the eastern terminal in its travels, a destination additionally served directly from Avenue Amelias 4, Syntagma Square, the latter taking 20min for the trip.

Terminals: The eastern building handles all except Olympic and is divided into two halves for arrivals and departures. Also within the building is a section dealing with charter movements. There are no modern devices such as airbridges at either of the two terminals, buses taking all passengers to and from the stands.

Spectator facilities: A terrace exists on the southern end of the western terminal, but because the position overlooks the military area, photography is not encouraged. There is therefore very little scope for shots at this point. On the other hand the international building (eastern terminal) has a good roof terrace but offers only limited opportunities for photographs. The attractiveness of this vantage point diminished considerably following action by the authorities in a belated and rather futile attempt to restore confidence in the airport. Away from the terminals, the threshold of runway 33R on the southeastern perimeter is an ideal position, but the area tends to be monitered by the local law enforcers who normally dislike the sight of cameras. Under the circumstances it may be prudent to forsake this well trodden corner of the airport for the safer havens in one of the several ideally situated hotels. The Fenix is by the Glyfada to Athens main road to the southwest of the 33R threshold, but not far away is the Emmantina which now regularly advertises its attractive position. This is certainly a good vantage point which also enjoys the advantages of a pool, bar and refreshments on its rooftop terrace. Providing sleep is of little consequence, a profitable time can be spent at the hotel. Both viewing and photography present no problems.

Operators: Scheduled services by Aeroflot (Tu-134/154, IL-86), Air Algerie (Airbus A310, Boeing 737), Air Canada (Boeing 767), Air France (Boeing 727, Airbus A310), Air Malta (Boeing 737), Airmust (DC-9/10), Air Portugal (Boeing 737), Air Zimbabwe (Boeing 707/767), Alitalia (DC-9), Austrian Airlines (DC-9), Balkan (Boeing 737, Tu-134/154), Bangladesh Biman (DC-10), British Airways (Boeing 737/757/767), Cyprus Airways (Airbus A310/320, One-Eleven), Czechoslovak Airlines (Tu-154), Egyptair (Boeing 737), El Al (Boeing 737/757/767), Ethiopean Airlines (Boeing 727), Finnair (DC-9), Gulf Air

(Boeing 737), Iberia (Boeing 727, DC-9), Iraqi Airways (Boeing 727), Japan Airlines (DC-10), Kenya Airways (Airbus A310), KLM (Airbus A310, Boeing 737), Kuwait Airways (Airbus A310, Boeing 727/767), Libyan Arab (Boeing 727), Lufthansa (Boeing 737, Airbus A300/A310/320), Luxair (Boeing 737), Malev (Tu-134/154, Boeing 737), Middle East Airlines (Boeing 707), Olympic Airways (Airbus A300, Boeing 727/737/747), Olympic Aviation (ATR-42, Dornier 228, Short SD3-30), Pakistan International (Airbus A300, Boeing 747), Polish Airlines (Tu-134/154), Qantas (Boeing 747), Royal Air Maroc (Boeing 727/737), Sabena (Boeing 737), SAS (DC-9), Saudia (Airbus A300), Singapore Airlines (Boeing 747), Sudan Airways (Boeing 737), Swissair (Airbus A310, DC-9), Syrianair (Boeing 727, Caravelle), Tarom (Tu-54, One-Eleven), Thai International (Boeing 747, DC-10), Trans World (Boeing 747/767, TriStar), Tunisair (Boeing 727/737), Turkish Airlines (Airbus A310, Boeing 727, DC-9), United Airlines (Boeing 727), Yemenia (Boeing 727) and Yugoslav Airlines (Boeing 737). *Charter and IT operators:* These include Aer Lingus (Boeing 737), Aero Lloyd (DC-9), Air Belgium (Boeing 737), Air Berlin (Boeing 737), Air Holland (Boeing 757), Appollonian Airways (DC-9), ATI (DC-9), Braathens (Boeing 737), Britannia (Boeing 737/757/767), Caledonian (Boeing 757, TriStar), Conair (Airbus A320), Condor (Boeing 737/757/767), Corse Air (Boeing 737), CTA (DC-9), Dan-Air (One-Eleven, Boeing 727/737), Hapag Lloyd (Airbus A310, Boeing 737), Finnair (DC-9), LTU (TriStar, Boeing 757/767), Lauda Air (Boeing 737), Maersk (Boeing 737), Martinair (DC-9, Airbus A310), Monarch (Airbus A300, Boeing 737/757), Nationair (Boeing 757, DC-8), Scanair (DC-10), Sobelair (Boeing 737), Sterling (Caravelle, Boeing 727/757), Tower Air (Boeing 747), Transavia (Boeing 737) and Transwede (DC-9). Athens also has an active military base which regularly attracts visits from other air arms. There is therefore a good variety of movements.

Movements (1990): Total air transport 112,700. Total passengers 10,077,000.
Runways: 15L/33R (11,483ft/3,500m), 15R/33L (10,334ft/3,150m),03/21 (6,000ft/1,828m). Normally only 15L/33R is used, the other two being used as taxiways or aircraft storage.
Radio frequencies: 118.1MHz, 122.1MHz (Tower), 118.3MHz (Radar), 121.7MHz (Ground).
Telephone: (01) 9699111.
Operator: Civil Aviation Authority.

Atlanta (Hartsfield International)
Ga USA

In the mid-1920s the city authorities exercised considerable foresight by taking up the offer of a disused speedway track for development into a flying field. Once the lease was signed a start was made on transforming the site by laying two short dirt runways, both equipped with lights to enable operations to continue at night. By 1926 the airfield also possessed two hangars and was linked with Miami by Florida Airways. While mail was already handled on a small scale, 1928 marked Atlanta's real entry into this sphere of activity. Pitcairn Aviation, the forerunner of Eastern Air Lines, plus St Tammany-Gulf Coast Airways both began scheduled services which extended the airport's route network northwards to take in New York and Chicago, while New Orleans was added to the coverage in the south.

Although commercial air transport was still in its infant stage, the future looked promising for the growing airport, but it very much depended upon the city's willingness to buy the field from the owner. Faced with the imminent expiry of its lease, a special session of the council was convened in early April 1929 to discuss the matter. With an unusual display of speed and determination by such a body, agreement was quickly reached, no doubt helped by the promise of a discount for cash. One week later a cheque for $94,400 was exchanged for the Deeds of the property thereby preparing the way for an impressive expansion programme.

There were few signs of this plan when the newly recruited airport manager arrived in the summer. An experienced pilot and engineer, Jack Gray found that his office was an abandoned 10ft x 8ft wooden shed and that his many duties also included the handling of the runway lights when any night movements were likely. At least he was not overburdened by staff problems because only four labourers and two mules were on the payroll at the airport. Undeterred, Gray set about extending the runways, improving the taxiways and generally clearing the approaches to the airfield where necessary. Fortunately an abundance of crime in the

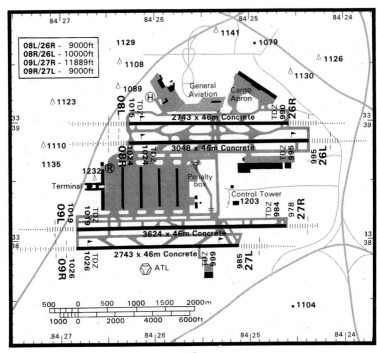

Above:
Delta's 737-232 N329DL taxis to its stand at Atlanta. *A. S. Wright*

Below:
Atlantic Southeast operates into Atlanta with its remaining Dash Sevens, in this case N720AS. *A. S. Wright*

area ensured that there was an ample supply of convict labour to support his meagre workforce.

As a result of this effort new routes were steadily opened, until by the beginning of the next decade Atlanta possessed the second highest number in the country. In addition to Lockheed having a manufacturing facility on site, the airport also became the maintenance and operations headquarters for Eastern Air Transport, the new name for Pitcairn. Needless to say, despite the undoubted success story there lurked a problem. There was no passenger terminal to accommodate the growing number of passengers; neither was there any money to pay for this important feature.

It could have been a major setback in the airport's progress, but help was at hand. American Airlines agreed to honour its rental obligations 10 years in advance, which enabled work to start immediately upon the erection of a modern building in 1932. When completed it was desirable to furnish the interior, but funds were still less than adequate to cover the outlay. In order to assist in the purchase of waiting room furniture, the airport manager persuaded Eastern to lend him a machine to fly sightseeing trips over nearby Stone Mountain.

During 1933 the nation's airlines were dealt a mortal blow by the government when it cancelled all the mail contracts. Since these contributed a significant amount to the companies' income, many of the smaller carriers were forced out of business before tenders were invited prior to the redistribution of the routes in 1934. Ironically the Fort Worth-Atlanta sector was then regained by Delta at the expense of American, which did not reappear at the airport until 1983. Hopefully it received a rebate of the unused rent advance.

During the remainder of the 1930s, the Roosevelt adminstration funded many projects including the development of Atlanta. Several million dollars were spent on lengthening and widening the existing runways which were also paved to take them to the same standard as the newly-laid strips. To facilitate these improvements, the overall size of the airport constantly grew by absorbing additional ground within the boundaries.

Even before America's active involvement in World War 2, Atlanta was declared an Air Base on 4 October 1940 which marked the beginning of another important phase in the airport's history. Recognising the opportunites which now presented themselves, the authorities applied for a $1 million grant to pay for yet more improvements to runways and lighting. It was duly paid in full by the central government without conditions.

During the war years Atlanta's airport almost doubled in size as it spread itself in three directions. Not surprisingly during this period it managed to collect a number of records including the distinction of becoming the country's busiest airport in terms of movements, achieved during the course of one day in 1942 with a figure of 1,700. During the same year there was much satisfaction when it was learned that a healthy profit was to be announced.

It meant that with peace restored the airport was well placed to handle the anticipated growth in air transport. Demobbed servicemen quickly launched airlines to supply the demand which confirmed the belief that a larger terminal was becoming a matter of some urgency. However, an element of caution was advisable in view of the probable rash of financially embarrassed carriers, a contagious disease still rife today. As an interim solution the authorities converted a surplus wartime hangar which entered service on 9 May 1948.

Elsewhere on the site work proceeded with the laying of three much longer and completely new runways. The three main carriers were Delta, Eastern and Southern, all of which were constantly adding services to their networks. With private flying also on the increase, there was obviously every need for the latest expansion when the 1948 figures showed that more than 1 million passengers and 360,082 aircraft movements had been handled by Atlanta Municipal Airport.

Once again the management was faced with the need to make a decision on the future terminal. It was by no means easy in view of the ever-changing specifications for airliners with enormous capacity. After much hestitation and not before over 2 million passengers had passed through the inadequate facility in 1955, a start was made on the new building two years later. It coincided with the award of a title it still holds today as the busiest connecting hub in the world. When opened on 3 May 1961, the modern edifice erected at a cost of $21 million, was the largest terminal building in the country. It boasted 48 gates for the use of the seven carriers serving the airport with parking for 52 aircraft. Designed to handle 6 million passengers annually, it was confidently expected to meet Atlanta's needs until at least the mid-1980s. However, it transpired that forecasting proved not to be high on the list of success stories. Even in the first year of operation over 3.8 million passengers, assisted by 5.7 million visitors, passed through the doors - an ominous sign indeed.

By the time that the badly needed runway was opened on the south side in December 1964, airlines were once more hunting for space and air traffic was being forced to stack incoming flights as a result of serious congestion.

Observing this alarming development, the city commissioned studies to determine Atlanta's long-term needs. For several years there was little progress while the planners endulged in internal disagreements, but finally work began on a master plan in 1967. It involved financial participation by the airlines, in exchange for which they were able to play an active part in the project. This was a satisfactory arrangement until February 1969 when the estimated cost of the package was released. A cost of some $300 million was now in prospect, a figure which understandably sent a shiver of fear through many airline financial controllers. Support was quickly withdrawn from the entire enterprise which in turn was unable to continue. Various alternative schemes were considered and discarded until in 1971 some of the reluctant airlines agreed to restore their commitment to the new Atlanta, renamed Hartsfield Atlanta International two months after the death of its founder (William B. Hartsfield). Nevertheless, another four years passed before all interested parties were in agreement and the future of the project was assured.

Construction began in January 1977 with a target for completion in 3½ years. Although an entirely new site, it was surrounded by the active runways and taxiways that had to remain working at all times. It was a formidable task, but on 21 September 1980 a convoy of 25,000 employees in hundreds of vehicles moved from the old terminal to the new premises where full-scale operations were re-established within two hours. In order to reduce taxying time and its associated expense, the terminal is located between the runways. There are parallel concourses interconnected by an underground transit system which carries over 65,000 passengers each day. Learning from their original under-estimates, the planners have allowed for the design capacity of 55 million passengers per year to grow to at least 75 million annually. This has meant that since the opening several major modifications have been incorportated including a 9,000ft fourth parallel runway in December 1984 and the extension of another to an impressive 11,889ft.

Despite its enormous size, additional runway capacity is still the most critical need at the airport. Already the planners are studying the possibility of providing one or more short strips for the use of general aviation and the growing volume of commuter services. Interestingly over 65% of the travellers use connecting flights and do not visit the main north and south buildings but merely change concourses. When the need arises the latter will be increased to five for domestic use but in the meantime Hartsfield can cope by using its existing facilities.

When the master planners designed the new airport, flexibility in cargo movement was considered an important priority. Consequently Atlanta has one of the largest freight complexes in the world to be ranked among the top 15 centres. It is also ideally situated to be a major participant in the international air courier and parcel industry.

Location and access: Situated 10 miles (16km) south of Atlanta between I-85, 75 and 285. Together they give major highway connections to the city and the entire southeast region. Ample parking exists adjoining the north and south terminals with a total of 19,400 spaces. There are three different charge rates which should be chosen to suit the length of stay. Coaches run at frequent intervals to all districts of Atlanta with a free shuttle bus to all airport hotels. The Metropolitan Atlanta Rapid Transit Authority (MARTA) covers the Fulton and DeKalb Counties with scheduled services to and from the airport. The trains operate every 12min taking 15min for the journey to the centre of the city.

Terminal: Two main buildings (north and south) are served by one international and four domestic concourses all equipped with ample snack bars, shops and bars.

Spectator facilities: None provided. From within the various concourses aircraft parked at many of the 146 gates can be seen and photographed despite the presence of tinted windows, although this can be a problem for those using colour film. There are few suitable vantage points around the perimeter, but fortunately many of the likely subjects can be found elsewhere with less difficulty.

Operators: Aeropostal (DC-9), Air Jamaica (Boeing 727), American Airlines (Boeing 727/747/767, DC-9), Atlantic Southeast (Brasilia, Bandeirante, Dash Seven), British Airways (DC-10), Cayman Airways (Boeing 737), Continental Airlines (Boeing 727/737, DC-9), Delta Air Lines (Boeing 727/737/757/767, DC-9, TriStar), Japan Airlines (Boeing 747), KLM (Boeing 747), Lufthansa (Boeing 747), Northwest Airlines (Boeing 727, DC-9), Midwest (DC-9), Sabena (DC-10), Swissair (DC-10), Trans World (Boeing 727/767, DC-9), United Airlines (Boeing 727/737, DC-9), USAir (Boeing 737, DC-9, Fellowship, Fokker 100).

Cargo flights by: Airborne (DC-8/9), Burlington Express (Boeing 707, DC-8), DHL (Metro, Boeing 727), Emery Worldwide (DC-8/9, Boeing 727), Federal Express (Boeing 727/747, DC-10, MD-11), Mountain Air (Caravan, Friendship), Southern Air Transport (DC-8), United Parcel Service (Boeing 727/757, DC-8) and Zantop (Convair 580, Electra).
Movements (1990): Total 569,400. Total passengers 48,015,000. This compares with 665,900 and 43,312,000 respectively in 1989.

Runways: 09R/27L (9,000ft/2,743m), 09L/27R (11,889ft/3,624m), 08R/26L (10,000ft/3,048m), 08L/26R (9,000ft/2,743m).
Radio frequencies: 119.5MHz (Tower north), 119.1MHz (Tower south), 125.7MHz Departure north), 125.0MHz (Departure south), 121.9MHz (Ground north), 121.75MHz (Ground south).
Telephone: (404) 530 6600.
Operated by: Department of Aviation, City of Atlanta.

Auckland International New Zealand

The site now occupied by Auckland's international airport first became involved in aviation in 1928 when the local aero club earmarked the field for its future use. Two years later 80 acres were purchased allowing the aerodrome to take shape. Throughout the 1930s it played a part in many historic events, particularly the epic trips made by Jean Batten in the Percival Gull G-ADPR. When World War 2 interrupted such pastimes, the facilities came under the control of the Royal New Zealand Air Force for the duration, before returning to the Auckland Aero Club in 1946. Thereupon civil flying was resumed for a short time, but the sale of the land to the government ended this phase in its career, because in March 1954

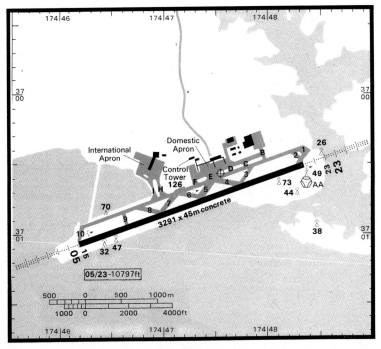

it was announced that an international airport was to be built.

Preparatory work began in 1960, but four years elapsed before construction really began. In the meantime some 160 acres of Manukaua Harbour were reclaimed so that the minimum amount of valuable farmland was swallowed up by the complex. Stage 1 of the airport's development was completed in November 1965, allowing operations to begin. The first commercial airliner to use the facilities was a Qantas Boeing 707, although the official opening was held with all due pomp on 29 January 1966.

Almost immediately there was confirmation that the venture would be successful because in its first two weeks in service, the airport handled over 10,000 passengers. It was a marked improvement over the unsuitable conditions at Whenuapai, the RNZAF base used hitherto. Subsequent expansion at Auckland has been gradual, commencing in March 1973 with the extension of the runway to its present 10,820ft (3,300m) length, a task carried out mainly to meet the demands of the Boeing 747s and DC-10s then entering service.

At the end of another four years the Jean Batten International Terminal was opened, thereby releasing the accommodation previously employed to deal exclusively with domestic traffic. There was then a long period before a third building was introduced in 1987, this time for the use of Ansett New Zealand's domestic customers. Towards the end of the decade the international facilities were extended, followed more recently by refurbishment and a complete upgrade of the amenities.

To meet the strong growth in both passenger and aircraft movements through the airport, the authorities have a substantial area of land reserved for future expansion. The existing runway is likely to reach its full capacity in about 2005, so to minimise delays a second strip will be needed. Since the proposed site is on land, it will avoid the environmental impact of reclaiming yet more of Manukau Harbour. By spacing the two runways nearly 2,000m apart, there will be enough land available for a major development of the terminals with long-term potential for up to 90 aircraft gates. In due course, the international building will be extended and two new piers incorporated into what will become a consolidated passenger terminal handing both types of traffic.

Location and access: Situated 14 miles (22km) south of Auckland. A combination of State Highways 1, 12 and 20 can be used to reach the city. The Airporter bus operates to and from the airport at 30min intervals throughout the day with a journey time of about 40min.

Terminals: All three buildings offer various shops, catering facilities and other services, although there is a much wider selection in the international terminal.

Spectator facilities: There is a viewing deck located on the second floor of the International Terminal. It provides a good view of all movements, but the glass front makes photography difficult in sunny conditions.

Operators: Aerolineas Argentinas (Boeing 747), Air Caledonie International (Boeing 737), Air Nauru (Boeing 737), Air Nelson (Metro, Saab SF340), Air New Zealand (Boeing 737/747/767, Friendship), Air Pacific (Boeing 767), Air Vanuatu (Boeing 727), American Airlines (DC-10), Ansett New Zealand (BAe 146, Dash Eight, Nomad), Bell Air (Beech 99), British Airways (Boeing 747), Britannia Airways (Boeing 767), Canadian Airlines International (DC-10), Cathay Pacific (Boeing 747), Continental Airlines (Boeing 747, DC-10), Eagle Air (Bandeirante), Garuda Indonesia (DC-10), Great Barrier Airlines (Islander), Japan Airlines (Boeing 747), Malaysian Airlines System (DC-10), Mt Cook Airlines (HS748, Navajo), Northern Commuter Airlines (Navajo), Pacific Midland (Navajo), Polynesian Airlines (Boeing 727), Qantas (Boeing 747/767), Singapore Airlines (Boeing 747), Soloman Airlines (Boeing 737), Thai International (DC-10), Tranzair (Bandeirante), United Airlines (Boeing 747) and UTA (DC-10).

Cargo services: Federal Express (Boeing 747, DC-10), Singapore Airlines (Boeing 747) and Southern World Airlines (DC-8).

Movements (1990): Total 85,994. Total passengers 5,374,382.

Runway: 05/23 (10,797ft/3,291m).

Radio frequencies: 118.7MHz (Tower), 120.5MHz, 124.3MHz, 129.6MHz (Approach), 121.9MHz (Ground).

Telephone: (09) 275-0789.

Operated by: Auckland International Airport Ltd.

Baltimore/Washington International, Md USA

Although a flying field was established at Baltimore in the autumn of 1921, the growth of commercial aviation later in the decade convinced the city authorities that it was inadequate. Plans for a municipal airport were produced, but because progress was somewhat leisurely it was not until 1941 that the site was ready to receive traffic. In the meantime the size and quantity of aircraft had increased dramatically, so almost immediately the newly opened complex was in need of some development. There was little action taken during the course of the war, but in 1946 a plan was formulated for a modern facility located 10 miles south of Baltimore and 30 miles north of its near neighbour, Washington DC. This time work proceeded with a greater sense of urgency, until on 24 June 1950 the airport was duly named Friendship International (FIA) and declared open by President Harry S. Truman.

Throughout the 1950s, FIA served the needs of the two cities and the five million-strong population in the surrounding area. It was prominent in the early days of the jet transports, remaining, until 1962, the only airport in the area capable of handling types such as the Boeing 707. At the end of the 1960s the authorities recognised that once again some major expansion was necessary if the airport was to maintain its position of importance. Even rough calculations indicated that the cost of such a project would be too great a strain on the city's finances, so another source had to be found. After much debate, in July 1972 the State of Maryland agreed to purchase FIA from Baltimore for $36 million.

The new owner immediately began to review the airport's intended role, in due course announcing a massive modernisation programme in a bid to attract more business from the nation's capital. To emphasise the point, the name Baltimore/Washington International (BWI) replaced the Friendship title displayed for over 20 years. Non-US passengers now knew roughly where they had landed.

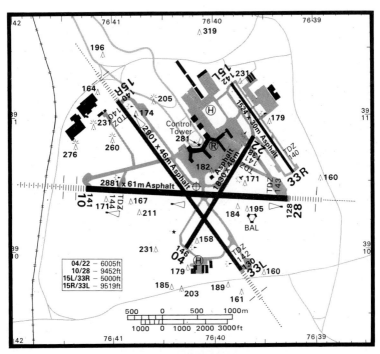

04/22	— 6005ft
10/28	— 9452ft
15L/33R	— 5000ft
15R/33L	— 9519ft

One of the most important features of the proposed expansion was the terminal. It was some 75% larger than the original building and made considerable use of glass and steel in its design to produce an atmosphere of spaciousness and light. Work began in October 1974, continuing apace until its completion in 1980. At the same time it was appreciated that any increase in passenger numbers must be accompanied by improved access. Accordingly a railway station was built on airport property some 1½ miles from the terminal, but linked by frequent shuttle buses. Opened in 1980, it gave BWI the distinction of becoming the first US airport to possess such a facility. Ten years later, a new four mile stretch of road was completed to give an uninterrupted connection with Interstate 95, the main artery between Washington and Baltimore. Not only does the latest section cut travelling time to the airport, it also extends the local catchment area to include south central Pennsylvania, all of Maryland, the Washington suburbs and the capital itself.

Despite the effects of the Gulf hostilities and general recession in the early part of 1991, BWI enjoyed a very positive first quarter against the worldwide trend. International traffic was responsible for the passenger total increasing by 35%, a result helped by the new services inaugurated by such as KLM and Icelandair. A daily average of 675 flights were being handled at BWI, with the corresponding increase in travellers to over 10 million annually, a figure expected to more than double by 2005. In addition to this healthy growth rate, BWI ranks among the top US airports in cargo work. Both domestic and international markets are served by the freight complex which now has of 300,000sq ft of floor space spread between eight buildings.

Location and access: Situated 10 miles (16.1km) south of Baltimore and 30 miles (48.28km) north of Washington, DC via I-95 and I-195. A regular bus service operates to Annapolis, Baltimore and Washington. There is an AMTRAK and MARC rail service from the airport station to Baltimore (Penn), the journey taking 20min. Similarly Washington (Union) can be reached in 30min. Car parks are charged hourly or daily.
Terminal: There are five piers extending

from the main building, four handling domestic traffic while the fifth is used for international flights. Altogether there are 65 gates available, of which 47 can be used by jets and 18 by commuter aircraft. There are numerous facilities for snacks or full meals in the building, while various shops are located either on or near the piers.
Spectator facilities: None provided, but reasonable views can be obtained through the terminal windows. Unfortunately the architect's preference for heavily tinted glass prohibits all photography. As an alternative there are vantage points around the perimeter which compensates to some extent although much depends on the wind direction. In any case most of the likely subjects can be found in far better locations elsewhere.
Operators: Scheduled services by Air Jamaica (Airbus A300, Boeing 727), American Airlines (Boeing 727, DC-9, ATR42), America West (Boeing 737), Continental Airlines (ATR-42, DC-9), Delta Air Lines (Boeing 757, DC-9), Icelandair (Boeing 757), KLM (Boeing 747), Ladeco (Boeing 757), Northwest Airlines (Boeing 727, DC-9), Trans World (Boeing 727/767), United Airlines (Boeing 727/737/757), USAir (Boeing 727/737/767, DC-9, Fokker 100, F-28) and USAir Express (Short SD3-30/3-60, Jetstream, Beech 1900, Dash Seven, Dash Eight).
Charter services: are provided by Aerocancun (DC-9), Carnival Air (Boeing 727/737) and Trump (Boeing 727).
Cargo flights: These are operated by United Parcel Service (Boeing 727/757, DC-8), Emery Worldwide (Boeing 727, DC-8), Federal Express (Boeing 727), Zantop International (Convair 640, Electra) and Burlington Express (DC-8).
Movements (1990): Total 302,248. Total passengers 10,245,049. These figures compare with 303,800 and 10,356,548 respectively in 1989.
Runways: 10/28 (9,452ft/2,881m), 15R/33L (9,519ft/2,901m), 15L/33R (5,000ft/1,524m), 04/22 (6,005ft/1,830m).
Radio frequencies: 119.4MHz (Tower), 133.75MHz (Departure) 121.9MHz (Ground).
Telephone: (301) 859 7100.
Operated by: Maryland Aviation Administration.

Berlin (Tegel/Templehof) Germany

Located in the centre of Berlin, Templehof became one of the busiest airports in Europe between the wars. Regular air services began on 8 October 1923 to link the city with Munich, intermediate stops being made at Dessau, Leipzig and Nuremberg. Growth was such that in the following year it had to be extended, the most impressive aspect of the project being the enormous hangars that could house 60% of the German commercial fleet during the non-flying winter months. In the 1930s the particularly impressive terminal was built, which in its day was one of the most modern to be found anywhere. In 1938 there were over 63,000 movements and a throughput of 247,000 passengers, no mean achievement but one which demanded more expansion. This was underway at the outbreak of the war which quickly halted all work of this nature. Routes radiating from the capital were then reduced in variety, but still connected Berlin with major cities in neutral, friendly or occupied countries. In fact commercial flying did not completely end until early in 1945.

Once the conflict was over, a survey of the scene revealed that most of Templehof had been destroyed, but remarkably the new buildings had survived, albeit in a badly damaged state. Under the control of the US forces, a few services were gradually introduced by American Overseas Airlines, but there were few passengers because Germans were still unpopular anywhere but in the Fatherland. In any case anyone willing to ignore this situation also had great difficulty in obtaining the necessary permits. Suddenly movements dramatically increased. On 24 June 1948 the Soviet Union introduced a total blockade of West Berlin leaving only one solution: an airlift of supplies for the population. Templehof and the RAF base at Gatow became the reception points, but it was soon obvious that the combined capacity was still insufficient to handle the volume of traffic which in turn was bound to slow down the effort.

To remedy this situation an additional runway was built in the Jungfernheide, near

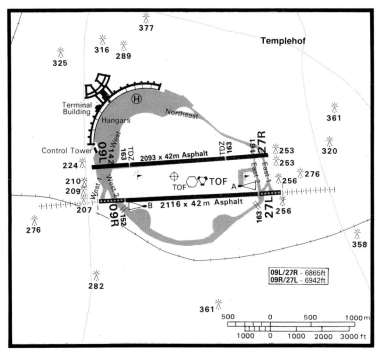

23

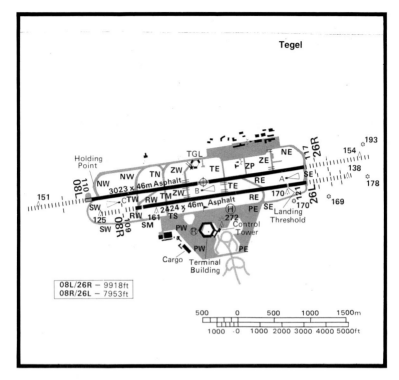

Tegel

Holding Point

NW NW NW
SW SW SW
CTW RW RW RW
SM TM ZW B TE
ZW TGL TE ZP ZE NE
TN TS TE RE A
3023 x 46m Asphalt
2424 x 46m Asphalt
RE
PE SE
PW PE
Cargo Terminal Building
PW PE
Control Tower
Landing Threshold

110 180
08L
08R 09
26L 26R
170 170
151
125
272 161
272
193
154
138
178
169

| 08L/26R — 9918ft |
| 08R/26L — 7953ft |

500   0   500   1000   1500m
1000   0   1000 2000 3000 4000 5000ft

Tegel, in the northern part of the city. At the time its 7,874ft (2,400m) length made it the longest in Europe, yet it was completed in only three months, an amazing achievement. Over 19,000 Berliners were employed in the levelling of the 300,000sq m site and the subsequent building operations. Although formally opened on 1 December 1948, a USAF C-54 became the first aircraft to land when it arrived on 5 November. It was not until 6 October in the following year that the blockade was lifted to allow the reintroduction of the normal land routes. During those hectic months there had been 277,728 movements shared between the three airfields, with some 2,326,205 tonnes of supplies flown to the city.

In the summer of 1951 a section of Templehof was handed over for civilian traffic, in effect officially opening the complex started in 1939. The national airlines of the three western Allies (Pan Am, BEA and Air France) introduced schedules from the airport using DC-3s, DC-4s and Languedocs. For a time the airport was able to cope with the relatively small number of commercial movements, but the number of passengers rose faster than expected to reach 320,000 by the end of the first year. Even this figure exceeded the design capacity of the improvised facilities, but two years later a throughput of 833,000 was recorded. Fortunately the USAF released more buildings in 1959, but an enormous amount of repair work had to be done before the terminal had attained an acceptable standard.

By the early 1960s Templehof had become an important centre, but it was December 1964 before it handled the first jet airliner: a Boeing 727 belonging to Pan Am. This type gradually replaced the carrier's DC-6B fleet in Berlin, while BEA withdrew the Viscounts and Comet 4Bs in favour of One-Elevens. By 1970, eight years after the opening of the new passenger terminal, the airport was once again seriously congested despite the move of all charter and IT traffic to Tegel in 1968.

It was realised that Templehof had reached its ultimate capacity and that it was impossible for the runways to be extended in order to cope with the larger aircraft coming into service. As a result the decision was taken to transform Tegel into a brand new airport, a task duly completed in November 1974. By the following September all commercial traffic had moved from Templehof to leave it a quieter place for some years, until in the 1980s commuter airlines began using the neglected facilities once more.

Although Tegel proved invaluable during the period of the airlift, immediately the operation ended in 1949 there was very little activity for over a decade. As the airlines began to introduce larger types towards the end of the 1950s, so it became apparent that the vast expanse of Tegel could be usefully revived. So on 2 January 1960 civilian traffic appeared with the arrival of an Air France Super Constellation. Two weeks later the same company introduced the Caravelle and it was not many months before all of the French carrier's flights were maintained by this type.

Naturally more sophisticated buildings were needed and duly provided, but passenger traffic to Berlin was rapidly increasing which meant some more interim measures before something more permanent could be available. Work began on a complete reconstruction of the airport in June 1969, a task which continued until the official opening on 23 October 1974. Already the base for Air France, Dan-Air and Laker, in 1975 it was decreed that these pioneers would be joined by the remainder of the carriers still operating from Templehof. The ruling caused some difficulties initially because Tegel was conceived as an additional facility and not as a replacement for the older airport. These problems were resolved in due course and Berlin now has an excellent airport well up to the customary German high standard.

Most of the nation's terminal designs offer some originality and that chosen for Tegel is no exception. Arranged in hexagonal form, the 620m-long structure is fitted with 14 airbridges, 10 fixed and four that swivel to allow their use by wide-bodied types. For every pair of jetties there is an arrivals room with its own conveyor belt and customs facility. This admirable idea eliminates the need for central baggage handling and helps to reduce the risk of items going astray. For those travelling in the opposite direction, each departure point again has its own passport and customs control point, a large waiting room and a duty-free shop. In the middle of the hexagon is a short-term parking area, which can reduce the walking distance involved from car to check-in to as little as 20m.

Location and access: Tegel is situated 5 miles (8km) northwest of Berlin to which it is connected by a network of multi-lane roads free of intersections. City Bus route 9 runs between the city centre (Budapesta Strasse) and the airport taking 30min for the journey. It also calls at the main railway station en route. Route 8 links the underground station (U-Bahn) on Kurt-Schumacher-Platz with the airport. Templehof is 4 miles (6km) southeast of the centre and is served by U-Bahn 6. Bus routes 104, 119, 184 and 341 also visit the airport from various parts of the city every 15min or so.

Terminal: (Tegel) Connected to the front of the hexagonal structure is the main building within which are located the various airlines' desks, bank and the usual shops. On the upper floors most of the space is devoted to offices of both the carriers and airport authority, but on the third level there is a restaurant capable of seating 340 people. (Templehof) The famous curved, canopied terminal fronts the main building which contains the usual concessions.

Spectators facilities: German airports are among the relative few still to possess a traditional terrace. Tegel has the roof of the hexagonal terminal allocated for this purpose, resulting in an excellent vantage point with the entrance to the left of the main building. Parked on the roof are a few items from the Air Classik Collection, the actual types on site changing from time to time as the aircraft are moved to and from other locations. Opening hours for the terrace are from 10.00 to 19.00 in the summer months, closing one hour earlier in the autumn. It is closed during the winter. A less mobile exhibit is the retired 707 painted as D-ABOC, alongside which is also a reasonable spot to view the movements. There are no facilities at Templehof, neither are there many vantage points.

Operators (Tegel): Scheduled services by Aeroflot (Tu-154), Aero Lloyd (DC-9), Air Algerie (Boeing 737), Air France (Airbus A300/320, Boeing 737), Air Portugal (Boeing 737), Alitalia (DC-9), Austrian Airlines (DC-9), British Airways (Boeing 737), Dan-Air (BAe 146, One-Eleven), Delta Air Lines (Boeing 767, TriStar), EuroBerlin (Boeing 737), Finnair (DC-9), Iberia (DC-9), Istanbul Airlines (Boeing 737), KLM (Boeing 737), Lufthansa (Airbus A310, Boeing 737), Olympic Airways (Boeing 727/737), SAS (DC-9), Swissair (DC-9), Turkish Airlines (Airbus A310), Trans World (Boeing 727) and United Airlines (Boeing 727).
Charter and IT operators: Aero Lloyd (DC-9), Air Berlin (Boeing 737), Air Charter (Boeing 737), Air Portugal (Boeing 737), British Airways (Boeing 737), Condor (Boeing 737), Dan-Air (Boeing 727/737,

One-Eleven), EuroBerlin (Boeing 737), German Air Cargo (Boeing 737/747, DC-8), Germania (Boeing 737), Hapag Lloyd (Airbus A310, Boeing 737), Istanbul Airlines (Boeing 737), Sultan Air (Boeing 737), Sun Express (Boeing 737) and Tunis Air (Boeing 737).

Operators (Templehof): Scheduled services by Berlin Spezialflug (Let 410), Crossair (Saab SF340), Delta Air (Saab SF340), Lufthansa (Boeing 737), Hamburg Airlines (Dash Eight), Lufthansa CityLine (Fokker 50), Interot Airways (Beech 1900), Luxair (Brasilia), NFD (ATR-42), RFG (ATR-42), RWL (Beech 1900) and Sabena (Brasilia).
Charters: Crossair (Saab SF340), Lufthansa CityLine (Fokker 50), and RFG (ATR-42).

Movements (1990) (Tegel): Total 106,068. Total passengers 6,719,684. These compare with the 1989 figures 98,878 and

5,951,885 respectively.

Movements (Jan-June 1991) (Templehof): Total 16,924. Total passengers 128,285. These compare with the figures for the same period in 1990 of 3,667 and 39,955 respectively.

Runways (Tegel): 08L/26R (9,918ft/3,023m), 08R/26L (7,953ft/2,424m).

Runways (Templehof): 09L/27R (6,865ft/2,093m), 09R/27L (6,942ft/2,116m).

Radio frequencies (Tegel): 118.7MHz, 119.7MHz (Tower), 119.3MHz, 132.65MHz (Departure), 121.75MHz (Ground).

Radio frequencies (Templehof): 122.1MHz (Tower), 119.3MHz, 132.65MHz (Departure), 121.9MHz (Ground).

Telephone: (Tegel) 4101-1. (Templehof) 6909-1.

Operated by: Berliner Flughafen-Gesellschaft mbH.

Boston (Logan International), Ma USA

Unlike many communities, Boston has its airport conveniently close to the city. It was on 8 September 1923 when a 189 acres of reclaimed mud flats were dedicated for the use of aviation. Originally the site was intended for the development of the local waterfront facilities, but this scheme was dropped in favour of the flying field. Two 1,500ft (457m) cinder runways were laid prior to the first landing by an aircraft of the 101st Squadron belonging to the Massachusetts National Guard. The event heralded the arrival of the entire unit because the area was leased to the US Government for five years until 1928. Prudently, an agreement was negotiated which ensured that private and commercial flying remained unaffected, so in 1927 the first scheduled passenger service began. Instigated by Colonial Air Transport, the regular flights linked Boston with New York.

By this time several hangars had been built on the growing airport, which, between 1928 and 1939, was operated by the Boston authorities. Through these years the Boston authorities maintained a programme of expansion using public funds for the purpose, but it eventually reached a stage when it could no longer carry the financial burden. Therefore in 1941 the State Department of Public Works assumed responsibility for operating and developing the facilities. Very quickly expansion began with the

help of more reclaimed land, until over 2,000 acres were available for the construction of a new apron, terminal buildings and large hangars for American, Eastern amd Northeast Airlines.

By 1959 most of the projects had been completed, including the new control tower and runway which had been added to the list at a late stage. However, in the process the Board had managed to accumulate debts of some $31 million, a situation not improved by the fact that passenger volume lagged far behind the growth of air transport generally. It was an opportune moment to hand over control to another operator, this time the Massachusetts Port Authority (Massport), itself created in 1956. During the same year Boston's airport had been officially renamed the Lieutenant General Edward Lawrence Logan International Airport, in memory of the officer's meritorious service in the military earlier in the century. Fortunately this title was quickly abbreviated to Logan. Massport launched a massive construction programme spread over almost 20 years. The International Terminal (now known as Terminal D) became the first reward for all the effort, followed by the North Terminal (C) in 1967. Two years later the Southwest Terminal (A) was ready for service, a year earlier than the Volpe International Terminal (E). Finally the contractors completed the South Terminal (B) in 1976, to mark the end of a lengthy phase in Logan's development. Elsewhere various accommodation was erected on land reclaimed from 90 acres of Boston harbour between 1964 and 1973.

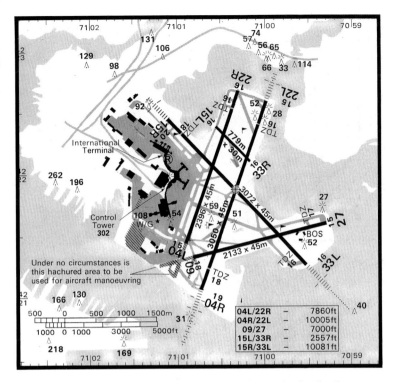

04L/22R	–	7860ft
04R/22L	–	10005ft
09/27	–	7000ft
15L/33R	–	2557ft
15R/33L	–	10081ft

Under no circumstances is this hachured area to be used for aircraft manoeuvring

International Terminal

Control Tower 302

The small airfield perched on some mud-flats in the 1920s has progressed a long way to become an important factor of New England's economy. In so doing it has become not only one of the nation's busiest airports, but has also achieved a similar status amongst those of the world.

Location and access: Situated 3 miles (5km) northeast of the city on a peninsula adjacent to Boston harbour. The Blue Line rapid transit system links the airport with the city centre every 10min or so. Shuttle buses offer a free journey between the airport station and all terminals with service 22 visiting Terminals A and B, while 33 calls at C, D and E in the course of its travels. In addition shuttle service 11 links all terminals but does not stop at the station. There is also a water shuttle between Logan and downtown Boston (Rowes Wharf) which runs every 15min. Free buses complete the journey from the airport boat dock and all terminals.
Terminals: Both B and C Terminals have two concourses projecting from the centre

two-level structure, but the other three consist of the main building only. Needless to say a vast selection of services are offered ranging from a Dunkin' Donut cart to a Legal Seafood market. These are mainly on the upper floors, with the exception of Terminal D. This building is used primarily by charter passengers who apparently do not warrant such pampering.
Spectator facilities: None specifically provided. As at many other locations, the Concourses' windows are equipped with tinted glass, but at least it is possible to observe many of the movements. During 1990 a rule that only ticketed passengers are allowed through the check-points at Logan effectively eliminates these opportunities. Good photographs can be obtained from Level 5 of the multi-storey car park located on top of Terminal B, with the choice of taxying and stationary subjects. There are few other suitable external vantage points due to the absence of public roads around the perimeter.
Operators: Aer Lingus (Boeing 747), Air Alliance (Dash Eight), Air Atlantic (Dash

Above:
Flagship Airlines operate the ATR-42 N144DD on American Eagle services into Boston.
A. S. Wright

Below:
Take-off shots at Boston are possible from the top of the car park as shown by the departure of the 727 N914TS with the Trump Shuttle. *A. S. Wright*

Eight), Air Canada (Boeing 727, DC-9), Air France (Boeing 747), Air Nova (Dash Eight), Air Portugal (Airbus A310), Alitalia (Boeing 747), American Airlines (Airbus A300, Boeing 727/757/767, DC-9), American Eagle (ATR-42, SD3-60), America West (Boeing 757), British Airways (Boeing 747/767), Canadian Airlines International (Dash Eight), Cape Air (Cessna 402), Continental Airlines (Boeing 727/737, DC-9), Delta Air Lines (Boeing 727/757/767, DC-9, TriStar), Delta Connection (Beech 1900, SD3-60, Saab SF340), El Al (Boeing 747), First Air (HS748), Lufthansa (Boeing 747, DC-10), Midwest Express (DC-9), Mohawk Airlines (Beech 1900), Northwest Airlines (Airbus A320, Boeing 747/757, DC-9/10), Northwest Airlink (Beech 1900, Metro), Precision Airlines (Dornier 228), Sabena (Boeing 747, DC-10), Swissair (Boeing 747, DC-10), Trans World (Boeing 727/767, DC-9, TriStar), Trans World Express (Saab SF340, Beech 1900), Trump (USAir) Shuttle (Boeing 727), United Airlines (Boeing 727/737/757) and USAir (Boeing 727/737, DC-9, Fellowship, Fokker 100, Friendship, Beech 1900).

Movements (1990): Total air transport 367,000. Total passengers 22,878,000.

Runways: 04L/22R (7,860ft/2,396m), 04R/22L (10,005ft/3,050m), 15L/33R (2,557ft/779m), 15R/33L (10,080ft/3,072m), 09/27 (7,000ft/2,134m).

Radio frequencies: 119.1MHz, 128.8MHz (Tower), 133.0MHz (Departure), 121.9MHz (Ground).

Telephone: (617) 561-1818.

Operated by: Massachusetts Port Authority.

Brussels National (Zaventem) Belgium

When constructed after the war, Brussels' new airport was known as Melsbroek, the name of a nearby village. At this stage the terminal was situated at the northern side of the field, but plans for the future development of the site proposed a parallel runway layout with the main buildings between them. Work proceeded apace and the new passenger terminal was duly opened on 29 June 1958 to be renamed Brussels National. Initially two piers, each with eight gates, extended from the central block, although provision was made at the outset for more to be added when required. Unfortunately fire destroyed much of the new accommodation in 1962 necessitating the use of temporary facilities until the rebuilt terminal was ready for use once again.

In 1973 a satellite spur was added towards the south, linked to the main area by an elevated walkway equipped with travelators. Airbridges were installed on this new circular extension which was sufficient to contain the growth at the airport until the late 1980s. Land limitations restrict the ability to expand to some extent, but the first stages of a long-term development programme, designed to handle the forecast traffic of 20 million passengers by the early 21st century, are now underway. Two new concourses in the centre area will be linked to each other and the main terminal building by travelators. Their completion will permit the long overdue refurbishment of the exist-ing facilities in the mid-1990s, followed by the provision of a third concourse to replace the satellite.

The entire complex will be served by the existing three runways which are considered to be adequate for the foreseeable future. However, all will be upgraded by the addition of a number of fast exits, together with parallel taxiways where appropriate. There is a remote possibility that a fourth runway could be built to the south, but this is very much a long-term prospect and would not be a popular decision.

In common with all other airports, Brussels has its professional group of protestors ready to oppose any expansion. During the summer of 1991, they were successful in forcing a ban on all night movements, a mortal blow indeed to the overnight courier companies dependent upon the hub for the exchange of parcels, etc. Plans are already in hand to contain any noise by the erection of either concrete walls or earth banks at strategic points around the perimeter.

Some of the growth at Brussels has been created by the presence in the city of the administrative headquarters of the European Economic Community, an organisation which is expected to become even more active after 1992. Another factor has been the airport's emergence as an important centre for air freight in recent years. A large cargo centre was built at the beginning of the 1980s which has since become responsible for the steady increase in tonnage handled. Chosen by Federal Express for its European hub, the airport is regularly visited by the American parcels carrier which routes its eastbound DC-10 sorties via Stansted to drop off items destined for the UK. Mean-

Restricted views are possible from the terminal at Brussels, but sometimes the subject is too close as with the TEA 737-3M8 OO-LTM. *AJW*

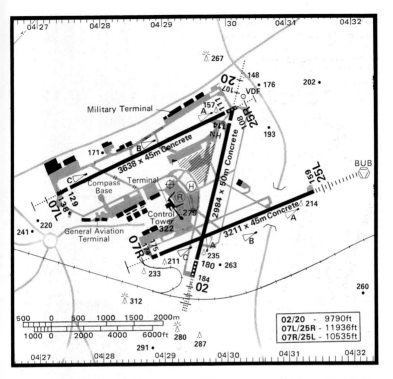

Map labels:

04|27 04|28 04|29 30 04|31 04|32

267

20
148 • 176 202 •
107 VDF

Military Terminal
157
A 111
114
HN
193
25R

171 •
B
3638 × 45m Concrete
159
25L
BUB

C
138
129
Compass Base
Terminal
H
214
2984 × 50m Concrete
A

07L
241 • 220
General Aviation Terminal
Control Tower
279
R
322
3211 × 45m Concrete
B
A

07R
175
A
235
C
180 • 263
211
233
184
02

312

500 0 500 1000 1500 2000m
1000 0 2000 4000 6000ft
280
287
291 •
260 •

02/20 - 9790ft
07L/25R - 11936ft
07R/25L - 10535ft

04|27 04|28 04|29 04|30 04|31 04|32

---

while feeder services ensure that consignments for the return trip are assembled in readiness for the transatlantic journey. DHL is another company conducting a similar European operation from Brussels, but in this case a fleet of Convair 580s provides the transport.

Location and access: Situated 8 miles (13km) northeast of the city. Adjacent to the Brussels ring road and the interchange with the E10 motorway to Antwerp and beyond, the airport is easily reached by private or public transport. A rail link with the city's North and Central stations takes 14min and 18min respectively. SNCV bus route 578BZ from North station travels via Diegem taking about 35min for the trip, whereas the 358 and 358B visit Woluwe on their way to the airport which is reached after an elapsed time of 45min. Other direct bus services are available from Antwerp, Ghent and Liege.

Terminal: One large building with two levels; one devoted to each of arrivals and departures with the latter floor containing most of the facilities. Prices are high in the buffets, so either a period of fasting is to be recommended or suitable snacks should be acquired before arrival at the terminal. Another surprise can await the unsuspecting in the toilet area since the female attendants clean the premises regardless of the occupants.

Spectator facilities: None specifically provided nowadays. A number of aircraft stands can be seen through the glass overlooking the apron, but this restricted view is virtually useless for photography. Europe's, if not the world's, largest collection of sticky fingermarks is to be found at this location which unfortunately appears to have been removed from any cleaning programme. In any case the entire area is usually congested and hot. There are several spots around the perimeter of the field which offer better prospects than anywhere in or near the terminal. One of these is by the threshold of 25L which is reached from the village of Kortenburg situated to the south of the airport. Good landing shots can be obtained. Such vantage points may disappear in the near future due to the erection of earth banks and the planting of shrubs and trees in order to forestall any native uprisings against noise.

Operators: Scheduled services by Aeroflot (Tu-154, IL-86), Aer Lingus (Boeing 737, Fokker 50), Air Algerie (Boeing 737), Air France (Boeing 727/737, Fellowship), Air Littoral (Brasilia), Air Meuse (Brasilia), Air Portugal (Airbus A310), Air Vendee (King Air), Air Zaire (DC-10), Alitalia (DC-9), American Airlines (Boeing 767), Austrian Airlines (DC-9), Balkan (Tu-134), British Airways (BAe ATP, Airbus A320, Boeing 737/757, One-Eleven), British Midland (BAe ATP), Brymon Airways (Dash Seven), Crossair (Saab SF340), Cubana (IL-62), Czechoslovak Airlines (Tu-134), Delta Air Transport (Fellowship, Brasilia, BAe 146), El Al (Boeing 737/757/767), Egyptair (Airbus A300, Boeing 767), European Air Transport (Convair 580, Metro), Finnair (DC-9), Garuda (Boeing 747), Iberia (Airbus A320, Boeing 727, DC-9), KLM CityHopper (Saab SF340, Fokker 50), Lineas Aereas Paraguayas (Boeing 707, DC-8), Lufthansa CityLine (Metro, Fokker 50), Lufthansa (Airbus A310/320, Boeing 727/737), Luxair (Brasilia, Fokker 50), Malaysian Airlines System (Boeing 747, DC-10), Malev (Boeing 737, Tu-134/154), Middle East Airlines (Boeing 707), Nationair (Boeing 747/757, DC-8), NFD (Metro, ATR-42), Olympic Airways (Boeing 727/737), Polish Airlines (Tu-134/154), Royal Air Maroc (Boeing 727), Royal Jordanian (Airbus A310), Sabena (DC-10, Boeing 737/747, Airbus A310), SAS (DC-9), Schreiner Airways (Dash Eight), Singapore Airlines (Boeing 747), South African Airways (Boeing 747), Swissair (DC-9, Fokker 50/100), Tarom (Tu-134/154, One-Eleven), Trans World (Boeing 767), Tunis Air (Boeing 727/737), Turkish Airlines (Boeing 727, Airbus A310), United Airlines (Boeing 767) and Yugoslav Airlines (Boeing 737, DC-9).

Charter and IT operators: Air Belgium (Boeing 737), Delta Air Transport (Fellowship), Sobelair (Boeing 737) and Euro Belgian Airlines (Boeing 737).

Movements (1990): Total air transport 100,000. Total passengers 8,025,000.

Runways: 07L/25R (11,936ft/3,638m), 07R/25L (10,535ft/3,211m), 02/20 (9,970ft/2,984m).

Radio frequencies: 118.6MHz (Tower), 127.15MHz (Departure), 121.875MHz (Ground).

Telephone: (02)-722311.

Operated by: Brussels Airport Authority.

Chicago (Midway), II USA

From modest beginnings as an air park in the early 1920s, the site was rapidly developed after officially becoming Chicago Municipal Airport in December 1927. There were five grass runways available, each equipped with up-to-date lighting for night operations, while no fewer than 12 hangars had been built by 1928. Scheduled airlines were beginning to develop so by the early 1930s United, American, Trans World, Eastern, Northwest, Chicago and Southern, Braniff and Pennsylvania Central were all serving the city. Between 1935 and 1941 the continued airport improvement programme had dealt with drainage, lighting, parking areas and runway extensions, the latter necessitating the removal of a railway track inconveniently bisecting the field. Even in 1936 there were 114 scheduled flights per day, so it is not surprising that Municipal was unquestionably the world's busiest airport at that date.

On 30 June 1941 the modernised facilities were unveiled to reveal that there were now four pairs of parallel runways to permit simultaneous arrivals and departures on the strips that ranged in length from 5,275ft (1,608m) to 7,438ft (2,267m). World War 2 brought increased activity with military movements added to the commercial traffic, while the Army Air Corps unit already in occupation became the Illinois National Guard and moved to Orchard Place to the northwest of Chicago. Thereafter its main occupation was to tow targets over Lake Michigan for the benefit of trainee airgunners.

After the war a new terminal building was opened together with a modern control tower which then became the responsibility of the FAA instead of the military. It was also decided to rename the airport, so after 22 years Chicago Municipal was dropped in favour of Chicago Midway to commemorate the famous wartime battle in the south Pacific.

By 1959 Midway was served by 19 scheduled carriers and enjoyed its busiest year to date when handling 10,040,353 passengers. However, it was not to last. The jet types being delivered needed longer runways and these were already available at rival O'Hare. The latter proved too great an attraction for the airlines so with almost

Above:
Bizjets such as Citation N60JD can be easily photographed at Chicago/Midway. *A. S. Wright*

Below:
Seen at Chicago/Midway, this 737-2T4 was leased from GPA as EI-BRN but was later reregistered N703ML. *A. S. Wright*

indecent haste operations were transferred. Symbolically, on 9 July 1962, United became the last to leave Midway having been the first to arrive at the old Municipal many years earlier.

A lengthy period of relative quiet began, although throughout the 1960s the authorities tried to stir up some interest in the little-used complex. After much effort United was persuaded to return, but the carrier's stay was short-lived because the 1973 oil crisis ended all new projects. Another five years or so passed before deregulation produced the locally-based newcomer, Midway Airlines, which began commercial services on 1 November 1979. Initially four cities were served by the carrier's three DC-9s, but both the fleet and route network rapidly expanded during the first year. After an unsuccessful venture trading as Midway Express and Midway Metrolink in 1984, the company reverted to its original title one year later, by which time 22 cities were linked to the Chicago hub. Commuter services using 19-seat Dornier 228s were introduced in 1987 under the marketing name of Midway Connection, a development which further increased the traffic passing through Midway Airport.

Meanwhile O'Hare was beginning to show signs of strain. Through the years, proposals to provide additional runways had always brought successful lawsuits from the surrounding suburbs, part of the settlements invariably stipulating that no such work could be undertaken before mid-1995. Some relief could undoubtedly come from greater utilisation of Midway which still has ample spare capacity. However, limitations on runway length will not permit the large types, such as wide-bodies, to use the facility, while its built-up urban surroundings prevents any thought of expansion without a major political and legal battle. Any improvements at the airport must therefore remain within the present boundaries although this still leaves ample scope. There has been a suggestion that the construction of a brand new airport for Chicago would mean the closure of Midway due to conflicting traffic patterns. This depends largely upon the eventual choice of the location, but in any case both of the existing facilities will have to cope with the city's air transport business for the next 20 years or so.

Location and access: Situated 10 miles (16km) southwest of Chicago and 15 miles (24km) southeast of O'Hare airport. There are bus services to the city and a coach link between Midway and O'Hare. The road access to the airport has been modernised and additional parking facilities provided. A free courtesy bus runs between the long-term park and the terminal every 15min. A more convenient method of reaching Midway was due to be introduced in October 1992 with the completion of the Transport Authority's new elevated rapid transit system to downtown Chicago. Access from the airport station to the terminal is via a bridge with a travelator.

Terminal: The main building has three concourses projecting from its west and south-facing sides. All the necessary concessions are to be found including a shop, restaurants and a bank. On an average day the building handles 23,300 passengers with peaks on Fridays and Sundays.

Spectator facilities: None provided. Views through the concourse windows are not particularly exciting, neither is photography easy. There are various vantage points around the square plot some of which give excellent opportunities for landing and taxying shots plus reasonable views of the general and light aviation aprons.

Operators: Scheduled services by ComAir (Saab SF340, Brazilia), Direct Air (Metro), Northwest Airlines (DC-9), Southwest Airlines (Boeing 737), United Airlines (Boeing 727), USAir (Fokker 100), USAir Express (Jetstream). There are approximately 200 general aviation aircraft based at Midway.

Movements (1990): Total air transport 128,000. Total passengers 8,541,000.

Runways: 04L/22R (5,509ft/1,679m), 04R/22L (6,102ft/1,860m), 13L/31R (5,078ft/1,548m), 13R/31L (6,519ft/1,987m).

Radio frequencies: 118.7MHz (Tower), 121.7MHz (Ground).

Telephone: (312) 767-0500.

Operated by: Chicago Department of Aviation.

Chicago (O'Hare),
II USA

During World War 2 the farm land to the northwest of Chicago was earmarked for the construction of an assembly plant under the control of the Douglas Aircraft Corporation. Allocated the name Orchard Place, work started on the site in June 1942 and included the erection of the largest wooden-roofed building in the world. When com-

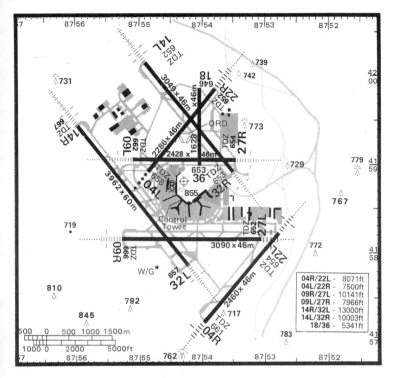

pleted in August 1943, the factory began production of C-54 transports, 655 of which were assembled and delivered before the facility was closed in 1945. Although the military retained part the main buildings, it was prepared to release over 1,000 acres for redevelopment, an offer quickly taken up by the Chicago City Council which had already been studying various options for a second field to augment the Municipal Airport, later renamed Midway. After more land acquisition, reconstruction began in earnest at Orchard Place with new aprons, taxiways and terminal buildings included.

In June 1949, the new airport officially became known as O'Hare in honour of Lt-Cdr Edward H. O'Hare, a local naval officer killed in action in 1943 after shooting down five aircraft. Interestingly the association with Orchard Place has been retained by the continued use of the identifying code ORD. Officially Chicago's new airport opened in 1955, but by this time O'Hare had already handled some 900,000 movements and 2 million passengers. One year later there were 17 airlines operating into the air-

port, a growing total which included several foreign carriers.

It soon became apparent that to cope with the forecast traffic increases, some extensive expansion was necessary. A new international terminal was opened in August 1958, the occasion being marked by the arrival of a TWA flight non-stop from Paris. This was only the start of the programme which included runways, hangars, additional terminal buildings and numerous support facilities. The first stage in O'Hare's development was completed in 1961 and in the following year all scheduled services were transferred from Midway thereby elevating its replacement into the status of the world's busiest airport.

Although the runways could generally handle the traffic, by the mid-1970s the passenger accommodation was becoming congested at peak times. A development team was appointed to consider methods by which the growing problem could be alleviated, with the result that a Master Plan was produced to cover the years until 1995. Once approved, no time was lost in action-

United DC-10s are to be found at Chicago/O'Hare, this example being N1833U. *A. S. Wright*

ing the proposals which commenced with a new concourse for Delta. This was completed in 1984 and was followed by the interim International Terminal 4 and the United Airlines' 'Terminal for Tomorrow'. By February 1991, 83% of the improvements listed in the 1982 plan had been introduced with the remainder either underway or in the detailed planning stage. Construction of the new International Terminal 5 began in July 1990, with its scheduled completion in February 1993 marking the conclusion of O'Hare's major expansion work for the time being. Meanwhile the creation of a Cargo City has been underway since the summer of 1985, with many of the individual carrier's already installed in their premises. However, facilities for Air France, Japan Airlines and Lufthansa were still on paper in early 1991, but construction was due to start in the spring.

For over 25 years, O'Hare has remained the commercial aviation capital of the world and the hub of national air transport in the US. Some 170,000 passengers are handled each day which amounts to over 60 million per annum. There are an average of 110 aircraft movements every hour, many of which are those of the 50 or so airlines using the airport on a regular basis. Impressive statistics indeed.

Location and access: Situated 21 miles (35km) northwest of the city. Chicago Transport Authority runs an elevated subway train service to link Downtown (The Loop) with the airport taking 35min for the journey. Greyhound Airport Express bus services operate from a number of towns and cities in the vicinity. Needless to say there are numerous car parks, but visitors are encouraged to use the remote sites from which courtesy buses run to the central area. These operate about every 15min and take 5min for the trip. They are due to be replaced by a high-speed transit system in mid-1992 which will include three miles of elevated guideway and six station stops. It is designed to promote further the use of the more distant car parks and decrease the number of private vehicles in the central core terminal roadway.

Terminals: Terminal 1 (United Airlines' 'Terminal for Tomorrow') consists of two parallel concourses, each making extensive use of glass both for decorative and light-giving purposes. The buildings are joined by a tunnel equipped with a 815ft-long travelator. Built on the site of the original International Terminal 1, the facility was designed for passenger convenience and efficient aircraft movement. Terminals 2 and 3 are both used for domestic passengers while Terminal 4 is now employed for international traffic. No airbridges are provided so all arriving and departing travellers are conveyed by wide-bodied buses to and from the aircraft stands. This building will be replaced by the new 20-gate Terminal 5 when it is opened in the summer of 1993.

Spectator facilities: None specifically provided, but good views of most movements are possible through the glass from within the various terminals. This also applies to photographs which can be adversely affected by reflections. Such is the size of the complex that a considerable amount of walking is involved with many movements inevitably missed while in transit. An airport tour programme is offered, but normally reservations have to be made by groups of at least 20 people one month in advance. However it is possible to negotiate at short notice. Some good vantage points are to be found around the airport which are suitable for taxiway and runway shots.

Operators: Scheduled services by Aer Lingus (Boeing 747), Air Canada (Boeing 727, DC-9), Air France (Airbus A310), Alitalia (Boeing 747), American Airlines (Boeing 727/757/767, DC-9/10), American Eagle (Short SD3-60, ATR-42), America West (Boeing 737/757), British Airways (Boeing 747), Continental Airlines (Boeing 727/737, DC-9), Delta Air Lines (Boeing 727, Saab SF340, TriStar), Ecuatoriana (Boeing 707), El Al (Boeing 747), Great Lakes (Beech 1900), Iberia (Boeing 747), Japan Airlines (Boeing 747), KLM (Boeing 747), Korean Air (Boeing 747), Polish Airlines (Boeing 767), Lufthansa (Boeing 747, DC-10), Mexicana (Boeing 727), Northwest Airlines (Airbus A320, Boeing 727/747/757, DC-9, Friendship), Polish Airlines (Boeing 767), Sabena (DC-10), SAS (Boeing 767), Sun Country (Boeing 727), Swissair (Boeing 747, DC-10), Trans World (Boeing 727/747 DC-9, TriStar), United Airlines (Boeing 727/737/747/757/767, DC-8/10), United Express (BAe 146, ATP, Friendship), USAir (Boeing 737, DC-9, Fokker 100, Fellowship), Varig (DC-10) and Yugoslav Airlines (DC-10).
Cargo flights: Airborne Express (DC-9), DHL (Boeing 727), Emery Worldwide (Boeing 727, DC-8), Federal Express (Boeing 727, DC-10), Mountain Air (Short SD3-30), Nippon Air Cargo (Boeing 747), Qantas (Boeing 747), Southern Air (Hercules, DC-8), United Parcel Service (Boeing 757, DC-8) and Zantop (Convair 640, Electra).
Movements (1990): Total air transport 657,600. Total passengers 60,118,000.
Runways: 04L/22R (7,500ft/2,286m),

Above:
Air Wisconsin uses 146s on services into Chicago/O'Hare on behalf of United Express, although N604AW is no longer in its fleet. *A. S. Wright*

Below:
Executive types mingle with the airliners at O'Hare, this Gulfstream being N684FM. *A. S. Wright*

04R/22L (8,071ft/2,460m), 09L/27R (7,966ft/2,428m), 09R/27L (10,141ft/3,090m), 14L/32R (10,003ft/3,049m), 14R/32L (13,000ft/3,962m), 18/36 (5,341ft/1,628m).
Radio frequencies: 126.9MHz (Tower north), 120.75MHz (Tower south),

125.0MHz, 125.4MHz, 127.4MHz (Departure), 121.675MHz, 121.75MHz, 121.9MHz (Ground).
Telephone: (312) 686-2200.
Operated by: Chicago Department of Aviation.

Cologne/Bonn
Germany

Aviation received enthusiastic support in Germany from the very early days, with many cities anxious to be associated with this new form of transport. Consequently when the first Zeppelin airship cruised over Cologne on 9 August 1909 it caused considerable excitement resulting in the local officials seeking an agreement with the operating company, Deutschen Luftschiffahrts, to ensure that the city was included in the airship's services. Nevertheless there were problems to overcome because the military authorities objected to the slow moving machines passing over the district.

Progress could not be halted and in 1911 the city announced its plans for the construction of a permanent airfield at Butzweilerhof. However, on 15 September 1912, the land was leased to the military but the change did not mean an end to the site's aviation connection. In fact after a grass strip was prepared and various buildings erected, units of Fliegerbataillon 3 moved into what was now an airfield. When the war began both ground and flying crew were trained at the base, an occupation which ended with the signing of the armistice in

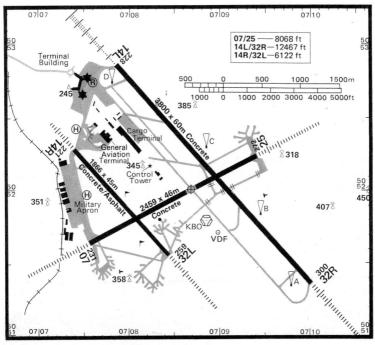

November 1918. For the next few years Butzweilerhof was in the hands of the British occupation forces, but at last the troops departed on 1 January 1926 allowing the city to take over the airfield for development.

Within a short time there were regular flights between Cologne and destinations in Britain, France and Switzerland in sufficient numbers to justify expansion. On 23 April 1935 a start was made on the construction of new buildings which duly became ready for operations about one year later, in July 1936. By the standards of the day, Cologne now had a world-class airport, attracting more than half of all the aircraft movements in the Rhineland-Westphalia region. As an international centre, it tied with Berlin as the second largest in Germany, Frankfurt taking the premier position.

Once again war interrupted Cologne's progess and later occupation forces took control as they had done many years before. For some reason the city was excluded from the immediate postwar aviation expansion, but during the late 1940s it became necessary to reconsider the district's economic situation. Links with national and international markets were essential so the city's officials began negotiations to win approval for an airport to serve jointly Cologne and the newly-created federal capital at Bonn. Eventually the Civil Aviation Board of the occupying forces issued a licence for the combined use of Wahn by the two cities. Before the war the area had been an artillery range, but in 1938 it was converted into an airfield for the Luftwaffe, its operators until taken over by the allies in 1945 whereupon it became an active RAF fighter base.

Initially consent had been given for only one year which did not give a great deal of security. Although the administration of the fledgling airport passed into German hands on 1 February 1951, development was halted early in 1952 when once again the facilities reverted to British control. This situation lasted until 1957 when finally, on 18 July, the site was handed over for the use of civil aviation. Being associated with Bonn meant that many international movements could be expected, so a programme of improvements was begun in 1958 to allow the airport to handle the largest of the new range of airliners then coming into service. By the mid-1960s traffic was out-growing the terminal capacity resulting in the construction of a new building which was eventually opened on 20 March 1970.

An interesting design was chosen to incorporate several novel features. Instead of one large hall for the completion of formalities, passengers pass directly to one of two star-shaped satellites each containing six gates complete with their own check-in desk. Even the main six-storey building succeeds in avoiding the rectangular box arrangement so often found. Instead each floor is stepped back to give an attractive sloping effect, a design continued by the two angled side wings although these have only four levels. By avoiding the conventional layouts at the planning stage, Cologne/Bonn has made the arrival and departure processes much easier for travellers. It also has the benefit of keeping aircraft turn-around times to a minimum since everything is accomplished as close as possible to the appropriate gate. Due allowance was made in the early stages for future expansion when the traffic exceeded the 3.5 million passengers capacity of the airport. Two additional satellites will be built and connected to the two side wings of the terminal, but this point has still to be reached. However, this may be earlier than anticipated if some services are diverted from Düsseldorf in order to relieve the latter's busier facilities.

In addition to the civil activities, the Luftwaffe's transport fleet is also in evidence. Germany now has an enviable selection of airports built to imaginative designs for practical efficiency and appearance, Cologne/Bonn certainly maintaining the trend.

Location and access: Situated 9 miles (14km) southeast of Cologne and 12 miles (20km) north of Bonn with a direct spur from the motorway linking the two cities. Car parks are arranged conveniently for each level of the terminal Express bus route 170 runs regularly from Cologne Central Station with a journey time of 20min. It takes 25min for bus service 670 to travel from Bonn Main Station to the airport, a trip undertaken every 30min.

Terminal: Shops and refreshment facilities are located on both levels, all being within easy reach.

Spectator facilities: An open-air terrace extending along the front of the building has been much reduced in size to leave only a small area available at the end. From this often congested vantage point it is possible to photograph aircraft on the apron, but this view is also possible from within the terminal, a spot which is less crowded although fronted by tinted glass. Ideally Runway 14L needs to be in use to justify a visit because all taxying traffic then passes the main building.

Operators: Scheduled services by Air France (ATR-42, Boeing 737), Alitalia (DC-9), Avianova (ATR-42), British Airways (Airbus A320, Boeing 737, One-Eleven), Crossair (Saab SF340, Fokker 50), Cubana

(IL-62), Delta Air (Saab SF340), El Al (Boeing 757), EuroBerlin (Boeing 737), Interot Airways (Dash Eight, Beech 1900), Lufthansa (Airbus A300/310/320, Boeing 737), Lufthansa CityLine (Fokker 50), Maersk (Fokker 50), Malev (Boeing 737), NFD (Dornier 228, Metro, ATR-42), Polish Airlines (Tu-134/154), Sun-Air (Bandeirante, Jetstream), Swissair (DC-9, Fokker 100), TAS Airways (Gulfstream 1) and Turkish Airlines (Airbus A310, Boeing 727).
Charter and IT operators: Aero Lloyd (DC-9), Air Atlantis (Boeing 737), Air Charter (Boeing 737), Air Malta (Boeing 737), American Trans Air (TriStar), Arkia (Boeing 707), Balkan (Tu-154), Condor (Boeing 737/757, Airbus A310), Germania (Boeing 737), Hapag-Lloyd (Boeing 737, Airbus A310), LTE International (Boeing 757), Malev (Tu-154), Tarom (IL-62) and Yugoslav Airlines (Boeing 727, DC-9).
Movements (1990): Total air transport 98,900. Total passengers 3,087,000.
Runways: 14L/32R (12,467ft/3,800m), 14R/32L (6,122ft/1,866m), 07/25 (8,068ft/2,459m).
Radio frequencies: 118.9MHz, 120.5MHz (Tower), 120.25MHz (Approach), 121.05MHz (Radar), 121.85MHz (Ground).
Telephone: 0 22 02/401.
Operated by: Flughafen Köln/Bonn GmBH.

Copenhagen (Kastrup) Denmark

A field only one mile or so from Copenhagen's Town Hall Square was used as an aerodrome in the days before World War 1. Located at Klovermarken near Christianhavn, the rudimentary facilities served both military and civil flying needs until the 1920s. Even by the beginning of that decade the authorities had become resigned to the fact that the site was too small and that another location was needed for a new airport. Some farmland in Kastrup on the east side of the island of Amager was considered satisfactory for the purpose, especially since it also lent itself to the operation of both flying boats and airships.

On 20 April 1925 Kastrup was opened to become the world's first exclusively civil airport. An interesting terminal building was constructed entirely of wood with a red tiled roof, quickly becoming known as the 'wooden castle' or 'summer house'. The latter was particularly appropriate because flying normally only took place during the summer months and even then was restricted to the periodic spells of fine weather conditions. As intended, a quay was provided for waterborne machines although its use was strictly limited. Between 1925 and 1932 the build-up of traffic was gradual, but from this point until the outbreak of World War 2 there was a sharp upturn in movements. From a total of 6,000 in the early 1930s, by 1939 the figure had risen to 50,000.

As early as 1936 it became obvious to the planners that the airport was too small, especially since it had become the focal point for aviation in northern Europe. Consequently following a design competition, a brand new terminal was built in time for opening in April 1939. Unfortunately it was barely a year later that the Germans took possession, although a small number of civil movements continued on routes to Sweden, Berlin and Vienna. During this period a concrete strip some 4,600ft (1,400m) long was laid to become the airport's first hard runway. Before the end of the war another three had joined this pioneer; a system of taxiways ensuring that Kastrup was a fully up-to-date international centre when the occupation ended in 1945. Fortunately the airport had suffered little damage, so it was soon ready for the new challenges.

Trans-Atlantic services were started in 1946 by the newly-formed Scandinvian Airlines System, thereby helping to boost traffic still further. Kastrup had become the third busiest airport in Europe by 1947, achieving a figure of 280,000 pasengers per year. Terminal extensions kept the construction industry busy, because no sooner was one project completed then it was inadequate. One of the most ambitious programmes was begun in 1956 with lengthened runways, an entirely new terminal and numerous other improvements incorporating modern technology. It all restored Copenghagen's airport to its position as the most advanced in Europe. Nevertheless it was necessary to construct two separate terminals later in the 1960s; one for domestic use in 1969 and the second to serve as an arrivals hall from 1971. Another runway was also laid parallel to 04/22 to permit simultaneous landings and take-offs since these had aready risen to 180,000 per year despite the use of larger aircraft types.

Throughout the 1970s there was no further expansion because plans were already well advanced for the construction of a new airport on the island of Saltholm to the east of Amager. Before a start could be made on its provision, a committee was set up to

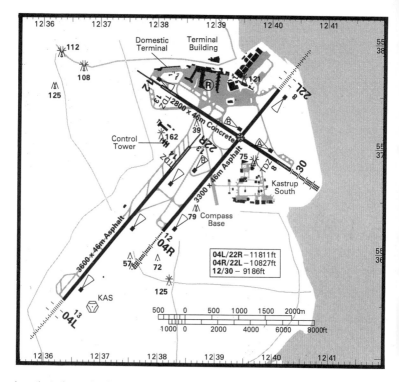

investigate the merits of the project which by now appeared to be somewhat unnecessary in view of the traffic figures being appreciably lower than forecast. As is often the case, the scheme was therefore suspended indefinitely, with Kastrup remaining the international airport for Denmark's capital city. There was no need to alter the runway system which was quite capable of coping with even the 22 million passengers forecast for the year 2000. Building extensions were also straightforward, so the conclusion reached was that it was far cheaper to retain the well-established facility rather than spend an astronomical sum on the conversion of an uninhabited island.

Accordingly work started on a modernised transit hall during 1982/83, followed in the next two years by the rebuilding of Pier C to make it suitable for the handling of wide-bodied aircraft. Financial restraints created a delay in the programme, but eventually a new Pier B was constructed in the 1980s, while 1989 saw a new domestic terminal built alongside the existing facility. Useful improvements were made on the

landside by redesigning the road system and parking area, the surrounds becoming the home for numerous shrubs and trees during a planting spree. Elsewhere a new cargo centre began to take shape on the eastern perimeter in 1989, which was due to be joined by two other units for DHL and SAS in 1992. There are plans outstanding for Pier A to be replaced, followed by the construction of a fourth pier (D) and a second international departure terminal in the future.

Location and access: Situated 6 miles (10km) southeast of Copenhagen. A shuttle bus links the terminal with the city centre (Central Station) every 15min. There are six other public bus routes including Hovedstadens Trafikselskab service 32 which runs from the city centre to the airport with a journey time of 30mins. A direct rail link is to be provided in the future.
Terminal: There are 18 restaurants, buffets and bars shared by the two terminals. Also within the complex are 30 shops plus the usual banks and service centres.

42

Spectators facilities: Another airport that possesses a long-closed roof terrace. In this case there are no real alternatives and very little can be seen of airside activities unless a passenger. Once through the security checks, there are numerous spots for viewing and photography available so an early check-in is sensible. Away from the terminal complex, an excellent vantage point exists within the grounds of a cafe, although a 45min walk is required. It is reached by bearing left from the airport along the main road until the first access is reached. At this point another left turn followed by more walking will eventually produce the welcome sight of the refreshment emporium. It is suitable for viewing or photography. While many of the movements are carried out by SAS, those of the Scandinavian charter companies such as Maersk, Conair and Sterling also contribute to the statistics.

Operators: Scheduled services by Aer Lingus (Boeing 737), Aeroflot (Tu-134/154, IL-62), Air France (Airbus A320, Boeing 727/737, Fellowship), Air Malta (Boeing 737), Air Portugal (Boeing 737), Alitalia (DC-9), Atlanta Icelandic (Boeing 737), Atlantic Airways (BAe 146), Austrian Airlines (DC-9), Balkan (Tu-134/154), Birmingham European (One-Eleven), British Airways (One-Eleven, Boeing 737/757), Business Flight (Beech 1900), Canadian Airlines (Boeing 767), Cimber Air (Nord 262, ATR-42), Czechoslovak Airlines (Tu-134/154), Egyptair (Boeing 767), El Al (Boeing 737/757), Finnair (DC-9), Golden Air (Metro, Saab SF340), Iberia (DC-9, Boeing 727), Icelandair (Boeing 737), Iraqi Air (Boeing 727), Japan Air Lines (Boeing 747), Kenya Airways (Boeing 757), KLM (Boeing 737, Airbus A310), Linhas Aereas de Mozambique (DC-10), Lufthansa (Airbus A310/320, Boeing 727/737), Lufthansa CityLine (Fokker 50, Dash Eight), Luxair (Fokker 50), Maersk Air (Boeing 737, Fokker 50), Malev (Boeing 737), Middle East Airlines (Boeing 707), Midtfly (Metro), Muk Air (Bandeirante, SD3-30, Metro), Norsk Air (Brasilia), Northwest Airlines (Boeing 747), Olympic Airways (Boeing 737), Pakistan International (Boeing 747), Polish Airlines (Tu-134/154), Royal Air Maroc (Boeing 737), Royal Jordanian (Airbus A310), Sabena (Boeing 737), Salair (Saab SF340), SAS (Friendship, Fokker 50, DC-9, Boeing 767), Singapore International (Boeing 747), Sterling Airways (Caravelle, DC-9), Swissair (DC-9), Swedair (Saab SF340), Syrian Arab (Boeing 727), Tarom (Tu-154, One-Eleven), Thai International (Boeing 747), Tower Air (Boeing 747), Trans World (TriStar), Tunis Air (Boeing 737), Turkish Airlines (Boeing 727), Varig (Boeing 747) and Yugoslav Airlines (Boeing 727/ 737).

Regular charter and IT operators: Business Flight (Beech 1900, Friendship), Conair (Airbus A320), Maersk Air (Boeing 737), SAS (DC-9), Scanair (DC-10), Star Air (Friendship), Sterling Airways (Caravelle, Boeing 727/757) and Transwede (DC-9).

Movements (1990): Total 212,712. Total passengers 12,473,667. These compare with the 1989 figures of 212,979 and 12,456,190 respectively.

Runways: 04L/22R (11,811ft/3,600m), 04R/22L (10,827ft/3,300m),12/30 (9,186ft/2,800m).

Radio frequencies: 118.1MHz, 118.575MHz, 119.9MHz, 121.6MHz (Tower), 119.8MHz (Approach), 120.25MHz (Departure), 121.9MHz (Apron)

Telephone: 45 31 50 93 33.

Operated by: Copenhagen Airports Authority.

Dallas/Fort Worth International, Tx USA

It is a well known fact that Texas is a large State, so if any problems existed for the airport planners it was not the lack of space. Although the close proximity of the two cities made the idea of a joint facility a logical step to take, in the first instance both Fort Worth and Dallas developed separate sites. The former began to construct Meacham Field for commercial purposes in 1927, an example followed by its neighbour a year later when it purchased Love Field from the military. When both cities sought financial support from the government in the early 1940s, the latter once again indicated that it would prefer a combined approach, but no action was taken. During the next 20 years or so both airports steadily grew, until in 1961 the subject of a new jointly controlled airport was revived. This time the Federal authorities were more positive in their comments which led to some detailed talks between the interested parties. There seemed a marked reluctance to end these meetings, because another four years elapsed before agreement was reached to pave the way for the Dallas/Fort Worth (DFW) Regional Airport Board to be created. Once this was set-

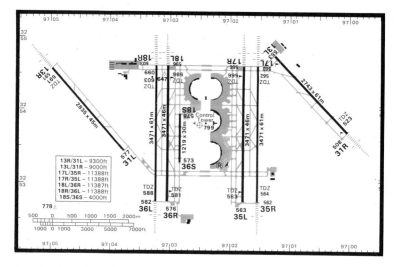

tled it then took a further three years to prise the necessary funds from the Texas coffers. Eventually work began on the site in December 1968, the first phase becoming operational five years later on 13 January 1974.

At least the designers were able to learn from the experiences of other major complexes when considering the options. A vast area was allocated to them, much of it reserved for future expansion, but for the first stage three runways were laid with four semi-circular terminal buildings located either side of a main multi-carriageway spine road. Ultimately the long-term plans made provision for 13 terminals and 11 runways so that the forecast traffic could be handled at the rate of 178 movements per hour. In the event, with the help of some extensions the original buildings proved adequate during the airport's first 17 years, although the number of runways doubled in the same period. Already the largest airport in the US, by 1989 it had passed Atlanta in terms of passenger totals to become number two to Chicago O'Hare.

Both American and Delta have established hubs at DFW which generate a considerable proportion of the airport's business. In an effort to maintain its policy for providing superior services, the Airport Board decided that American needed to be relocated from its present facilities in Terminals 2 and 3 on the east side, to a new concourse complex to the west. On completion of the first stage there will be 55 gates available, but this number will eventually reach 102 at the conclusion of the development in 1996. Delta's increased traffic has necessitated the airline adding a nine-gate satellite to its existing Terminal 4 accommodation.

In order to keep pace with this growth, plans for two additional runways were prepared in 1989. The first of these was due to be in service during 1992, while its partner's introduction is provisionally set for 1997, although this date was left flexible to meet any unforeseen demands. In the meantime two of the main parallel strips are in the process of being lengthened to 13,400ft with completion scheduled for 1993. Ground movements are also the subject for continued improvement by augmenting the taxiways and apron systems. Despite all the ongoing expansion and its position as the second busiest airport in the world, DFW experiences virtually no delays, an enviable claim to fame indeed.

Location and access: Situated 15 miles (24km) northwest of Dallas, 18 miles (29km) northeast of Fort Worth. From the south US Highway 183 is used, while Texas State Highway 114 and Interstate 635 serve travellers from the north. Trailways Bus Service links the airport with downtown Dallas with a journey time of between 45min and 75min. Fort Worth Airport Bus Service takes between 40min and 60min to reach the city's downtown area. An automated transit system operates between the airport terminals, long-term car parks and the on-site hotel. Stations are located on the lower level of each building.

44

Terminals: All buildings were designed to afford the utmost in passenger convenience. The lower level roadway is used by those departing with the upper level dedicated to arrivals. All terminals are self-sufficient and contain the usual shops, restaurants and services.

Spectator facilities: None specifically provided, but viewing and photography is possible through the glass from within the various terminals. Both the north and south employees' car park provide good vantage points but otherwise the airport is so vast that it is difficult to observe all movements, the majority being those of American and Delta.

Operators: Scheduled services by America West (Boeing 737/757), American Airlines (Airbus A300, Boeing 727/737/747/757/767, DC-9/10), American Eagle (Gulfstream 1, Jetstream, Metro, CASA 212, SD3-60, Saab SF340, ATR-42/72), Atlantic Southeast (Bandeirante, Brasilia), British Airways (DC-10), Conquest Airlines (Beech 1900), Continental Airlines (Boeing 727/737, DC-9), Delta Air Lines (Boeing 727/737/757/767, DC-9, TriStar), Emery Worldwide (Boeing 727, DC-8), Evergreen International (Boeing 747, DC-8), Exec Express (Navajo, Beech 99), Federal Express (Boeing 727/747, DC-10, MD-11), Lufthansa (Boeing 747), Mexicana (Boeing 727), Midwest Express (DC-9), Southwest Airlines (Boeing 737), Trans World (Boeing 727, DC-9), Thai International (Boeing 747), United Airlines (Boeing 727/737) and USAir (Boeing 727/737, DC-9).

Movements (1990): Total air transport 546,200. Total passengers 48,515,000.

Runways: 17L/35R (11,388ft/3,471m), 17R/35L (13,400ft/4,084m), 18L/36R (13,400ft/4,084m), 18R/36L (11,388ft/3,471m), 13L/31R (9,000ft/2,743m), 13R/31L (9,300ft/2,835m), 16/34 East (8,500ft/2,591m), 16/34 West (9,900ft/3,017m), 18S/36S (4,000ft/1,219m).

Radio frequencies: 126.55MHz (Tower east), 124.15MHz (Tower west), 118.55MHz Departure east), 124.25MHz (Departure west), 121.65MHz (Ground east), 121.8MHz (Ground west).

Telephone: (214) 574-3694 (Visitor Information), (214) 574-8888 (Public Affairs).

Operated by: Dallas/Fort Worth International Airport Board.

Denver (Stapleton International), Co USA

Denver is one of the few major cities in the US not situated on a navigable waterway, yet the main reason for its existence and steady growth is its strategic location as a transport centre. In the early days it served as a base camp for the mining towns in the Rocky Mountains to the west, so there was considerable doubt about the wisdom of spending $143,000 to purchase 630 acres of prairie land just for the benefit of the few people involved in aviation. Fortunately for Denver the purchase was concluded despite the opposition. It was the autumn of 1929 when the site was officially opened with all the traditional celebrations, but the timing could have been better because one week later came the infamous Wall Street crash.

Regardless of the setback caused by this economic disaster, a commercial airport gradually emerged at Denver, consisting of four unpaved runways, a terminal building and a single hangar. These facilities were considerably better than many of those offered by some cities around the country, a position it has mananged to maintain. Until 1944 the airport was known as Denver Municipal, but at this point it was renamed Stapleton in recognition of the founder, Mayor Benjamin F. Stapleton. In 1966 the title 'International' was conferred upon the expanding centre, although links with other countries were anticipated rather than a reality. Nevertheless the name did bring a sense of importance and prepare the path for the future.

By the early 1970s the original terminal buildings had been replaced by a modern curved structure as the base unit for the concourses projecting from it. During the years these have increased in number until in 1991 five were in use and allocated for the use of specific carriers. The growth in domestic services had taken Denver into the top five of the busiest US airports by the mid-1980s, with a predicted move into third position by the year 2000. Peak traffic was reached in 1986 when over 35.5 million travellers were handled, but subsequently there has been a noticeable decline in numbers.

Naturally, a constant programme of expansion to the overall facilities has been necessary, much of it towards the southwest. Inevitably there was a limit to the amount of space available, so in the mid-1980s studies began into the feasibility of building a completely new airport. Located to the northeast of the city, the area chosen

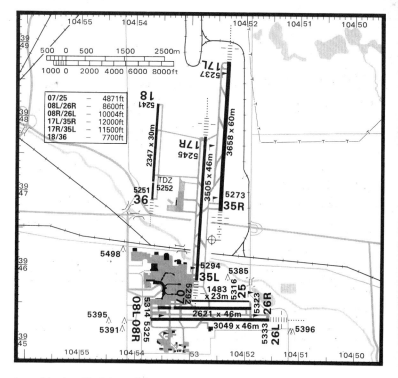

07/25	– 4871ft
08L/26R	– 8600ft
08R/26L	– 10004ft
17L/35R	– 12000ft
17R/35L	– 11500ft
18/36	– 7700ft

has minimal residential population so will cause little disruption. Denver International is expected to open during the period 1993-1995, but in the meantime Stapleton will continue to receive any modernisation and refurbishing necessary. For instance. all the concourses are earmarked for either internal improvements or extensions, much of the work likely to be on-going until the mid-1990s. It is already an important hub for both Continental and United, with the latter's flight training centre also housed at the airport. American has already expressed its intention to increase its presence when the new airport opens, in so doing providing employment for over 3,000 people.

Location and access: Situated 8 miles east of downtown Denver at an altitude of 5,330ft above sea level. Access is easily gained via Interstate 70. The bus operator is the Regional Transportation District (RTD) and services connect with most locations in the Denver area.

Terminals: The vast semi-circular building contains a huge variety of eating establishments, shops and other services such as shoe-shine points that are considered essential for travellers. Five concourses (A to E) share a total of 109 Gates, plus 12 associated with a remote satellite terminal completed in 1987 and somewhat confusingly known as A Plus. Shuttle buses ferry passengers to and from the main building. This mode of transportation is also used by those wishing to move from one Concourse to another. Walking is the alternative, which, although good exercise, could become a test of stamina for the unfit on some of the trips. An average time for the journey from the end of D Concourse to the main building is 15min, while 10min passes during the course of a similar trek from any of the other four.

Spectator facilities: None specifically provided. Concourses A and B offer some good views of the movements with photography possible through the glass. Concourse C is used by the international carriers, but frequent change of location is not to be recommended due to the long distances involved.

Operators: Scheduled services by America West (Boeing 737), American Airlines (Boeing 727/767, DC-9), Air Midwest (Metro), Continental Airlines (Airbus A300, Boeing 727/737/747, DC-9), Continental Express (ATR-42, Beech 1900, Dash Seven), Delta Air Lines (Boeing 727/757, DC-9), G.P. Express (Cessna 402), Mesa Airlines (Beech 1900), Mexicana (Boeing 727), Midwest Express (DC-9), Northwest Airlines (Boeing 727, DC-9), Trans World (DC-9), United Airlines (Boeing 727/737/757, DC-8/10), United Express (BAe 146, Beech 1900, Brasilia) and USAir (Boeing 727/737).
Freight or charter flights: these are operated by American Trans Air, Burlington, Casino Express, Casper Air, Corporate Air, DHL, Emery Worldwide, Federal Express, Flight International, Majestic, Southern Express, Sun Country and United Parcels.
Movements (1990): Total air transport 305,700. Total passengers 27,433,000.
Runways: 17L/35R (12,000ft/3,658m), 17R/35L (11,500ft/3,505m), 08L/26R (8,600ft/2,621m), 08R/26L (10,004ft/3,049m), 07/25 (4,871ft/1,483m — commuter use), 18/36 (7,700ft/2,347m — commuter use).
Radio frequencies: 118.3MHz (Tower east/west), 119.5MHz (Tower north/south), 123.85MHz, 128.05MHz (Departure), 121.9MHz (Ground).
Telephone: (303) 398-3844.
Operated by: City and County of Denver, Department of Public Works.

Detroit-Metropolitan (Wayne County), Mi USA

By 1927 the potential of the infant air transport industry was already being recognised in the US, Detroit being one of the major cities anxious to be included in any future route networks. During the following year the authorities allocated funds to acquire one square mile of land for use as a flying field, with the result that a landing strip was prepared and ready for operations in 1929. In addition a few basic buildings were erected, although these were mainly for maintenance purposes rather than passenger comfort. Nevertheless, despite the primitive nature of the facilities, the Thompson Aeronautical Corporation inaugurated a service on 1 April from what had become known as Wayne County Airport. It also became a stop for the night mail run between Bay City and Cleveland with most of the sorties being in the hands of Stinson SM-1s. This situation did not last for very long because after a series of takeovers and mergers, American Airlines assumed responsibility for the operations.

Throughout the 1930s civil activities continued, although in 1931 the Michigan Air National Guard set up its base at the airfield. Soon after the outbreak of war, control of Wayne County passed into the hands of the military so that the ever-growing number of heavy bombers and transports destined for Europe could be processed. Many of these aircraft were built locally at the Ford plant, but since the prewar airport was unable to handle the influx, a brand new airfield was constructed at nearby Willow Run.

At its peak in 1943, the enormous factory employed 42,000 workers and in its 3½ years of operations, a total of 8,685 B-24s rolled off the lines. Equipped with six runways of impressive length for that period, it was not surprising that the superior facilites also attracted the commercial operators.

In 1945 the military announced its intention to return Wayne County to its original owner, thereby paving the way for it to be developed into Detroit's main airport once again. Towards the end of the 1940s work started on a major expansion programme designed to treble the size of the site. It was sufficient to attract several of the larger carriers including Pan American and BOAC, both companies launching new services from the renamed Detroit-Wayne Major Airport. A further financial boost was received in 1956 which allowed the redevelopment work to continue uninterrupted, while during the year a contract was signed with American Airlines whereupon the company agreed to move its operations from Willow Run. In fact it was the first of the seven airlines remaining at the latter airfield to make the move to the rejuvenated Wayne.

Detroit became one of the first to receive long range radar in readiness for the forthcoming jet age, which was also responsible for the erection of a brand new terminal building and a 10,500ft (3,048m) runway. In due course this led to the airport being certified by the Civil Aeronautics Administration in 1958 as being suitable for international jet services. At the same time there was yet another, but final, name change to Detroit Metropolitan Wayne County, but any protests were soon silenced when Federal Funds met 50% of the construction costs.

Detroit is the location of this Airborne Express YS-11 freighter, this specimen being N910AX.
A. S. Wright

48

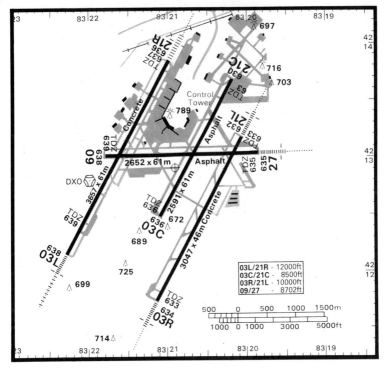

03L/21R - 12000ft
03C/21C - 8500ft
03R/21L - 10000ft
09/27 - 8702ft

Throughout the next decade growth was slow but steady, but had reached an annual figure of some 3 million passengers by the end of the 1960s. A second terminal was built in 1974 to absorb the increasing traffic, while the last of the three parallel runways was completed in 1977. However, substantial reductions in passenger traffic were experienced in the years between 1979 and 1982 due to the national and local economies, the controllers' strike and airline deregulation. By 1984 the prospects were much brighter and led to an update of the Master Plan which specified several necessary future developments. Further changes were incorporated in 1989 but the five main points of the project concerned the provision of a second East-West runway, the extension of Runway 3L, the construction of a south airport access roadway, a new terminal complex situated on the southern side of the airport and the provision of a fourth parallel North-South runway.

From its humble beginnings in 1928, Detroit Metroplitan has become an international gateway to the State of Michigan.

Some 25 carriers currently operate domestic and international services to take the number of daily movements to over 1,000. Nowadays Northwest carries the majority of the passengers using scheduled flights, accounting for about 67% of the total. Although no longer involved with regular services, Metro's near-neighbour at Willow Run continues to flourish in the interests of general avaition and as a busy cargo centre.

Location and access: Situated 20 miles (32km) south of Detroit close to Interstate 94. Greyhound Express Bus Services operate from the major cities in Michigan. Ample car parking with 13,000 spaces available served by free shuttle bus to terminal.

Terminals: There are two buildings named L. C. Smith (south) and J. M. Davey (north) linked to create an 'L' shaped complex. Seven piers are spaced at intervals either side of these terminals and are allocated to various carriers. An independent building (M. Berry terminal) equipped with three small piers serves the needs of international

Above:
ComAir's Saab SF340 N358CA leaves its Detroit stand for another commuter service. *A S. Wright*

Below:
Ryanair's One-Eleven EI-CCW arrives at Dublin. *AJW*

carriers. The majority of the shops and other public services are located in the north and south terminals, but adequate facilities are also available in the long-haul building. It takes about 15-20min to walk from one end of the terminal area to the other.

Spectator facilities: An observation deck allows most movements to be seen if not photographed. Neither the sun nor wire mesh aids the latter activity, but it is by no means impossible to obtain reasonable shots. Elsewhere there are other vantage points in car parks offering alternative opportunities.

Operators: Scheduled services by American Airlines (Boeing 727/757/767, DC-10), American Trans Air (TriStar), British Airways (Boeing 747), Comair (Metro, Braslia, Saab SF340), Continental (Boeing 737, DC-9), Delta Air Lines (Boeing 727/737/757), Drummond Island Air (Navajo), Great Lakes Aviation (Beech 1900), Meseba (Metro, Friendship), Midwest Airlines (DC-9), Northwest Airlines (Airbus A320, Boeing 727/747/757, DC-9/10),

Skyway (Beech 1900), Southwest Airlines (Boeing 737), Trans World (Boeing 727, DC-9), United Airlines (Boeing 727/737, DC-10), USAir (Fellowship, Boeing 727/737, DC-9).

Non-scheduled: These are operated by Alitalia (Boeing 747), Britt Airlines (Metro), Condor (DC-10), Key Airlines (Boeing 727), LOT Polish Airlines (IL62), Lufthansa (Boeing 747, DC-10). Cargo flights by Alitalia (Boeing 747), Federal Express (Boeing 727), United Parcels (DC-8).

Movements (1990): Total air transport 276,700. Total passengers 21,942,000.

Runways: 03R/21L (10,000ft/3,048m), 03C/21C (8,500ft/2,591m), 03L/21R (12,000ft/3,657m), 09/27 (8,702ft/2,652m).

Radio frequencies: 118.4MHz (Tower east), 135.0MHz (Tower west), 125.525MHz (Departure west), 132.025MHz (Departure east), 119.45MHz (Ground east), 121.8MHz (Ground west).

Telephone: 942-3607.

Operated by: Wayne County Department of Public Services.

Dublin (Collinstown) Eire

In the early days of commercial flying, the military airfield at Baldonnell, situated some 14 miles from Dublin, was employed for the limited number of movements by the small capacity airliners. Supposedly a temporary expedient, nevertheless very little serious effort was made to find an alternative until the launch of Aer Lingus in 1936. There was then more urgency, so site investigations were undertaken, one of those short-listed being the area previously used by the Royal Flying Corps/Royal Air Force at Collinstown. This had been one of four airfields chosen to become Training Depot Stations during World War 1, but the end of the conflict was in sight before the base was ready for its intended role. Collinstown continued to house token RAF units for some years until the final withdrawal of the forces from Ireland at the end of 1922. Thereafter the facilities were allowed to gently deteriorate until 1931 when Irish Aviation was formed with the intention of operating internal flights from the airfield, mainly with mail and newspapers. This enterprise did not last beyond the end of the year, so once again Collinstown was left to its own devices.

Finally, on 9 December 1936, the government announced that it proposed to develop the derelict airfield as Dublin's new civil airport. When the plans were released it could

be seen that all of the existing dilapidated military buildings were to be demolished to make way for the terminal, hangars and other accommodation. Probably one of the main factors to influence the decision was Collinstown's excellent weather record and its obstacle-free position 10 miles from the nearest mountains. Four grass strips were prepared, the longest being 5,250ft (1,600m), but although a few test flights were undertaken by the military in October, it was over two years later before the buildings were completed with the official opening taking place on 19 January 1940.

Dublin's new airport was then generally considered to possess the most impressive terminal in Europe. Designed by 25-year old Desmond Fitzgerald, it had won him the award of a gold medal from the Royal Institute of the Architects of Ireland. Sadly few travellers could appreciate the building's excellence as the number of routes plied were now in the singular. Aer Lingus managed to maintain the link with Merseyside by using both its DH86s or the newly acquired DC-3, intended as the basis for a modern fleet. Luckily it had just managed to evade the German forces as they advanced on Amsterdam, where it was being prepared for delivery by Fokker. Otherwise it would undoubtedly have been destined for a career with the Luftwaffe had it survived the aerial attacks.

With the war at an end, the rapid increase in aircraft movements and size made a hard runway layout essential if the airport was to be able to handle the newer types successfully. Consequently three concrete strips were laid, the longest stretching for over 5,000ft (1,524m) and completed in 1950. As forecast, traffic steadily increased, until by 1950 over 150,000 passengers were using Dublin annually. Throughout the decade it was necessary to continue this programme of expansion which meant new hangars were built and those existing thoroughly modernised.

In 1957 the launch of scheduled services by British European Airways, BKS and Sabena brought the time nearer when the terminal would need some attention. This point was reached during the next year because by now the national carrier had begun trans-Atlantic services, a development which helped to ensure that the new North Terminal was opened on 8 June 1959 as an arrivals area. By this time the jet-age was looming, so once again both runways were extended until by the end of the 1960s Dublin's two main strips had grown to 6,800ft and 7,500ft in readiness for the

imminent arrival of the first of the latest monsters, the 747.

An enormous increase in cargo tonnage in the early 1970s led to the construction of a new freight centre to cope with nearly 40,000 tonnes per year. Passenger figures were now exceeding 1.6 million annually so inevitably yet another terminal complex was opened in 1972, this time capable of handling 4 million travellers. Very little growth was apparent in the 1980/85 period at Dublin, where the airport regularly recorded a throughput of some 2.6 million passengers. However with the advent of greater competition, particularly on the London routes, numbers climbed to 2.9 million in 1986 and over 3.5 million in the next year. This impressive performance not only represented an additional 600,000 passengers or a 20% increase on 1986, but an amazing 1 million greater than 1985.

Such an influx demanded some general reorganisation of the terminal arrangements including a passageway to link the main departures area with Pier A in an effort to ease congestion. A more important develop-

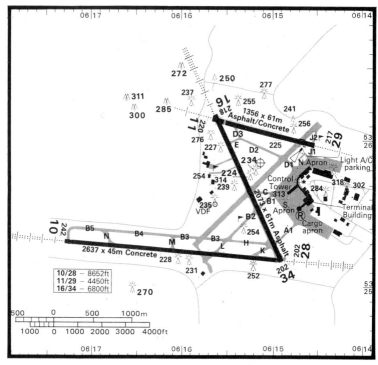

ment for the airport was the provision of the brand new runway 10/28. This was duly opened on 21 June 1989, but in fact the first official departure did not take place until eight days later, the distinction going to the Aer Lingus Commuter Fokker 50, EI-FKB. The introduction of the new strip allowed resurfacing work to proceed elsewhere and the general upgrade of the landing aids to proceed. Eventually it was possible to relegate Runway 05/23 to taxiway standard during daylight hours, a necessary restriction because of the absence of lights.

Location and access: Situated 5.5 miles (8.8km) north of the city off N1. A coach operates between the airport and Central Bus Station running every 20- 35min with a journey time of 20min. Taking 35-40min for a similar trip, a variety of Dublin City buses visit the airport in their travels, some of which find their way to the city centre (Eden Quay). It is considerably cheaper if somewhat slower, but the time can be spent pondering why one-man-operated buses have a conductor.

Terminals: These contain an excellent restaurant, plus self-service snack bars. A selection of shops provide for most immediate requirements including those anxious to acquire a new tie. There is a security checkpoint on the approach road to the buildings.

Spectator facilities: A viewing gallery exists in the main terminal which affords good views of the proceedings although photography is not entirely satisfactory through the tinted glass. Neverthless it is by no means impossible with care. As an alternative the nearby multi-storey car park serves as a good vantage point but of course security precautions may encourage the police to evict casual onlookers. At the end of the walkway between the main terminal and Pier A a small area lends itself for viewing the activity on this apron and the

movements along the near taxiway. Photography is possible, but this time it is through untinted glass liberally decorated with finger marks. A similar handicap is experienced when using the usefully positioned windows in the main terminal. These overlook the stands on the east side of Pier B and are convenient for obtaining the occasional shot. Several vantage points also exist around the perimeter and these have the advantage of offering fresh air and no glass.

Operators: Scheduled services by Aer Lingus (Boeing 737/747, Saab SF340), Aeroflot (Tu-134), Air France (Airbus A320, Boeing 737), Air Portugal (Boeing 737), Alitalia (DC-9), British Midland (Boeing 737, DC-9), Brymon (Dash Seven/Eight), Delta Air Lines (Boeing 767), Iberia (DC-9), Lufthansa (Airbus A310/A320, Boeing 737), Manx Airlines (Short SD3-60, BAe 146, BAe ATP), Ryanair (One-Eleven, ATR-42), SAS (DC-9) and Viva Air (Boeing 737, DC-9).
Charter and IT operators: Adria Airways (Airbus A320), Aer Lingus (Boeing 737/747), Aero Lloyd (DC-9), Air Atlantis (Boeing 737), Air Canada (Boeing 747/767), Air Charter/Euralair (Boeing 727/737), Air Columbus (Boeing 727), Air Europa (Boeing 737/757), Air Malta (Boeing 737), Air Sul (Boeing 737), Air Transat (TriStar), Cyprus Airways (Airbus A310/320), Futura (Boeing 737), Oasis Air (DC-9).
Cargo flights: Aer Turas (DC-8), Air Bridge (Merchantman, Electra), Iona (Friendship), TNT (BAe 146) and United Parcels (DC-8).

Movements (1990): Total air transport 94,900. Total passengers 5,510,000.
Runways: 10/28 (8,652ft/2,637m), 11/29 (4,450ft/1,356m), 16/34 (6,800ft/2,073m).
Radio frequencies: 118.6MHz (Tower), 121.1MHz (Approach), 128.0MHz (Radar), 121.8MHz (Ground).
Telephone: (01) 379900.
Operated by: Aer Rianta-Irish Airports.

Düsseldorf
Germany

With the opening of Düsseldorf's airport on 19 April 1927, Deutsche Luft Hansa introduced scheduled services on routes within Germany to link the city with Berlin and Hamburg plus an international sector to Geneva. It was not the district's first contact with aviation because as early as 19 September 1909 a Zeppelin airship landed on Golzheimer Heath, an area later destined to become a base for such devices. During the 12 years to the outbreak of war in 1939,

expansion was at a leisurely pace as reflected in the relatively modest passenger total of 87,333 recorded in this period. It was not surprising that civil flying was suspended at the outbreak of war, the airfield becoming the scene of military movements for the duration. No longer featuring in the timetables of the civil operators, it did however appear as one of the chosen targets for the RAF throughout the war, the frequency of the visits increasing by 1943. More accurate bombing was possible when the Pathfinder Force was introduced, both Mosquitos and Lancasters marking the tar-

Malev Tu-154 HA-LCR landing at Dusseldorf. AJW

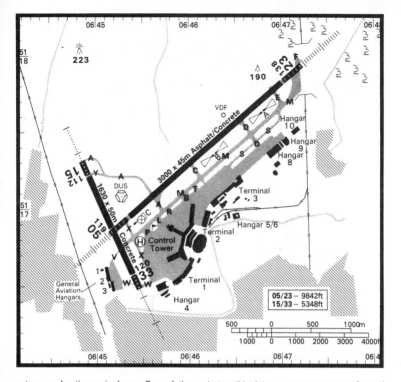

get areas for the main force. One of the heaviest attacks took place on the night of 2/3 November 1944 when 992 bombers were despatched to the city with good effect. There was little left of the prewar airport by the end of the year.

Reconstruction was slow to begin, but in 1948 a temporary terminal was provided and a makeshift 3,937ft/1,200m runway (17/35) was laid using steel plates for the purpose. This method had been perfected during the war when there was a necd for rapid completion of landing grounds. Scheduled flights were resumed on 4 April 1949 when British European Airways introduced a service from Northolt including both Hamburg and Düsseldorf in its journey, while SAS started to fly between the latter and Copenhagen. These carriers were quickly joined by Sabena, KLM and Air France to link the airport with the capitals of Belgium, Holland and France, by which time work had started on the construction of Runway 06/24, the future main 3,700ft/1,128m runway. Until 1 December 1950 control had been vested with the Allied administration,

but on this date a new company was formed by the city to take-over the responsibility for the complex.

At the beginning of the 1950s a permanent runway was laid to replace 17/35, the new strip becoming 16/34 and 4,750ft/1,450m in length. In those days aircraft were not as tolerant of cross-winds as they are in the 1980s so it was necessary to provide something suitable. With this requirement no longer so important, nowadays its use is restricted to light aircraft. While this was in progress 06/34 was being lengthened to 8,100ft/2,475m and the airport also gained taxiways and additional apron area. When the postwar Lufthansa began operations in April 1955, Düsseldorf was already developing as one of Germany's major air transport centres, a role in which it has continued through the years. Nevertheless expansion was not too rapid in the 1950s but by the next decade the need for an enlarged terminal was becoming apparent. It was to be 1967 before the design was finalised and two years later before work actually began. Planned to be undertaken in stages, the first phase was completed in 1973 to allow the new Terminal 2 to be opened for operations. It brought immediate relief but was still only an interim solution pending the completion of the second phase in early 1977, Düsseldorf 's 50th anniversary year which was duly celebrated on 19 April.

Throughout this time the original terminal had remained in service, but in 1982 work started on its replacement by providing another extension to Terminal 2 complete with the brand new Pier C. When opened in 1986, a total of 28 air-bridges were available on the stands, many capable of handling wide-bodied types. Certainly there was less need to use buses between the building and the aircraft. Handling 11.9 million passengers in 1990, Düsseldorf is now Germany's second largest airport, with its traffic shared equally between scheduled and charter services. In fact the airport is now the nation's leading centre for air-tourism. About 18% of the passenger volume originates from around the city. North Rhine-Westphalia accounts for a further 68%, these travellers mainly coming from neighbouring centres such as Essen, Duisburg, Bochum, Wuppertal, Krefeld, etc. Only some 10% travel from outside this region, many of them residents from the eastern fringes of Holland. It is often quicker to use the German airport than to travel to Schiphol, but much depends upon the ulitmate destination.

According to the current forecasts for the aviation industry, the growth in demand is expected to increase the annual traffic figures to about 14 million passengers by the year 2000. To meet this challenge the Düsseldorf authorities have three major projects planned, including a new freight centre, a terminal extension and the provision of a parallel runway. Surface access has already been improved by a direct rail connection to the Ruhr region, but for road users a link to the A44 motorway due for completion by 1993 should remove much of the congestion. The future of the airport is also largely dependent upon its environmental compatability. A soundproof hangar capable of housing a 747 has been designed and built exclusively for ground running jet engines, a necessary practice but one which generates strong complaints. Once the building was completed in September 1990, tests showed that there was an appreciable reduction in noise when compared with the level reached with the previous protection barriers.

A decision has also been taken to relocate some of the regional flights at nearby Monchengladbach, thereby easing the load on Düsseldorf . This may also extend to the general aviation traffic, which although having its own dedicated terminal on the southwest side, frequently shares the runway with the commercial movements. Similarly more collaboration is planned with Cologne/Bonn in an attempt to streamline the air transport services in the North Rhine-Westphalia region.

Location and access: Situated 4 miles (6.5km) north of Düsseldorf it is well signposted from the nearby autobahns. Fast local trains on line S7 of the Rhine/Ruhr S-Bahn network connect the airport terminal to Düsseldorf Central station and Solingen-Ohligs. Rheinbahn bus route 727 plies between the airport, railway station and Düsseldorf -Eller, while other buses provide direct services to Essen (Route 153), Ratingen (759) and Krefeld (072).

Terminal: Departures are handled on the upper floor, arrivals at ground level with the urban railway station below. Numerous shops, restaurants, cafeterias and snack bars are located around the building. There are three piers; A has 11 passenger airbridges, B has 9 while C is equipped with 8. All have an additional gate from which buses convey passengers to more distant stands.

Spectator facilities: An excellent observation deck has been provided on the roof of Pier B. Being close to the taxiways photography is no problem, a wide-angle lens often being useful. For take-off shots on the main runway a 200mm telephoto lens is required. The interesting Air Classik museum collection has now been dispersed to other locations.

Operators: Scheduled services by Aer Lingus (Boeing 737), Aeroflot (Tu-134/154), Air Canada (Boeing 767), Air France (Boeing 737, Airbus A300/320), Air Meuse (Brasilia), Air UK (BAe 146), Alitalia (DC-9), American Airlines (Boeing 767), Austrian Airlines (DC-9), British Airways (One-Eleven, Boeing 737/757), Crossair (Saab SF340, Fokker 50), Delta Air Transport (Brasilia), Egyptair (Boeing 767), EuroBerlin (Boeing 737), Finnair (DC-9), Ghana Airways (DC-10), Iberia (DC-9, Airbus A320), Interot Airways (Beech 1900, Dash Eight), Japan Airlines (Boeing 747), KLM (Boeing 737), KLM CityHopper (Fokker 50, Saab SF340), LTU (Boeing 757/767, Tristar, MD-11), Lufthansa (Boeing 737/747, DC-10, Airbus A300/310/320), Lufthansa CityLine (Fokker 50), Luxair (Fokker 50), NFD (ATR-42, Metro), Olympic Airways (Boeing 727/737), RFG (ATR-42), Rheinland Air Service (SD3-60), Royal Air Maroc (Boeing 727/737), SAS (DC-9), Sabena (Dash Eight), Swissair (DC-9,

Above:
Good apron shots can be obtained from Dusseldorf's excellent roof facility, the subject being Brasilia OO-MTD of Air Meuse. *AJW*

Below:
Lufthansa dominates the scene at Dusseldorf with an ever-growing number of A320s in evidence. *AJW*

Fokker 100), Thai Airways (DC-10, Boeing 747), Tunis Air (Boeing 727/737), Tyrolean (Dash Eight) and Viva Air (Boeing 737, DC-9).

Charter and IT operators: Adria Airways (DC-9), Aero Lloyd (DC-9, Caravelle), Air Atlantis (Boeing 737), Air Columbus (Boeing 727), Air Europa (Boeing 737), Air Malta (Boeing 737), Aviogenex (Boeing 727/737), Balkan (Tu-154), Birgenair (DC-8), Braathens (Boeing 737), Britannia Airways (Boeing 737), Condor (Boeing 737/757/767, DC-10, Airbus A310), CSA (Tu-134/154), Dan-Air (Boeing 727, One-Eleven), Futura (Boeing 737), Germania (Boeing 737), German Cargo (DC-8, Boeing 737), Greenair (Tu-154, IL-86), Hapag-Lloyd (Boeing 737, Airbus A310), Istanbul Airlines (Boeing 737), LTE (Boeing 757), LTU/LTU-Sud (Boeing 757/767, TriStar, MD-11), Malev (Boeing 737, Tu-134/154), Meridiana (DC-9), Noble Air (Boeing 727), Pegasus (Boeing 737),Spanair (DC-9), Sun Express (Boeing 737), Tarom (One-Eleven), Tunis Air (Boeing 737/727), TUR (Boeing 727), Turkish Airlines (Boeing 727) and WDL (Friendship). LTU is based at the airport, the large Hangar 8 being used for TriStar maintenance.

Movements (1990): Total 155,147. (Air transport 139,031). Total passengers 11,934,604.

Runways: 05R/23L (9,842ft/3,000m), 05L/23R (8,858ft/2,700m), 15/33 (5,348ft/1,630m).

Radio frequencies: 118.3MHz (Tower), 119.4MHz (Approach), 121.9MHz (Ground).

Telephone: 0211 4211.

Operated by: Flughafen Düsseldorf Gmbh.

Frankfurt Main
Germany

Aviation was introduced to Frankfurt as early as 1909 when an International Air Show was staged. Hardly up to modern standards the main participant was indeed 'air', but it did mark the start of the city's involvement in flying which has continued to the present day. Two years later an aero club was formed in the locality at Rebstock from where commercial flights were introduced after the war. Such was the growth that in 1934 4,620 departures were recorded which accounted for 33,400 passengers, 552 tons of freight and 86 tons of airmail. Already the total capacity had been reached and with no room to expand plans were made to provide a new facility known as Rhein-Main Airport and Airship Port on the site that much later was to become the present centre.

Scheduled services were begun in May 1936 with the departure of both the mighty airships *Hindenberg* and *Graf Zeppelin* to Rio de Janeiro and Lakehurst, USA respectively. Two months later, on 8 July, Deutsche Lufthansa (DHL) launched its services with a Junkers Ju52, an event which quickly multiplied to take Frankfurt into the position of Germany's second largest airport after Berlin. Much of the traffic was provided by the successful German carrier which by the outbreak of World War 2 was the leading airline in western Europe. During the 1939-1945 period the airport was taken over by the Luftwaffe but in any case it received frequent visits from the Allied air forces to bring about its almost total destruction by the time the fighting ended.

After the war the reconstruction work became the responsibility of the Supreme Commander of the Allied Forces. Enough progress had been made by 14 August 1946 to give Danish Airlines (DDL) the distinction of operating the first postwar civil movement with a DC-3. In 1948 Frankfurt played an important role in the support of the aircraft taking part in Operation 'Planefare', the relief of beseiged Berlin. Such was the intensity of the movements by the heavily-laden transports employed on the airlift that the runway became seriously damaged. As a consequence a second parallel strip was laid in 1949 whereupon the control of the airport was transferred to a Germany company. Still the scene of considerable military activity by USAF transports, the southern side was devoted to such operations while the northern area was allocated to the growing commercial activities.

It was almost 10 years after the war before the reborn Lufthansa was allowed to recommence flying, its first service employing one of four Convair 240s for a domestic sector on 1 April 1955. Two weeks later international services began and by the year's end not only was Frankfurt linked with most of the European capitals, but Super Constellations had begun to visit New York. Jet-powered airliners were introduced to the airport on a regular basis in 1958 when BOAC Comets began to stage through on their way to Tokyo, but it was 1960 before Lufthansa's new Boeing 707s arrived to take over the daily trans-Atlantic runs. In common with many other airports, Frankfurt's traffic increased dramatically with the dawn of the new era to such an extent that in

A few of the aircraft displayed on the roof at Frankfurt can be seen behind the departing Turkish A310 TC-JCM. *A. S. Wright*

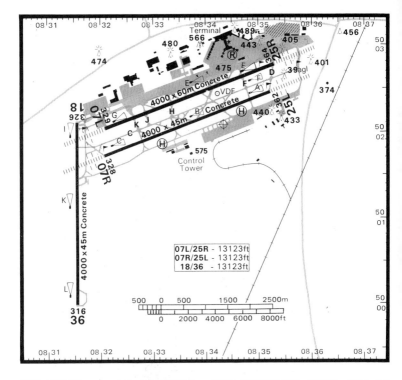

1965 4,875,850 passengers were handled. Once again the design capacity was being exceeded thereby demanding urgent expansion. Much planning work had already been completed on what was to become a massive new terminal so it was possible to lay the foundation stone in June 1965. It took six years of intensive activity by day and night to complete the building by which time its size had been doubled in anticipation of the arrival of the wide-bodied types. Finally, on 16 March 1972, operations were transferred from the original complex much to the relief of all concerned. Construction of a third runway (18/36) designed exclusively for take-offs was started in 1981, opening for traffic on 12 April 1984.

Frankfurt is the engineering base for the Lufthansa, German Cargo Services and Condor fleets and also the flag carrier's largest international connecting point. Boeing 747s are maintained in a custom built hangar capable of housing six of the type while another almost as large caters for the needs of DC-10s and Boeing 737s. Accommodation built much earlier is used for the

other narrow-bodied airliners. From the beginning, the importance of air cargo was recognised so a freight centre was established on the western perimeter with warehouses capable of storing containers of all sizes. As a result the airport handles a vast quantity of freight, 70% of which is actually in transit. In recent years the growth rate has been much less than anticipated due in part to the difficulty of obtaining slots and the fact that landing and handling fees are higher than at competitive airports. Therefore while dedicated cargo aircraft are still to be seen, 94% of the total cargo tonnage in 1990 was carried on scheduled flights. In addition each night the airport plays its part in Germany's mail system, although the modest growth recorded is related to domestic traffic. Airmail on the European routes has been declining for several years, trucks taking over to save costs and to ensure punctual delivery.

Despite the somewhat disappointing figures in the early 1990s, the overall trend is for the demand in air transport to grow rapidly. The traffic projections for the year

Royal Jordanian A310 F-ODVE arriving at Frankfurt. *A. S. Wright*

61

2000 prepared by the Frankfurt authorities in 1985 had already been exceeded after only four years, so an urgent revision of the airport's future expansion plan was required. As an interim expedient a number of measures were introduced to create more space within the existing buildings, but the most significant feature was the new East Terminal. Opening in 1994, it will be fitted out as an independent passenger facility to handle between 10 and 12 million travellers annually. A rapid transit system will be installed to link the two separate complexes so interlining will be no problem. Primarily the terminal will be used for intercontinental flights with the capability of accommodating the future extra large aircraft types expected early next century.

In planning the East Terminal, the designers ensured that it will be possible to extend the building towards the west to link with the existing Pier C. Once this stage has been completed, after the turn of the century, Pier A will be extended southwards to provide four extra gates. All of this additional traffic will continue to use the three runways currently available, although a number of improvements will be necessary. More fast exits and taxiways are to be provided, but any plans to lay a fourth strip have been dropped. Undoubtedly Frankfurt will be well placed to meet the demands of the single European market and the libralisation of air traffic when this programme is completed.

Location and access: Situated 5.6 miles (9km) southwest of Frankfurt at the Frankfurter Kreuz, the intersection of the A3 and A5 autobahns. There is a rail station under the terminal which is served by frequent trains. Line S15 connects with Frankfurt Central track 21 at 10min intervals taking 11min for the journey, while Line S14 runs every 20min between Wiesbaden, Mainz, Russelsheim, the airport, Central station and Konstablerwache. There are also intercity trains which link some 47 cities all over Germany. For the more adventurous a number of surburban bus services visit the airport's bus station located in front of the terminal. There are 15 stops numbered 10 to 24 allocated to the local routes that serve Walldorf-Morfelden, Kelsterbach, Russelsheim, Offenbach, Neu-Isenburg, Frankfurt-Sud and Frankfurt-Schwanheim. **Terminal:** Contains not only restaurants and buffets but over 100 shops covering a wide range of services. For entertainment those not impressed by aircraft can make use of the skittles alley or visit the cinema. **Spectator facilities:** Against all modern trends Frankfurt possesses a superb observation deck which is certainly one of

the best in Europe and is open from 1 April until 30 September between 08.00 and 21.00, closing time for the other six months being 18.00. Access is gained from the gallery on the departures concourse of Hall A. A strict security checkpoint has to be passed before entry to the roof is permitted and this can take some time if carrying the normal equipment essential for enthusiasts. Once cleared, the vast area available for spectators is amazing. Naturally a considerable number of Lufthansa aircraft parade before the onlooker at some time or other, but for variety the left side of pier B offers excellent views of the charter traffic, some of which is not often seen in the UK. With the terminal facing south, sunny days can present a few problems for photographers, but by taking up a suitable position this can usually be overcome. There are refreshment facilities on the roof but prices are high making it more economic to acquire food and drink in the basement supermarket. Fortunately re-entry to the terrace is permitted, making sorties into the terminal quite practical and worthwhile especially since the TV monitors not only give arrivals and departures as customary, but also the registration of the aircraft on the service. The admission charge includes the Historic Aircraft Collection which contains up to 20 exhibits. Airport tours, previously available for groups only, were extended to individuals in September 1990. These are run twice daily departing from the visitors' terrace Gate 33.

Operators: Scheduled services by Aer Lingus (Boeing 737), Aerolineas Argentinas (Boeing 747), Aeroflot (Tu-134/154, IL-62), Aero Lloyd (DC-9), Air Algerie (Boeing 737), Air Canada (Boeing 767), Air China (Boeing 747), Air France (Airbus A320, Boeing 737, Brasilia, Fellowship), Air India (Boeing 747), Air Lanka (TriStar), Air Malta (Boeing 737), Air Mauritius (Boeing 767), Air New Zealand (Boeing 747), Air Portugal (Airbus A310, Boeing 737, TriStar), Air Seychelles (Boeing 767), Air UK (BAe 146), Air Zimbabwe (Boeing 707/767), Alitalia (DC-9), American Airlines (Boeing 767, DC-10), ATI (DC-9), Austrian Airlines (DC-9), Austrian Air Services (Fokker 50), Avianca (Boeing 747), Avianova (ATR-42), Balkan (Tu-154), British Airways (Airbus A320, Boeing 737/757, One-Eleven), BWIA International (TriStar), Cameroon Airlines (Boeing 747), Canadian Airlines International (Boeing 767, DC-10), Cathay Pacific (Boeing 747), Continental Airlines (Boeing 747, DC-10), Crossair (BAe 146, Saab SF340), Czechoslovak Airlines (Tu-134/154), Cyprus Airways (Airbus A310/320), Delta Airlines (Boeing 767, TriStar), Delta Air (Saab SF340), Egyptair

(Boeing 747/767), El Al (Boeing 747/757/767), Emirates (Airbus A310), Ethiopian Airlines (Boeing 767), EuroBerlin (Boeing 737), Finnair (DC-9), Flandre Air (King Air), Garuda Indonesian (Boeing 747, DC-10), Gulf Air (Boeing 767, TriStar), Hamburg Airlines (Dash Eight), Iberia (Airbus A300/320, Boeing 727, DC-9), Icelandair (Boeing 737), Iran Air (Boeing 747), Japan Air Lines (Boeing 747), Kenya Airways (Airbus A310), KLM (Boeing 737), Korean Air (Boeing 747), Kuwait Airways (Airbus A310), Libyan Arab (Boeing 727), Lineas Aereas Paraguayas (DC-8), LTU (TriStar), LTU-Sud (Boeing 757), Lufthansa (Boeing 727/737/747, DC-10, Airbus A300/310/320), Lufthansa CityLine (Fokker 50), Luxair (Boeing 737, Fokker 50), Malaysian Airline System (Boeing 747, DC-10), Meridiana (BAe 146, DC-9), Middle East Airlines (Boeing 707), NFD (Dornier 228), Northwest Airlines (Boeing 747, DC-10), Olympic Airways (Boeing 727/737, Airbus A300), Pakistan International (Boeing 747), Qantas (Boeing 747), Somali Airlines (Boeing 707, Airbus A310), Philippine Airlines (Boeing 747), Polish Airlines (Tu-134/154, IL-62), RFG (ATR-42, Metro), Royal Air Maroc (Boeing 727/737), Royal Brunei (Boeing 757), Royal Jordanian (Airbus A310/320), Royal Nepal (Boeing 757), SAS (DC-9), Sabena (Boeing 737), Saudia (TriStar), Singapore Airlines (Boeing 747), Somali Airlines (Airbus A310),South African Airways (Boeing 747), Swissair (DC-9, Fokker 100), Syrian Arab (Boeing 727), Tarom (One-Eleven, Tu-154), Thai International (Boeing 747), Trans World (Boeing 747/767, TriStar), Tunis Air (Airbus A320, Boeing 727/737), Turkish Airlines (Boeing 727, Airbus A310), Tyrolean Airways (Dash Seven/Eight), United Airlines (Boeing 747/767), USAir (Boeing 767), Varig (DC-10, Boeing 747), Viasa (DC-10), Viva Air (Boeing 737, DC-9), Yemenia (Boeing 727), Yugoslav Airlines (Boeing 727/737, DC-9, ATR-42) and Zambia Airways (DC-10).

Charter and IT operators: Adria Airways (DC-9), Aero Lloyd (DC-9, Caravelle), Aviogenex (Boeing 737), Condor (Boeing 737/757/767, Airbus A310, DC-10), Dan Air (Boeing 727), Germania (Boeing 737), Hapag Lloyd (Airbus A310, Boeing 737), LTE (Boeing 757), LTU (TriStar, MD-11), LTU-Sud (Boeing 757/767) and Spanair (Boeing 767, DC-9).

Movements (1990): Total 324,400. Total passengers 29,631,400. These compare with the 1989 figures of 311,800 and 26,724,400 respectively.

Runways: 07L/25R (13,123ft/4,000m), 07R/25L (13,123ft/4,000m),18/36 (13,123ft/4,000m).

Radio frequencies: 119.9MHz, 124.85MHz (Tower), 120.8MHz (Approach), 120.15MHz (Departures), 121.9MHz (Ground).

Telephone: 069 690-1 (main switchboard) 069-690-3051 (information).

Operated by: Flughafen Frankfurt Main AG.

Geneva (Cointrin) Switzerland

Second only to Zurich in terms of traffic handled by the Swiss airports, Geneva began life in 1920 when a grass strip and wooden buildings were sufficient to cater for the scheduled services, the first being a link with Paris. These arrangements in fact sufficed until after the war, a period when the Swiss took the opportunity to lay a concrete runway in readiness for the predicted postwar boom in air transport. Together with a more substantial terminal, these facilities then served until well into the 1960s, but with the advent of much larger types, the Geneva Canton authorities took the decision to undertake a complete modernisation programme before the airport was overtaken by an embarrassing influx of passengers.

It was a very advanced scheme for its time, making use of three satellite buildings linked to the main terminal by underground tunnels. By this method the apron is not filled with buses or passengers walking to the aircraft. Instead the machines park radially around the satellites which contain a number of holding lounges for waiting travellers. All the normal formalities are carried out in the main building which also contains a departure lounge, but the majority of people prefer to proceed to the satellite immediately. This brings an added bonus for the authorities since congestion is then kept to a minimum. Because of the restricted area of land available for expansion, an exchange of territory was agreed with France in 1956 so that the runway could be extended towards the northeast. To simplify matters a 'French sector' was established within the terminal on the departures level, this being linked to a customs road leading directly into France at Ferney-Voltaire. Even by the early 1980s the Swiss had drawn up a plan which was entitled Horizon 2000. A major terminal development will introduce two Y-shaped piers at either end of the main building to be reached by the rapid transit system similar

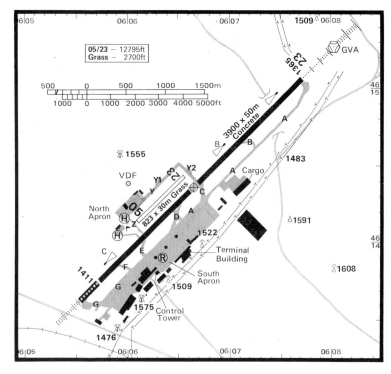

to that now employed between Gatwick North and South. From June 1987 access to the airport was greatly improved by the opening of the direct rail link making the airport station the terminus of the Lausanne-Geneva line. General aviation is handled on the far side of the runway although facilities exist for executive types beyond the cargo centre to the south of the terminal. CTA's hangar and adminstration offices are also situated in this area.

Location and access: Situated 2.5 miles (4km) north of city centre. Ample car parks are available and the Lausanne-Chamonix-Lyon motorway passes alongside the airport with access points provided. TPG trolleybus route 10 runs from the city centre (Bel-Air and Cornavin station) every 12min with a journey time of 20min. Every 15min an SBB train leaves the airport station for Geneva-Cornavin taking 6min for the trip.

Terminal: A whole range of shops are situated in the departures hall embracing a wide range of goods with everything on sale that is normally associated with the country.

Unfortunately the cost is prohibitive. A number of restaurants and buffets are to be found, but these too are extremely expensive.

Spectators facilities: An excellent open first-floor terrace extends along much of the apron with access from alongside the restaurant building. Opening hours are between 09.00 and 19.00, but occasionally the facility is closed when some high-ranking politician chooses the city as a suitable place for a chat with counterparts from other nations. From this admirable vantage point all movements can be seen and most photographed with ease. Geneva is an example of an airport that recognises the popularity of the public area and therefore has retained it by introducing a security check point at the entrance. By way of a change a saunter along to the holding point of runway 05 is worthwhile because although there is the usual fence, it contains a series of convenient holes. If this is not enough, then a nearby grass bank gives a higher elevation. This location also overlooks the Aeroleasing apron; a

Above:
Crossair's 146s are regular sights at Geneva where HB-IXC was shot from the terrace. *A. S. Wright*

Below:
Charter flights to Geneva were regularly made by Air Sul's two 737s before the airline ceased operations in 1992. In this case CS-TMB was the aircraft in use. *A. S. Wright*

company which specialises in long range airtaxi work. Airport tours are arranged but these are for groups of at least 15 persons. For bookings telephone the Authority on 022-981122.

Operators: Scheduled services by Aeroflot (Tu-134/154, IL-76), Air Afrique (Airbus A300, DC-10), Air Algerie (Boeing 727/737), Air Canada (Boeing 747/767), Air Exel (Brasilia), Air France (Airbus A310/320, Boeing 727/737), Air India (Boeing 747), Air Littoral (Metro), Air Malta (Boeing 737), Air Mauritius (Boeing 747/767), Air Portugal (Boeing 727/737), Air Vendee (Metro), Alitalia (DC-9), American Airlines (Boeing 767), Austrian Airlines (DC-9), British Airways (Airbus A320, One-Eleven, Boeing 737/757), Cameroon Airlines (Boeing 747), Crossair (BAe 146, Fokker 50, Saab SF340), Cyprus Airways (Airbus A310/320), Czechoslovak Airlines (Tu-134/154, IL-62, Yak-40), Delta Air (Saab SF340, Metro), Egyptair (Airbus A300, Boeing 767), El Al (Boeing 737/757), Finnair (DC-9), Iberia (Boeing 727, DC-9), Iran Air (Boeing 747), Iraqi Airways (Boeing 727), KLM (Airbus A310, Boeing 737), Lufthansa (Airbus A310/320, Boeing 737), Luxair (Fokker 50, Brasilia), Meridiana (ATR-42), Middle East Airlines (Boeing 707), Olympic Airways (Airbus A300, Boeing 737), Polish Airlines (IL-62, Tu-134/154), Royal Air Maroc (Boeing 727/737), Royal Jordanian (Airbus A310, TriStar), Sabena (Boeing 737), SAS (DC-9), Saudia (Boeing 747, TriStar), Swissair (Airbus A310, Boeing 747, DC-9/10, Fokker 100), TAT (Fokker 100), Tunis Air (Airbus A300, Boeing 727), Turkish Airlines (Airbus A310, DC-9), Trans World (Boeing 767), United Airlines (Boeing 727) and Viva Air (DC-9, Boeing 737).
Charter and IT operators: Adria Airways (DC-9), Aero Lloyd (DC-9, Caravelle), ATI (DC-9), Air Belgium (Boeing 737), Air Charter (Caravelle, Boeing 727/737), Air Europa (Boeing 737/757), Air Holland (Boeing 757), Air Liberte (DC-9), Air Littoral (Brasilia, Bandeirante), Air Malta (Boeing 737), Air Sul (Boeing 737), Air Sur (DC-9), Air UK Leisure (Boeing 737), Air 2000 (Boeing 757), Balair (DC-9/10), Balkan (Tu-134/154), Braathens (Boeing 737), Britannia (Boeing 737/767), British Midland (DC-9), Cimber Air (ATR-42), CTA (DC-9), Condor (Boeing 737), Corse Air (Caravelle), Dairo Air Services (Boeing 707), Dan-Air (Boeing 727, One-Eleven), Futura (Boeing 737), German Cargo (DC-8), Hapag-Lloyd (Airbus A310, Boeing 737), Inter European (Boeing 737), Linjeflyg (Boeing 737, Fellowship), LTU (TriStar), Maersk (Boeing 737), Malev (Tu-154), Martinair (DC-9, Airbus A310), Monarch Airlines (Boeing 737/757), Oasis (DC-9), Portugalia (Fokker 100), Rich International (DC-8), Scanair (DC-10), Sobelair (Boeing 737), Spanair (DC-9), Sterling Airways (Caravelle, Boeing 727), TEA Basle (Boeing 737), Transwede (DC-9), Tyrolean Airways (Dash Seven/Eight) and WDL (Friendship).

Movements (1990): Total 149,969 (air transport 98,594). Total passengers 6,020,355 (non-commercial 46,810). These compare with 148,383 (95,480) and 5,933,328 (49,690) during 1989.
Runways: 05/23 (12,795ft/3,900m), 05/23 (2,700ft/823m - grass).
Radio frequencies: 118.7MHz, 119.7MHz, 119.9MHz (Tower/Approach), 121.9MHz (Ground).
Telephone: 022-981122.
Operated by: Department of Public Economy of the State of Geneva.

Helsinki (Vantaa) Finland

When air transport was introduced in Finland, a city centre seaplane base was established at Katajanokka. Although convenient, this type of aircraft was very limited in scope so in 1938 a more conventional landplane airport was provided at Malmi. This continued in service until the present complex at Vantaa was officially opened on 26 October 1952, although it had been used during the course of that summer's Olympic Games. Nevertheless another 17 years passed before a permanent terminal was completed, a temporary wooden structure serving during the lengthy wait. At least the time was spent usefully by the planners because after 1969 no further work was necessary until the building was extended between 1980 and 1983. Vantaa's first runway was only 6,562ft (2,000m) long, but by 1956 a second had been constructed, both subsequently extended several times until the main strip now stretches for 11,286ft (3,440m). Although much superior to its predecessor, Vantaa's position was dictated by the need to accommodate jet-age aircraft so inevitably it is further from the city.

Weather conditions in these northern latitudes are frequently inhospitable, but the Finns are suitably equipped to handle vast deposits of snow and ice. Accordingly the airport possesses a large fleet of vehicles dedicated to keeping it open at all times with hardly a break in traffic. Needless to say it is a full time occupation during the long winter months.

Vantaa has been Finnair's main base since 1952, joined in due course by most of the country's other aviation companies such as Karair and Finnaviation. Altogether there are now 19 airlines operating scheduled services from Helsinki to 42 foreign and 21 domestic destinations.

In addition to the third runway to be provided in the latter half of the 1990s, several other major developments will take place at the airport during the decade. Work began in early 1991 on the construction of a new domestic terminal for completion in December 1992. At this point the existing premises will be refurbished and begin handling only international traffic. In association with this expansion a new multi-storey car park has been opened, while the surface areas have been considerably increased in size.

Location and access: Situated 12 miles from the city centre near to the Tuusula motorway. Charges vary in the car parks depending on whether short term, 48hr, long term, open air or under cover. Finnair buses operate from Helsinki's city air terminal to the airport at about 20 to 30min intervals depending on the time of day. Sirola bus route 615 also links the Central railway station, the journey taking between 30 and 35min.

Terminal: This contains four restaurants, two bars and three buffets. There are several shops and other services both in the transit hall and unrestricted areas. Although airbridges are used for loading, these all project from the main building rather than from piers.

Spectator facilities: A balcony originally provided for visitors' use has been closed for security reasons, but it is possible to use a large window in the departure hall from where all movements can be observed. From this vantage point photography is possible through the glass with care. Alternatively if Runway 15/33 is in use then the adjacent car park 11 can provide a reasonable spot albeit sometimes chilly. Finland's aviation museum is located at the airport and can be reached after a 15min

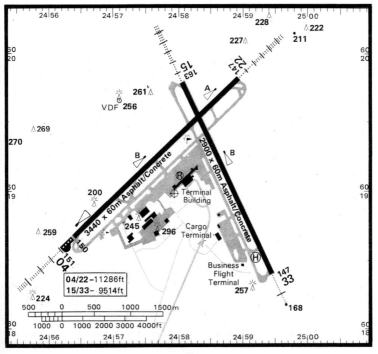

A murky day at Helsinki where Finnair's MD-87 OH-LMA awaits its next duty. *Helsinki Airport*

walk. It contains various vintage types plus other items and photographs relevant to the country's history.

Operators: Scheduled services by Aeroflot (Tu-134/154), Airbotnia (Bandeirante), Air France (Airbus A320, Boeing 727/737), Austrian Airlines (DC-9), Balkan (Tu-154), British Airways (Airbus A320, Boeing 737/757), Czechoslovak Airlines (Tu-154), Egyptair (Boeing 767), Finnair (ATR-42, DC-9/10, MD-11), Finnaviation (Saab SF340), Icelandair (Boeing 737), Karair (ATR-42, Airbus A300), KLM (Airbus A310, Boeing 737), Lufthansa (Airbus A320, Boeing 737), Malev (Tu-134/154), Polish Airlines (Tu-134/154), Sabena/Delta Air Transport (BAe 146), SAS (DC-9), Swissair (DC-9), Thai International (Boeing 747, DC-10), and Turkish Airlines (Airbus A310, Boeing 727).

Charter and IT operators: Adria Airways (DC-9), Air Europa (Boeing 737), Air Malta (Boeing 737), Airmust (DC-9/10), ATI (DC-9), Balkan (Tu-154), Busy Bee (Boeing 737), Conair (Airbus A320), Finnair (DC-9/10), Icelandair (Boeing 757), Karair (Airbus A300), Linjeflyg (Boeing 737, Fellowship), Maersk Air (Boeing 737), Martinair (DC-9, Airbus A310, DC-10), Monarch (Boeing 737), Royal Air Maroc (Boeing 737), Royal Jordanian (TriStar), Scanair (DC-10), Saudia (TriStar), Sobelair (Boeing 737), Sterling (Boeing 727, Caravelle), Tarom (One-Eleven), Thai International (DC-10), Transwede (DC-9), Yugoslav Airlines (Boeing 737, DC-9) and ZAS Airline of Egypt (DC-9).

Movements (1990): Total 132,918. Total passengers 8,007,776.

Runways: 04/22 (11,286ft/3,440m), 15/33 (9,514ft/2,900m). A third is planned for the 1990s.

Radio frequencies: 118.6MHz, 119.7MHz (Tower), 119.1MHz (Approach), 129.85MHz (Radar), 121.8MHz (Ground).

Telephone: (358-0) 82921.

Operated by: Helsinki Airport Authority.

Hong Kong (Kai Tak) Hong Kong

The airport's present site has been associated with aviation since 1929 when the local flying club rented some reclaimed land for its activities. Gradually the field was used by an increasing number of passenger carrying aircraft which prompted the Government to fund the development of an airport. By 1936 Imperial Airways was running a regular service to Penang to conveniently connect with that already linking England with Australia. The advent of World War 2 found Hong Kong infested with Japanese military tourists, but their presence at least meant that the airport was considerably enlarged to render some compensation for the years of oppression.

It was 1947 before Kai Tak began to appear on the route networks of international carriers, but if this attention was to be further encouraged some major redevelopment was essential. There was little scope for extending the existing pair of runways, so the Government decided that it was necessary virtually to start again, but using the same site. Work started on the ambitious scheme in 1954, much of the effort being directed at the construction of the new runway. This in itself was a major undertaking because of the extremely restricted space limitations imposed by the unfriendly terrain. To overcome the problem, the designers decided to build the runway into Kowloon Bay, a solution which certainly relieved the situation on the land.

When declared open in 1958, the new strip stretched 8,350ft (2,545m) across the water which was ample for the types then in service. As the wide-bodies began to appear in the 1970s, so more land was reclaimed to enable the runway to be extended in two stages, first to 10,000ft (3,048m) and then to 11,128ft (3,392m) in 1975. While these improvements were to be welcomed, one feature remained solidly in place, namely the mountain range guarding the northwest. This formidable obstruction has always prevented the long, flat approaches normally associated with airliners to be carried out at Kai Tak. Instead, a somewhat alarming, curved manoeuvre is necessary when using Runway 13, giving the impression that both mountains and high-rise buildings are close to the wingtip. Landings from the southeast over the sea are therefore less stressful for inexperienced passengers.

In addition to the land used for the runway and parallel taxiway, the apron is one of the most advanced in Asia. Occupying 46.5 hectares of reclaimed land, it accommodates 32 parking bays plus another five in the cargo area. When opened in 1976, the latter had a handling capacity of 340,000 tonnes, but after an expansion programme in 1984 this figure increased to 720,000 tonnes annually. Although constantly visited by up to five Boeing 747 freighters simulta-

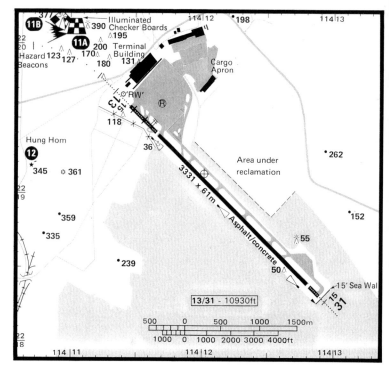

Map labels:
- Illuminated Checker Boards
- 11B
- 11A
- Hazard Beacons
- Terminal Building
- Cargo Apron
- 'RW'
- Hung Hom
- 12
- Area under reclamation
- 3331 × 61m
- Asphalt/concrete
- 13/31 - 10930ft
- 15' Sea Wall

Numbers: 377, 390, 195, 200, 170, 180, 131, 123, 127, 118, 36, 345, 361, 359, 335, 239, 198, 262, 152, 55, 50, 262

Scale: 500 0 500 1000 1500m / 1000 0 1000 2000 3000 4000ft

Coordinates: 114|11, 114|12, 114|13

neously, the majority of the cargo is still carried in the holds of passenger aircraft. This business is very important to Hong Kong's economy, so every effort is made to encourage growth. For this reason the construction of a second cargo terminal began in 1989, which, when completed some two years later, more than doubled the annual freight handling capability with its possible 1.4 million tonnes throughput.

The Government accepted the recommendations of a consultant in 1988 to proceed with a $2.4 billion programme of development, which was intended generally to improve the airport's facilities and realise its ultimate capacity. The project included a two-stage extension to the main apron so that when finished a total of seven additional wide-bodied aircraft could be parked. Enhancement of the terminal and road access was also high on the list of priorities, so a completion date in July 1992 was arranged.

Meanwhile serious thought was being given to the building of a replacement airport for Kai Tak. A Master Plan published in 1981 had indicated that the most suitable site would be at Chek Lap Kok off the north coast of Lantau Island. After lengthy studies, in 1989 the Governor formally announced that a new facility would be constructed at this location for an operational debut in 1997. Interestingly, another significant event is scheduled to take place in the same year, namely the return of the Colony to China. Not surprisingly the latter expressed concern about the responsibility for the financial burden and even justification for the project, bearing in mind that two other new airports in the immediate vicinity will be in service long before Hong Kong's replacement. However, once the debate had ended, the interested parties were in general agreement that the Lantau project should go ahead.

Location and access: Situated on the east of the Kowloon peninsula, 3 miles (5km) from Victoria. Kowloon Motor Bus Co service A1 (Circular) leaves Star Ferry Terminal every 15min and takes 54min for the trip calling at various hotels en route. Service A2 runs from Central Hong Kong

Island (Macau Ferry Bus Terminus) via Cross Harbour Tunnel with a journey time of 40min. There is a multi-storey car park for those arriving by road.

Terminal: Operated on a two-level system, with arrivals on the ground floor and departures on the level above. The latter area contains the shops, restaurants and other services. Airline offices and airport administration occupy the upper floors with the control tower located on the roof.

Spectator facilities: A large rooftop gallery offers good views of the movements, but the quality of the glass leaves something to be desired when considering photography. As an alternative the top deck of the multi-storey car park is a good vantage point for landing shots, but suitable locations at ground level are scarce. Some interesting pictures can be obtained from several spots on the hillsides which are at the appropriate level as the aircraft carry out the curved approach to the runway. The quality of the subjects is worth the effort especially with backgrounds that are unique to the area.

Operators: Scheduled services by Air China (Boeing 707/747/767), Air France (Boeing 747), Air Hong Kong (Boeing 707/747), Air India (Airbus A310), Air Lanka (TriStar), Air Mauritius (Boeing 747), Air New Zealand (Boeing 747), Air Niugini (Airbus A310), Alitalia (Boeing 747), All Nippon Airways (TriStar), American Airlines (Boeing 747), British Airways (Boeing 747), Canadian International (DC-10), Cathay Pacific (Boeing 747, TriStar), China Airlines (Airbus A300, Boeing 747), China Eastern (Airbus A300, DC-9), China Southern (Boeing 737/757), Federal Express (Boeing 747), Garuda Indonesia (Airbus A300, DC-10), Gulf Air (Boeing 767), Dragon Airlines (Boeing 737), Japan Airlines (Boeing 747/767, DC-10), Japan Asia Airways (DC-10), KLM (Boeing 747), Korean Air (Airbus A300, Boeing 747), Lauda Air (Boeing 767), Lufthansa (Boeing 747), Malaysian Airlines System (Airbus A300, Boeing 747, DC-10), Nippon Cargo Airlines (Boeing 747), Northwest Airlines (Boeing 747), Philippine Airlines (Airbus A300, DC-10), Qantas (Boeing 747/767), Rosenbalm Aviation (DC-8), Royal Brunei (Boeing 757), Royal Nepal (Boeing 757), Singapore Airlines (Boeing 747), South African Airways (Boeing 747), Swissair (Boeing 747), Thai International (Airbus A300, Boeing 747), United Airlines (Boeing 747), United Parcel Service (DC-8) and World Airways (DC-10).

Charter and IT carriers: Air Hong Kong (Boeing 707/747), Air Swazi Cargo (Boeing 707), American International Airways (DC-8), American Trans Air (TriStar), Ansett Airlines (Boeing 767), Cargolux (Boeing 747), Condor (DC-10), Hapag Lloyd (Airbus A310), Hawaiian Air (TriStar, DC-8), HeavyLift Cargo Airlines (Belfast, CL-44, Boeing 707), Linea LAN Chile (Boeing 707), Martinair (DC-10) and Tradewinds Airways (Boeing 737).

Movements (1990): Total air transport 105,800. Total passengers 18,688,000.

Runway: 13/31 (11,128ft/3,392m).

Radio frequencies: 118.7MHz (Tower), 119.1MHz (Approach), 121.6MHz (Ground), 121.3MHz, 123.7MHz (Area Control).

Telephone: 867 4203.

Operated by: The Civil Aviation Department of the Hong Kong Government.

Honolulu International, Hi USA

Although the Hawaiian Islands are some 3,000 miles from the nearest continent, aviation reached the area at a surprisingly early stage. An enterprising aviator provided a brief glimpse into the future when he demonstrated his flimsy machine to the local population on New Year's Eve 1910, but another eight years passed before a flight successfully linked the islands. Encouraged by this achievement, the military established a landing strip in Honolulu during 1919; a development envied by the civil authorites. Eventually the latter raised sufficient funds to acquire some land alongside Keehi Lagoon, the site chosen for the future commercial airport which was opened on 21 March 1927. It adopted the name of John Rogers, a naval officer who had piloted the first aircraft to reach Hawaii, albeit disguised as a sailing boat following an unintentional landing in the Pacific some distance short of his destination.

Thereafter there was steady growth in the airline industry leading to the formation of Inter-Island Airways in 1929. On 11 November a scheduled passenger service was launched to link Honolulu with the outer islands of the group, resulting in Maui, Hilo and Kauai being visited regularly while Molokai and Lanai were request stops. This was made possible by employing a pair of Sikorsky S-38 amphibians, each configured with eight seats. As the popularity of the operation increased during the 1930s, so the fleet was augmented by the larger S-43. Meanwhile, on 16 April 1935, Pan American operated the first flight from the US mainland, the lengthy trip from San Francisco to Pearl Harbor taking 17 hr 14min.

After the Japanese attack on 7 December 1941, the airport was taken over by the military thereby ending all civilian flying until a local freight run was introduced with three DC-3s in March 1942. Just prior to this event, Inter-Island Airways had changed its name to Hawaiian Airlines, a title the company has retained to the present day. Interestingly, in-flight entertainment was introduced in the 1940s with ukelele and song-sheet-equipped stewardesses performing both song and dance on board the company's DC-3s. Nevertheless Hawaiian's air transport monopoly was lost after World War 2 when Trans-Pacific Airlines (later renamed Aloha Airlines) was given permission to commence operations. After numerous legal battles, the new carrier won approval to offer scheduled services in competition with Hawaiian to the benefit of the local travellers.

During the 1950s the number of passengers handled by the airport steadily increased until the terminal building was unable to cope. This became even more obvious with the introduction of jet services in 1959, so construction of a new complex began which eventually opened for business on 15 October 1962. Subsequently Honolulu International has been developed into one of the world's most attractive airports covering 4,480 acres. There are now four active runways, one of which was the first major strip to be built entirely off-shore.

Passengers are accommodated in the much-enlarged terminal buildings and transported to the appropriate Concourses and Gates by Wiki Wiki buses. This method will become inadequate when the new international terminal is completed in 1994. At this point the walking distance from one end of the airport to the other will increase by some 50%. At present it takes 23min to transfer on foot from the main concourse to the Hawaiian Airlines terminal; a time which will become 32min in the mid-1990s. To improve matters, the authorites are planning an automated people mover system as a practical means of transporting passengers quickly between the Main, International and Interisland buildings. Detailed design work began in 1991 with construction due to start in May 1992. Hopefully the completion will coincide with the opening of the International terminal extension two years later.

Interisland passenger traffic at HIA has also increased significantly over the last decade, a trend that is expected to continue. In 1980 5.8 million such travellers passed through the gates, a total that by 1989 had risen to 8.6 million. Forecasts indicate that by 2016 this figure will have doubled so preparations are already in hand to deal with this enormous influx with work beginning on the provision of a new multi-level domestic complex in November 1989.

As new markets in Europe, Japan and elsewhere are found for Hawaii's products, inevitably there will be a general increase in cargo operations. Two areas are being developed for the use of this traffic. One, known as Cargo City, is designed to handle freight carried in the holds of passenger aircraft and comprises the existing United and Northwest Airlines' complexes. A second phase targeted for completion in April 1992 will allow further expansion of this business. Meanwhile, the South Ramp Cargo Facility on the southeastern side of HIA has been earmarked for the use of pure freighters, with the individual operators responsible for the erection of their own warehouses. United Parcel Service became the first to complete its accommodation by the end of 1990, at which time a similar facility was already well underway for Federal Express. Parking positions for four Boeing 747s have been constructed in front of the South Ramp area, while the road access has been greatly improved.

It seems amazing that in 1940 a total of 1,153 passengers used the airport. Twenty years later it had only risen to 1,609,041 but by 1980 15,155,337 were being handled annually. If this growth is maintained then the anticipated 42 million in 2012 does not appear to be an unreasonable forecast.

Location and access: Situated 9 miles (14.4km) west of Waikiki Beach and 4 miles (6.4km) west of central Honolulu. City Bus Service (MTL) 19 (eastbound) runs from the airport to Kalihi Kai and downtown Honolulu before terminating at Waikiki. The westbound route takes the bus to nearby Hickam AFB. Service 20 (eastbound) takes a similar track but travels via Kalihi (Dillingham) before proceeding to the same terminus as the 19. In this case the westbound service 20 travels from the airport via the Arizona Memorial, Aloha Stadium, Aiea until finally Pearlridge is reached. This public transport is considerably cheaper than the airport coach, but of course takes longer. In all cases the exact fare is required. For those with cars the parking charges are graduated.

Terminals: A main pier with two branches at each end extends from the central terminal. A wide range of shops, restaurants and snack bars are scattered throughout the buildings.

Spectator facilities: There is a good observation area at the front of the international terminal, but it has its limitations for photography due to its south-facing aspect and the obstruction caused by visiting 747s which are invariably parked on near stands. Elsewhere around the perimeter it is possible to find suitable spots, especially near the thresholds of the runways.

Operators: Air Micronesia (Boeing 727), Air New Zealand (Boeing 747/767), Aloha Airlines (Boeing 737), Aloha Islandair (Twin Otter), American Airlines (DC-10), China Airlines (Boeing 747), America West (Boeing 747), Canadian International (DC-10), Circle Rainbow (Islander), Continental Airlines (Boeing 727/747, DC-10), Delta Air Lines (TriStar), Garuda (DC-10), Hawaiian Airlines (Dash Seven, DC-8/9, TriStar), Japan Airlines (Boeing 747), Korean Air (Boeing 747, DC-10), Malaysian Airlines System (Boeing 747), Northwest Airlines (Boeing 747, DC-10), Panorama Air (Navajo), Philippine Airlines (Boeing 747), Qantas (Boeing 747), Singapore Airlines (Boeing 747), Trans World (Boeing 747), United Airlines (Boeing 747, DC-10). Military movements are to be seen as Hickam AFB shares the runways with the airport. Hawaiian National Guard aircraft are among those based at this site.

Movements (1990): Total air transport 251,900. Total passengers 22,300,000.

Runways: 08L/26R (12,360ft/3,767m), 08R/26L (12,000ft/3,657m), 04R/22L (9,000ft/2,743m), 04L/22R (6,950ft/2,118m).

Radio frequencies: 118.1MHz (Tower), 121.9MHz (Ground control), 118.3MHz, 119.1MHz, 124.8MHz (Approach/Departure).

Telephone: (808) 836-6411.

Operated by: State of Hawaii Department of Transportation.

London (Gatwick) United Kingdom

Officially the site became an airport on 6 June 1936 when it was formally declared open for commercial flying by the Secretary of State for Air. Six years earlier, in August 1930, flying had begun at Gatwick to become very popular with the horse racing fraternity due to its close proximity to the course. When the airfield was earmarked for development the planners incorporated several novel features into the design including an underground passageway to the adjacent railway station and the provision of a circular terminal building with covered walkways to the parked aircraft. Although several operators moved into the newly created facility, unfortunately Gatwick suffered from waterlogging from time to time causing some to forsake their new home.

A military presence began in 1937 when the Tiger Moths and Harts of No 19 E&RFTS took up residence, an occupation which speeded up the provision of additional buildings. This training establishment was closed at the outbreak of war, an event which also decreed that civil flying was suspended for the duration. Initially RAF Blenheims became the occupants, but in September 1940 the station came under the control of Army Co-Operation Command. Thereafter Lysanders and Tomahawks became a familiar sight until replaced with Mustangs in 1942; this type taking part in the Dieppe operation in August. In the middle of the following year Gatwick became a part of No 11 Group so the local scene was thereafter dominated by Spitfires as various squadrons spent short periods at the airfield. Most of the operational activity involved escort duties or sweeps along the Channel, an occupation which continued until after D-Day in 1944. In the run-up to the invasion of France Gatwick had also become the base for photo-reconnaissance Mustang units charged with the task of providing up-to-date information on the disposition of the German forces. By August the war had moved on leaving the airfield with only non-operational activities for the remainder of its military career. Two years later the RAF relinquished its control which then passed to the Ministry of Civil Aviation.

Even at that early stage some thought was given to the possibility of Gatwick becoming a London airport, but it was by no means certain that another would be necessary to assist Heathrow. By 1952 there were no doubts left; Gatwick would be needed. When the plans were finalised the area selected was positioned to the north of the original site, the proposed single runway stretching for 7,000ft/2,133m towards the west. Access to the railway was still possible although a new station was required near to the box-like terminal building. It was on 9 June 1958 that the opening ceremony was performed by HM The Queen and Prince Phillip, a Heron of the Royal Flight bringing the distinguished visitors to the scene.

For several years the new airport was able to cope with its traffic, much of which was provided by the charter carriers, but

Above:
Landing shots are possible from the Gatwick roof, this subject being Philippine Airlines' 747 N744PR. *AJW*

Below:
Dan-Air's 146-300 G-BPNT prepares to push-back at Gatwick. *AJW*

with the creation of British United Airways in 1960, so the volume was considerably increased. Not far away, Heathrow was also feeling the strain, so it was decided to implement an expansion programme to relieve both airports. Gatwick's terminal was effectively doubled in size and the runway lengthened to 8,200ft/2,500m, but with the provision of a third London airport abandoned in the early 1970s, yet another even more ambitious development scheme was begun. Again a vast terminal expansion was involved including the addition of a satellite connected to the main building by a rapid transit system. Access was further improved by a direct link with the M23 motorway and British Rail's train services became both frequent and fast. Airside changes included additional parking areas and taxiways, while an emergency runway was laid parallel to the existing strip with completion in October 1985. Ideally Gatwick would benefit from its regular use to facilitate simultaneous landings and take-offs, but unfortunately the separation distance does not comply with the safety limits. By this time the main runway had been extended once again, this time taking it to 10,363ft/3,159m in length.

After the removal of most charter flights from Heathrow, Gatwick became the main terminal for such operations in the London area although scheduled movements also steadily increased as more and more airlines opened up services. Both British Caledonian and Dan-Air contributed considerably to the growth, but the advent of trans-Atlantic flights by wide-bodied types was largely responsible for the need for yet more terminal space. It was not possible to provide this around the original building, so a second complex was planned on the north side which was duly opened for business in March 1988. All British Airways flights were transferred to the new facility to be joined gradually by other refugees from the south terminal.

In the 1980s Air Europe became a major force at Gatwick as its involvement in scheduled services became greater. Together with its IT work, the airline accounted for some 10% of the traffic at the airport, so when the company collapsed in March 1991 it had a marked effect on the traffic figures. Fortunately it was only temporary because there were more than enough eager carriers willing to takeover the commitments. The decision to give newcomers the opportunity to have access to Heathrow was responsible for a number of moves from Gatwick, but the void was soon filled by others keen to serve London whichever gateway was allocated. The growing shortage of runway space in the southeast of England was responsible for a survey into the various options available, but it seems very unlikely that a second strip will now be laid at Gatwick.

Location and access: Situated 28 miles south of London with a direct link to the M23 motorway at Junction 9. Short term multistorey car parking with open long term serve north and south terminals, both with graduated charges. Since these are expensive, it is cheaper and almost as quick to use the off-airport organisations. If an extended stay is contemplated it is more economic to use public transport. By rail the Gatwick Express runs nonstop between London Victoria station and the airport's south terminal every 15min during the day taking 30min for the journey. During the night the trains are hourly and take up to 15min longer to complete the trip. An alternative Thameslink service runs halfhourly from Kings Cross, St Pauls, Blackfriars and London Bridge taking some 35min for the trip from the latter. There is a direct transit link from Gatwick station to the north terminal. Speedlink coaches connect Gatwick with Heathrow every 20min, each sortie scheduled to take 60min but this depends on the road conditions on the M25 motorway. Route 777 runs to Victoria coach station while the 747 visits Heathrow and Luton airports. Local services C1, C2, 405, & 422 operate to both Crawley and Horley. There is a bus information desk in the international arrivals hall at Gatwick (Tel: (0293) 502116).

Terminal: Both main terminals contain restaurants and snack bars. Shops and banks are also much in evidence.

Spectator facilities: A gallery situated on the roof of the south terminal building gives good views of all movements although some are rather distant. There is an admission charge and opening hours vary according to the season. A refreshment buffet is a welcome facility available, while the provision of TV monitors for checking arrivals and departures is very useful. As a photographic vantage point the terrace has its limitations, although shots are possible of some of the aircraft using the satellite and the nearer centre pier stands. Unfortunately many of the more interesting charter types are often banished to the far stands beyond the piers.

Operators: Scheduled services by Adria Airways (DC-9), Aer Lingus (Boeing 737), Aigle Azur (Bandeirante), Air France (Fokker 100), Air Littoral (Fokker 100, Brasilia), Air Malta (Boeing 737), Air New Zealand (Boeing 747), Air Seychelles (Boeing 767), Air UK (BAe 146), Air Vendee (Saab SF340), Air Zimbabwe (Boeing 767),

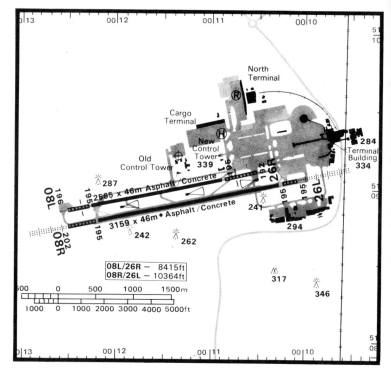

American Airlines (Boeing 767, DC-10), Brit Air (Bandeirante, Saab SF340, ATR-42), British Airways (DC-10, Boeing 737/747/757), Air China (Boeing 747), Cameroon Airways (Boeing 747), Cathay Pacific (Boeing 747), Cityflyer Express (Short SD3-60, ATR-42), Contactair (Jetstream), Continental Airlines (Boeing 747, DC-10), Cyprus Airways (Airbus A310/320), Dan-Air (One-Eleven, BAe 146, Boeing 737), Delta Air Lines (Boeing 767, Airbus A310, TriStar), Emirates (Airbus A300), Garuda International (Boeing 747), GB Airways (Boeing 737), Jersey European (Friendship, Short SD3-60), KLM (Saab SF340), Lauda Air (Boeing 737), Lucas Air Transport (Bandeirante, Beech 200), Lufthansa (Boeing 737), Maersk Air (Boeing 737), Malmo Aviation (BAe 146), Meridiana (BAe 146, DC-9), Northwest Airlines (Boeing 747), Norway Airlines (Boeing 737, DC-9), Philippine Airlines (Boeing 747), RFG (ATR-42), Royal Nepal (Boeing 757), SAS (DC-9), Sterling Airways (DC-9), Transavia (Boeing 737), Transwede (DC-9), Trans World (Boeing 767, TriStar), Uganda Airlines (Boeing 707), USAir (Boeing 767), Virgin Atlantic (Boeing 747), Viva Air (Boeing 737), and Yemenia (Boeing 727). *Charter and IT operators:* Aeroflot (Tu-134/154, IL-86), Adria Airways (DC-9), Air Atlantis (Boeing 737), Air Columbus (Boeing 727), Air Europa (Boeing 737/757), Air Malta (Boeing 737, Airbus A320), Air Sul (Boeing 737), Air Transat (TriStar), Air UK Leisure (Boeing 737), Air 2000 (Boeing 757), Alitalia (DC-9), American Trans Air (Boeing 757, TriStar), Arkia (Boeing 707), ATI (DC-9), Aviogenex (Boeing 727/737), Balair (DC-9), Balkan (Tu-154), Britannia Airways (Boeing 737/757/767), Caledonian Airways (Boeing 757, TriStar), Canadian Airlines International (Boeing 767, DC-10), Canada 3000 (Boeing 757), CTA (DC-9), Dan-Air (Boeing 727/737, One-Eleven, BAe 146), El Al (Boeing 707), Excalibur Airways (Airbus A320), Futura (Boeing 737), Kar-Air (DC-9, Airbus A300), Meridiana (DC-9), Monarch Airlines (Airbus A300, Boeing 737/757), Nationair (Boeing 747, DC-8), Pegasus Airlines (Boeing 737), Polish Airlines (Tu-134/154), Royal Air Maroc

(Boeing 737), Spanair (Boeing 767, DC-9), Tarom (IL-18, Tu-154), Sterling Airways (Boeing 727, Caravelle) and Transwede (DC-9, Caravelle).
Movements (1990): Total 203,098 (air transport 189,409). Total passengers 21,178,762.
Runways: 08R/26L (10,364ft/3,159m),

08L/26R (8,415ft/2,565m - used only in emergencies or if 08R/26L is closed; otherwise it serves as a taxiway).
Radio frequencies: 124.225MHz (Tower), 128.575MHz (Approach), 119.60MHz (Radar).
Telephone: (0293) 535353.
Operated by: Gatwick Airport Ltd.

London (Heathrow)
United Kingdom

Since its opening in 1946, Heathrow has become one of the world's leading international airports with over 70 airlines providing services to all parts of the world. Almost all of the movements are those of scheduled traffic, although executive aircraft are regular visitors and the cargo facility opened in 1968 continues to handle a considerable amount of business. Compared with some of its European counterparts, Heathrow presents a jumble of buildings of varying designs all packed into the restricted space available in the centre area. Even the much acclaimed Terminal 4 does little to redress the balance. Nevertheless the airports on the continent do not have to contend with the same volume of traffic as London so the emphasis has always had to be on the speedy movement of passengers rather than elegance. Much of the blame for the problem stems from its early days when it was planned as a standard RAF airfield with a triangular runway pattern. Even when this was quickly abandoned the choice of layout still favoured the centre island arrangement. Breaking away from this was the only solution when a new terminal was urgently needed at the end of the 1970s. Its opening in April 1986 certainly brought some relief because at that stage all of British Airways' inter-continental services together with the airlines's Paris, Amsterdam and Athens flights were all transferred from either Terminals 1 or 3. Also accommodated in the new Terminal 4 are KLM, Air Malta and Air Lanka.

A long-standing policy was changed in 1991 when the authorities agreed to allow new carriers access to Heathrow. This relaxation of the rules came after American Airlines and United Airlines bought trans-Atlantic routes from TWA and Pan Am respectively. A number of companies subsequently transferred their operations from Gatwick in the belief that travellers would prefer using London's premier airport. Charter operators were also allowed back after an absence of over 20 years, with several

tour companies offering Heathrow as an alternative departure point in their summer programmes. Needless to say this influx did nothing to improve the congestion both land and airside, so investigations began into the feasibility of a fifth terminal and another runway to the north of the Bath Road. The latter proposal revives the scheme originally planned for Heathrow in the 1940s, but abandoned as unnecessary at the time.

Location and access: Situated 14 miles (22.5km) west of central London with access direct from the M4 motorway at Junction 4 or the A4 to the centre area. Terminal 4 is alongside the A30 and can be reached from the M25. Each of the four terminals have their own short-term car park with rapidly escalating charges after the first two hours. Long-term parking is available on the northern boundary for those using Terminals 1, 2 and 3 while Terminal 4 has its own nearby. A courtesy bus shuttles backwards and forwards at frequent intervals. If a stay is likely to exceed two hours it is therefore more sensible to use this park. Bearing in mind the amount of public transport on offer, it is often cheaper to leave the car outside the airport and catch a bus or train. By using the Piccadilly Line from central London it is possible to make the journey in 47min. Trains stop at Hatton Cross on the boundary of the airport before travelling in a clockwise direction to Terminal 4 and Heathrow Central. The return to London takes the train around the remainder of the loop to Hatton Cross once again. Numerous local buses call at the central bus station, while coaches to most parts of the country either leave from Heathrow or via a direct link with Victoria coach station. Express services are operated on this route by Greenline's Fleetline 767 and London Transport's Airbus which also visits Euston railway station in its travels. A direct Speedlink coach links Gatwick and Heathrow every 20min, while Jetlink 747 has a similar purpose but includes Luton in its itinerary. As an alternative Rail/Air links are available with coaches ferrying passengers to and from Woking and Reading BR stations for onward

Several of BA's aircraft advertised The World's Biggest Offer in 1991, one to be seen at Heathrow being the 737-236 G-BKYK. *AJW*

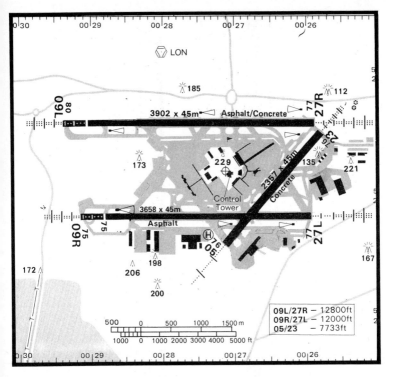

travel by InterCity or local trains to the west. In the future BR intends to build a line to the airport so that fast trains can be operated in a similar manner to those serving Gatwick.
Terminals: All four have lounge areas, shops, restaurants, bars, buffets, bank and post offices. Terminal 1 handles all British Airways' (European Division) flights plus all other UK airlines including Aer Lingus. As a result congestion is not unknown in the building particularly around the arrivals area. A major improvement scheme to enlarge the facilities on the northern side of Terminal 1 began in 1991. Following the opening of Terminal 4 several other carriers using the centre complex were relocated in order to achieve a better distribution of traffic in the terminals. As a result Cyprus Airways, El Al, Icelandair, Sabena and South African Airways are handled by Terminal 1. The remaining European airlines use Terminal 2 with the exception of SAS which is allocated to Terminal 3.
Spectator facilities: A large roof terrace is

provided over Queens's Building and Terminal 2. It has its own refreshment facilities and is open daily from 10.00 until dusk. There is an admission charge. It is a fine vantage point for viewing purposes, all movements being visible if somewhat distant at times. Unfortunately through the years the photographic opportunities have steadily declined mainly due to the number of buildings that have grown along the front of the buildings. However, while it is now more difficult to obtain reasonable ground shots of even BA aircraft, it is not impossible although luck plays a significant part. Without doubt a visit to Schiphol, Dusseldorf or Frankfurt is far more rewarding and less frustrating
Operators: Scheduled services by Aer Lingus (Boeing 737, Fokker 50), Aeroflot (Tu-154, IL-62/86), African International (DC-8), Air Algerie (Boeing 727/737), Air Canada (Boeing 747/767), Air France (Airbus A300/310/320, Boeing 727/737. ATR-42, Fellowship), Air India (Boeing 747), Air Lanka (TriStar), Air Malta (Airbus A320, Boeing 737), Air Mauritius (Boeing

747/767), Air Portugal (Airbus A310, Boeing 737, TriStar), Air UK (BAe 146, Friendship), Air Zaire (DC-10), Alitalia (DC-9, Airbus A300), All Nippon Airways (Boeing 747), American Airlines (DC-10, Boeing 767), ATI (DC-9), Austrian Airlines (DC-9), Balkan (Tu-154), Bangladesh Biman (DC-10), British Airways (Airbus A320, Concorde, TriStar, Boeing 737/747/757/767, One-Eleven), British Air Ferries (Friendship, Viscount), British Midland (DC-9, BAe ATP, Dash Seven, Boeing 737), British West Indian Airways (TriStar), Brymon Airways (Dash Seven/Eight), Cathay Pacific (Boeing 747), Crossair (BAe 146, Fokker 100), Cyprus Airways (Airbus A310/320), Czechoslovak Airlines (IL-62, Tu-134/154, Airbus A310), Delta Air Transport (Fellowship, BAe 146), Egyptair (Airbus A300), El Al (Boeing 747/767), Emirates (Airbus A310), Ethiopian Airlines (Boeing 767), Finnair (DC-9), Federal Express (Boeing 747, DC-10), GB Airways (Boeing 737), Ghana Airways (DC-10), Gulf Air (TriStar, Boeing 767), Iberia (DC-9, Boeing 727, Airbus A300/320, DC-10), Icelandair (Boeing 737), Iran Air (Boeing 747SP), Iraqi Airlines (Boeing 727/747), Japan Air Lines (Boeing 747), Kenya Airways (Airbus A310), KLM (Airbus A310, Boeing 737, Fellowship, Fokker 50), Kuwait Airways (Boeing 747), Lufthansa (Airbus A300/310/320, Boeing 727/737), Luxair (Fokker 50, Boeing 737), Malaysian Airlines System (Boeing 747), Malev (Tu-134/154, Boeing 737), Middle East Airlines (Boeing 707/747), Manx Airlines (BAe 146, BAe ATP), Nigeria Airways (Airbus A310, Boeing 747, DC-10), Olympic Airways (Boeing 727/737, Airbus A300), Pakistan International (Boeing 747), Polish Airlines (Tu-134/154, IL-62), Qantas (Boeing 747), Royal Air Maroc (Boeing 727/737/757), Royal Brunei (Boeing 767), Royal Jordanian (TriStar, Airbus A310), Sabena (Boeing 737, BAe 146, Fellowship), SAS (DC-9), Singapore International (Boeing 747), Saudi Arabian Airlines (Boeing 747), Sudan Airways (Airbus A310), Swissair (DC-9, Airbus A310, Fokker 100), Tarom (One-Eleven, Boeing 707), Thai International (Boeing 747), Trans Mediterranean (Boeing 707), Tunisair (Boeing 727), Turkish Airlines (Airbus A310, Boeing 707/727), United Airlines (Boeing 727/747/767), Varig (DC-10), Viasa (DC-10), Virgin Atlantic (Boeing 747), Yugoslav Airlines (DC-9, Boeing 727/737) and Zambia Airways (DC-10).
Charter operators: Air 2000 (Boeing 757) and Britannia Airways (Boeing 737/767)
Movements (1990): Total 390,393 (air transport 368,461). Total passengers: 42,950,832
Runways: 09R/27L (12,000ft/3,658m), 09L/27R (12,802ft/3,902m), 05/23 (7,733ft/2,357m).
Radio frequencies: 118.5MHz, 118.7MHz, 124.475MHz (Tower), 119.2MHz, 119.5MHz, 120.4MHz (Approach), 121.9MHz (Ground)
Telephone: (081) 759 4321.
Operated by: Heathrow Airport Ltd.

Los Angeles International, Ca USA

Aviation came to the Californian city in 1928 when a private airport known as Mines Field was opened on 640 acres of land acquired from a local ranch. It was a somewhat primitive facility possessing only a dirt runway and no buildings, but after noting that some 200,000 curious spectators had been attracted to the year's National Air Races, the City authorities decided to develop the site. Construction of two modern hangars commenced on the south side of the field, each capable of housing 20 aircraft. Further interest was aroused in 1929 when the German *Graf Zeppelin* airship paid a short visit following a trans-Pacific flight, but it was 7 June 1930 before America's latest aviation centre was formally opened.

Commercial airline services began for the first time in December 1946 using temporary passenger accommodation. Previously only private or charter flights had been handled, although during the war there were a considerable number of military movements. By this stage Los Angeles had become the official title, to which the word International was added in October 1949. An enormous growth rate was experienced in the postwar years which brought the need for constant expansion. It was met in 1957 by commissioning the construction of a brand new terminal designed especially for the new age jetliners. Dedicated on 1 June 1962, the complex used the satellite concept with the separate buildings linked to the centre area. This system helps to reduce congestion for the aircraft and travellers alike by decentralising the ground movements. Other work undertaken included the extension of the two main runways to 10,000ft and 12,000ft in 1959/1960, a considerable length 30 years ago.

Above:
Iberia began using its new A320s on some of its Heathrow services during 1991, EC-583 being delivered in July. *AJW*

Below:
Southwest 737s such as N29SW are to be found at Los Angeles. *AJW*

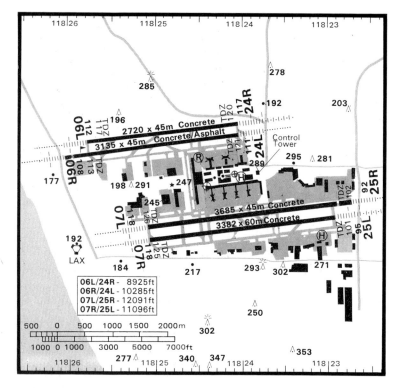

From 1961, the total number of passengers handled annually at Los Angeles (LAX) rose steadily from 7 million to almost 45 million. A major improvement programme was completed in 1984, most of the work being devoted towards the provision of the huge Tom Bradley International Terminal. Certainly the largest of its kind in the US, it can serve almost all of the overseas flag carriers with its 11 airbridge gates plus another 18 served by buses from remote stands. For several years preceding the opening, overseas travellers were processed in a leisurely manner within three air-supported halls. The plastic domes did not give a very good first impression, but were necessary as a short-term expedient.

In the centre of the area a notable landmark rises 135ft. Known as the Theme Building, its parabolic arches symbolise the futuristic aims of the airport. A restaurant is suspended some 70ft above the ground and has a tiered floor to give all of its 220 patrons an uninterrupted view through its expanse of glass.

Location and access: Situated 15 miles (24km) southwest of Los Angeles. Airport Bus Services operate from many of the surrounding towns and districts in the State. FlyAway Bus Service offers frequent non-stop transportation between LAX and the San Fernando Valley. A tram service links the various terminals within the complex. There are spaces for 26,000 cars in the central terminal parking area plus accommodation for another 16,000 in the long-term section. Charges vary according to the location and duration.

Terminals: A group of eight separate buildings cater for most of the scheduled carriers with only a few using the Imperial terminal on the south side. A pylon on top of, or adjacent to, the building, displays the relevant number of the structure. All terminals are equipped with cafeterias, snack bars, lounges, shops and other amenities.

Spectator facilities: The observation deck on top of the Theme Building offers a reasonable vantage point, although

Shot from one of the conveniently situated Los Angeles carparks, this 727 of Continental is N24728. *AJW*

needless to say everything is rather distant. By passing through the security checks at the approaches to each terminal, it is possible to obtain acceptable photographs through the glass, but opportunities are limited at any one point. Sadly, since the advent of the Gulf crisis, access has been restricted to passengers and seems unlikely to be restored. Nevertheless, as an alternative some useful spots can be found around the perimeter, especially in the outlying car parks from where some good landing shots can be acquired.

Operators: Services by Aerocalifornia (DC-9), Aerocancun (DC-9, Airbus A310), Aerolineas Argentinas (Boeing 747), Aeromexico (DC-9), Air Canada (Airbus A320, Boeing 767), Air China (Boeing 747), Air France (Boeing 747), Air Jamaica (Airbus A300), Air LA (Bandeirante), Air New Zealand (Boeing 747/767), Alaska Airlines (Boeing 727, DC-9), Alitalia (Boeing 747), Alpha Air (Beech 1900), America West (Boeing 737), American Airlines (Airbus A300, Boeing 727/737/767, BAe 146, DC-9/10, MD-11), American Eagle (Metro), American Trans Air (TriStar, Boeing 757), All Nippon (Boeing 747), Avianca (Boeing 767), Aviateca (Boeing 737), Britannia (Boeing 767), British Airways (Boeing 747, DC-10), Caledonian (TriStar), Canada 3000 (Boeing 757), Canadian Airlines International (Boeing 737/767), Cathay Pacific (Boeing 747), China Airlines (Boeing 747), Condor (DC-10), Continental Airlines (Airbus A300, Boeing 727/737/747, DC-9/10), Continental Express (Metro), Delta Air Lines (Airbus A310, Boeing 727/737/757/767, TriStar), Ecuatoriana (Boeing 707, DC-10), EgyptAir (Boeing 767), El Al (Boeing 747), Finnair (DC-10, MD-11), Garuda (DC-10, Boeing 747), Grand Airways (Metro), Hawaiian Air (TriStar), Iberia (Boeing 747), Japan Airlines (Boeing 747), KLM (Boeing 747), Korean Air (Boeing 747), LACSA (Boeing 727), LAN Chile (Boeing 767), LOT Polish Airlines (IL-62), LTU (TriStar), Lufthansa (Boeing 747), MGM Grand Air (Boeing 727, DC-8), Malaysian Airlines System (Boeing 747), Martinair (DC-10), Mexicana (Boeing 727, DC-10), Midwest Express (DC-9), Nationair (Boeing 747/757), Northwest Airlines (Airbus A320, Boeing 727/757, DC-9/10), Pacific Coast Air (Navajo), Qantas (Boeing 747), Philippine Airlines (Boeing 747), SAS (Boeing 767), Singapore Airlines (Boeing 747), Sky West (Metro, Brasilia), Southwest Airlines (Boeing 737), Sun Country (Boeing 727), Swissair (DC-10), TACA (Boeing 737/767), TAP Air Portugal (TriStar), Trans World (TriStar, Boeing 727/747/767), United Airlines (Boeing 727/737/747/757/767, DC-10), United Express (Jetstream, BAe 146, Bandeirante, Brasilia, Short SD3-60), USAir (Boeing 727/737/767, DC-9, BAe 146, Fellowship), USAir Express (Beech 1900), Varig (Boeing 747, DC-10), Virgin Atlantic (Boeing 747) and Yugoslav Airlines (DC-10).

Cargo services: These are operated by Airborne Express, Ameriflight, American International Airways, Challenge Air Cargo, DHL Express, Emery Worldwide, Evergreen International, Federal Express, Martinaire, Rosenbalm Aviation, Salair, Southern Air Transport, Union Flights, United Parcel Service and Zantop International.

Movements (1990): Total air transport 616,100. Total passengers 45,810,000.

Runways: 07R/25L (11,096ft/3,382m), 07L/25R (12,091ft/3,658m), 06R/24L (10,285ft/3,135m), 06L/24R (8,925ft/2,720m).

Radio frequencies: 120.95MHz (Tower south), 133.9MHz (Tower north), 124.3MHz, 125.2MHz (Departure), 121.75MHz (Ground south), 121.65MHz (Ground north).

Telephone: (213) 646-5260.

Operated by: Los Angeles Department of Airports.

Luxembourg (Findel) Luxembourg

Although a number of fields in Luxembourg were used by light aircraft from the earliest days of flying, it was 1937 before a serious attempt was made to attract commercial services to the country. In March the government announced its intention to build a new airport at Findel, some three miles from the capital. World War 2 intervened before the site was completed, although the Americans provided some temporary buildings during their presence in 1945. Two years later the runway was completely relaid and extended to 3,805ft, sufficient to allow the safe operation of DC-3s and the like. Further works in 1948 took the strip to 4,921ft with land earmarked to add another 1,600ft in the future. At the same time a brand new terminal was constructed to handle the modest flow of passengers, while nearby a hangar large enough to accommodate four DC-3s was provided.

When fully operational, Findel received 679 foreign aircraft during 1947, of which

Above:
The terminal area at Los Angeles presents problems for the visitor due to the distances involved. *Los Angeles Department of Airports*

Below:
Luxembourg offers the opportunity for photographs of Luxair's Fokker 50s and Brasilias. *Luxembourg Airport Authority*

90% were DC-3s. Many of the movements were originated by Sabena which inaugurated a scheduled run to Basle using this type. On 10 January 1948 Luxembourg Airlines was formed; a company in which Scottish Aviation had a financial interest and provided technical support. A month or so later the carrier commenced operations on routes that linked its headquarters with Frankfurt, Paris and Zurich, but in 1950 the British company withdrew and all services were suspended for a time. With the assistance of Seaboard and Western Airlines operations were restarted, but finally Luxembourg Airlines ceased trading in 1958.

In April 1962 a reorganised company known as Luxair resumed flying on the same three routes using a Fokker Friendship leased from the manufacturer. At this time the airport's capacity was not stretched, but with the emergence of the new flag carrier it was not long before plans were announced for a new terminal, cargo centre and maintenance facility. Target date for completion of the complex was the end of 1975 and in fact the terminal opened for business on 1 November of that year. In addition to the European flights offered by Luxair, Findel also became the departure point for low-cost trans-Atlantic charters which staged through Iceland on their way to America. Subsequently Icelandair has developed scheduled services over similar routes using DC-8s and more recently Boeing 757s. A good deal of freight passes through the airport, much of it carried in the Boeing 747s of locally-based Cargolux

Location and access: Situated 3 miles northeast of the city off road N1. Luxembourg Community Transport bus route 9 links the central railway station with the airport at regular intervals, taking 22min for the journey. There is ample car parking space with charges dependent on duration of stay. Both Belgian and Luxembourg currency is accepted.

Terminal: The single building is still adequate for the volume of traffic handled although there is a project to build three interconnected piers in the future. All the usual facilities such as buffet, shop and

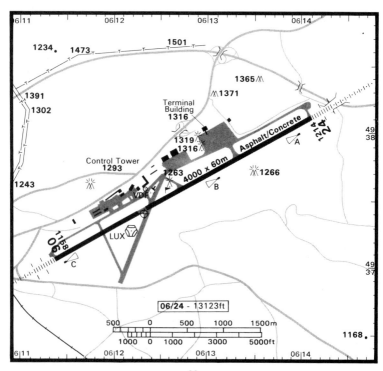

06/24 - 13123ft

bank are included within.

Spectator facilities: A fine rooftop terrace is provided giving excellent views of all movements. It is also a very good vantage point for photography although the sun can present a problem in the afternoons. There is now no charge levied for entrance to the facility. If at anytime it is closed there are terraces at either side of the terminal which can prove useful for some shots. For the patient there is the reward of some interesting subjects, but since movements are well spaced at times, a visit is more profitable if organised after checking airline schedules. It is also possible to obtain some good views of freight aircraft on the Cargolux apron including the regular visiting Aeroflot IL-76s and the 747F of China Airlines.

Operators: Scheduled services by Aeroflot (Tu-134/154), Air Portugal (Boeing 737), Avianova (ATR-42), British Airways (Boeing 737), Crossair (Saab SF340), Iberia (DC-9), Icelandair (Boeing 757), KLM CityHopper (Saab SF340, Fokker 50), Luxair (Brasilia, Boeing 737/747, Fokker 50), Sabena (Metro), Tarom (Boeing 707) and Tunis Air (Boeing 727/737). Charter operators Air Belgium (Boeing 737), Aviogenex (Boeing 737), Balkan (Tu-134/154), Luxair (Boeing 737) and Sterling Airways (Caravelle). There are regular cargo flights by Aeroflot (IL-76), Cargolux (Boeing 747) and China Airlines (Boeing 747).

Movements (1990): Total 62,714. (Scheduled 22,675/non-scheduled 5,504/general aviation 7,242). Total passengers 1,072,264.

Runway: 06/24 (13,123ft/4,000m).

Radio frequencies: 118.1MHz (Tower), 118.45MHz, 119.95MHz (Approach)

Telephone: 00352-47981.

Operated by: Administration de l'Aeroport.

Manchester International
United Kingdom

Manchester has been the UK's third busiest airport for many years, a position it is likely to retain. Package holiday flights in particular have contributed greatly to the impressive growth, attracting travellers from far and wide as the tour operators continued to offer a widening range of destinations for the sun-seekers. There has also been a significant increase in the variety of scheduled services on offer, including more trans-Atlantic flights. Fifty years ago the generation of the day was either happy with the nearby coastal resorts of northern Britain or stayed at home. No one could possibly have envisaged the change in habits at the time of the airport's opening on 25 June 1938.

Then known as Ringway, the first commercial arrival had been on the previous day when a KLM DC-2 completed its trip from Amsterdam. Once everything had settled down, schedules began to build up, but it was not to last. With the outbreak of war so the airport ended its brief association with civil aviation. Although not actually requisitioned by the Air Ministry, Manchester became the home of a number of military units, probably the best known being the Central Landing School from which emerged No 1 Parachute Training School. By the end of the war over 60,000 troops had passed through the gates to make over 500,000 jumps from Whitleys and Dakotas. In addition to this major activity, gliders were also in evidence until space forced a move to a less cramped locality. As if this was not enough, both Fairey and Avro flew their newly-built products from the airfield and RAF operational squadrons used Ringway for a while when defending the city.

Postwar commercial services were resumed in 1946, the first schedule being an international link with Paris flown by Air France. KLM was also quick to reappear with its Amsterdam service, but domestic operations were limited in the UK at this time. This was mainly because of much uncertainty and discontent following the decision that the newly created British European Airways would operate all services. In the event it was unable to commence work on many of the internal routes in 1946 due to lack of resources, so most were contracted to the smaller companies as an interim measure. Although the mainline sectors were taken over by the state airline in 1947, it was neither keen nor able to absorb the many seasonal links. Manchester therefore retained its connection with both Jersey and the Isle of Man; routes which produced such impressive load factors for the operator of the day that BEA decided that it was in its interest to take them over in future.

By the 1950s a new terminal had been built with all modern facilities, but despite the improvements there was still a reluctance by BOAC to introduce long-haul services from the airport. This omission was duly noted by the Belgian flag carrier, Sabena, resulting in the start of a new schedule to New York. BOAC was at last

This shot of the Air Charter/Euralair 737 F-GCLL was taken from the site of the new spectators' area proposed for the southwest side of Manchester airport. AJW

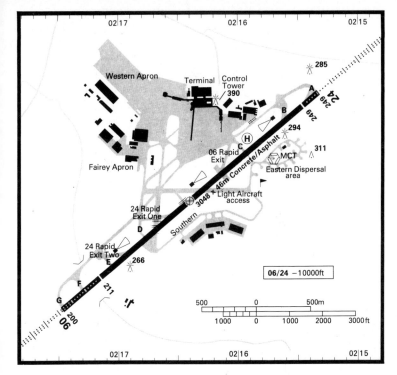

Western Apron

Terminal

Control Tower
390

Fairey Apron

06 Rapid Exit

Eastern Dispersal area

24 Rapid Exit One

Southern

3048 + 46m Concrete/Asphalt

Light Aircraft access

MCT

285

249

249

24

294

311

24 Rapid Exit Two

266

211

200

06

06/24 − 10000ft

| 500 | 0 | 500m |
| 1000 | 0 | 1000 | 2000 | 3000 ft |

forced to move its northern UK terminal to the growing Ringway, but it was not until 1954 that the first Stratocruiser departed for the American city, albeit via Prestwick. Meanwhile BEA had tended to ignore the potential of the European sectors, which had allowed airlines such as Aer Lingus and SAS to exercise their fifth freedom rights on routes passing through Manchester.

Traffic growth had begun to outstrip the capacity of the airport by the late 1950s, so plans were initiated for a brand new terminal to be constructed to modern standards. When opened in 1962 two piers projected from the impressive main building across the extensive apron. Its completion was not a moment too soon because over 1 million passengers were handled for the first time during that year. A significant impact was now being made by the inclusive tour flights, of which more and more were being offered by specialised airlines. At first these mainly linked the Mediterranean coastal areas with Manchester, but soon the more adventurous were taking advantage of the cheap trans-Atlantic charters on offer.

With the arrival of the so-called jumbo era, a new international pier complete with airbridges was built at the western end of the terminal, a project which was completed in 1974. In conjunction with this expansion, some major internal alterations were also carried out in the main building. Any of the new generation airliners could now be accommodated with ease, so to put the finishing touches to the airport the name Ringway was finally dropped by adopting the grander title of Manchester International.

Although traffic still increased each year, there still remained a certain reticence on the part of the national carrier to become too involved in the northern airport. In 1981 it actually suspended all its trans-Atlantic activities, at the same time severely trimming back both its European and domestic operations. Fortunately there were foreign airlines willing to introduce schedules although not all found them to be a commercial success. Subsequently BA reintroduced many of its links with the continent, but it still has a very limited range of long-haul services on offer. Instead it prefers to ferry passengers to Heathrow on the shuttle to connect with flights elsewhere.

Further extensions to the airport included a satellite area at the end of the international C pier and more recently the erection of a separate domestic terminal to replace the A pier previously employed. Costing £27 million, it was opened in the spring of 1989 and is completely self-contained with its own restaurants, shops and multi-storey car park. There is a linkway with the main concourse for the benefit of transfer passengers.

While this development was intended to handle 2.5 million travellers annually, in the long-term more substantial expansion will be needed before the end of the century if traffic continues to increase at the current rate. Therefore in 1988 plans were approved by the airport authority for a brand new terminal to be built on the northwest side of the present complex. Apart from that needed for the diversion of a local road, all the land is already owned by the airport.

An interesting design has been selected which calls for a fairly shallow two-storey building on the edge of the much-enlarged apron. The main concourse will be flanked on either side by long fingers along which the various gates will be positioned. Parallel, but some distance in front of this structure, will be a remote island pier reached by means of two underground passageways. It was expected that the new facility would be ready to assist with the anticipated 12 million passengers using Manchester in 1993, a total forecast to rise to 20 million by the end of the century. No doubt many will use the new airport rail station planned to open in the early 1990s, which will provide a direct link with the northern BR network and give speedy access to the city.

In the meantime Manchester will strive to win a fairer share of the long-haul market to the benefit of the north country inhabitants and the overcrowded London airports. This ambition came a little closer to fruition in mid-1991 when it was announced that a second runway was to be laid.

Location and access: Situated 10 miles (16km) south of Manchester, directly connected to the M56 motorway at Junction 5. A large short-term multi-storey car park adjoins the terminal, with an open park for longer visits with courtesy bus links. Bus service 44, 300 and 369 all visit the nearest railway station at Heald Green, the 44 travelling at 20min intervals on to the city which it reaches one hour after leaving the airport. Route 300 also calls at Wilmslow station which is on the London-Manchester main line. Express coach service 757 runs every half-hour from Manchester Victoria, Piccadilly Gardens and Chorlton Street coach station taking about 25min for the journey.

Terminal: Large modern building containing restaurant, buffets, bar and various shops. The new domestic terminal also contains a similar selection on a smaller scale. An elevated walkway connects the two complexes.

Spectator facilities: A roof terrace along the front of the building overlooks the apron between the domestic terminal and Pier B. Reached via an external stairway, it is all that remains of the original first class facilities. However, most of the movements can be seen although it tends to be come somewhat crowded with the curious and those wishing to wave. Photographs are not easy to obtain because of the narrow field of vision and in any case a 200mm lens is necessary for most shots. There is now no charge for entrance. Views of the international Pier C stands are not possible from the terrace, but the nearby multi-storey car park compensates. Plans were approved in the summer of 1991 to convert an old brickworks into a ground level viewing area. Located on the southwest side of the runway, the vantage point has been used unofficially for many years and is a good position for photography.

Operators: Scheduled services by Aberdeen Airways (Gulfstream 1), Aer Lingus (Boeing 737, Fokker 50), Aeroflot (Tu-154), Air Canada (Boeing 747/767), Air France (Airbus A320, Boeing 737, Fellowship), Air Hong Kong (Boeing 707/747), Air Littoral (Brasilia, Fokker 100), Air Malta (Airbus A320, Boeing 737), Air Portugal (Boeing 737), Air Transport Schiphol (Jetstream), Alitalia (DC-9), American Airlines (Boeing 767), British Airways (One-Eleven, Boeing 737/747/757, BAe 748/ATP, TriStar), Business Air Services (Bandeirante, Saab SF340), Canadian Airlines (Boeing 767), Cathay Pacific (Boeing 747), Cyprus Airways (Airbus A310), Dan-Air (One-Eleven, Boeing 737, BAe 146), Delta Air Lines (Boeing 767), El Al (Boeing 737/757/767), Emery Worldwide (DC-8), Emirates (Airbus A300/310), Finnair (DC-9, Boeing 737), GB Air (Boeing 737), Gill Air (Short SD3-30/3-60), Iberia (DC-9), Jersey European (Short SD3-60, Friendship), KLM (Boeing 737, Saab SF340), Loganair (Short SD3-60, BAe ATP), Lufthansa (Airbus A320, Boeing 737/727, Dash Eight), Manx Airlines (Short SD3-60, BAe 146/ATP), Newair (Jetstream), Pakistan International (Boeing 747), Polish Airlines (Tu-154), Qantas (Boeing 747), Sabena (BAe 146), SAS

(DC-9), Singapore International (Boeing 747), South African Airways (Boeing 747), Suckling Airways (Dornier 228), Swissair (DC-9, Airbus A310), Turkish Airlines (Boeing 727), Viva Air (Boeing 737) and Yugoslav Airlines (Boeing 727/737).

Charter and IT operators: These include Adria Airways (DC-9), Air Atlantis (Boeing 737), Air Charter (Boeing 737/727), Air Columbus (Boeing 727), Air Liberte (DC-9), Air Malta (Boeing 737), Air Sul (Boeing 737), Air Transat (TriStar), Air Toulouse (Caravelle), Airtours (DC-9), Air UK (BAe 146), Air UK Leisure (Boeing 737), Air 2000 (Boeing 757), American Trans Air (TriStar), Aviogenex (Boeing 727/737), Balkan (Tu-154), Birmingham European (One-Eleven), Britannia Airways (Boeing 737/757/767), British Air Ferries (Viscount, One-Eleven), Caledonian Airways (Boeing 757, TriStar), Canada 3000 (Boeing 757), Cyprus Airways (Airbus A320), Dan-Air (One-Eleven, Boeing 727/737), Excalibur Airways (Airbus A320), Futura (Boeing 737), Inter European (Boeing 737/757), Nationair (Boeing 747/757), Oasis (DC-9), Royal Air Maroc (Boeing 727), Spanair (DC-9) and Tarom (One-Eleven, IL-18).

Movements (1990): Total 154,817 (air transport 121,745). Total passengers 10,475,645.

Runway: 06/24 (10,000ft/3,048m).

Radio frequencies: 118.625MHz (Tower), 119.4MHz (Approach), 121.35MHz (Radar).

Telephone: 061-489 3000.

Operated by: Manchester Airport PLC.

Melbourne
Australia

Essendon Airport was established in 1922 to serve the City of Melbourne, a role it played until the 1950s when it was apparent that it was unable to cope with the postwar technical advances. It was surrounded by residential development thereby precluding any expansion a problem compounded by the existence of a jet curfew between 22.00 and 06.00. A number of alternative sites were investigated, but eventually an area around Tullamarine was chosen. Following government approval, the necessary land was acquired to enable construction to begin in September 1964.

When the new Melbourne Airport was commissioned in 1970, Victoria had been without direct international services for the previous five years because of Essendon's inability to handle aircraft of the 707 and DC-8 size. The first arrival on the opening day was scheduled to be an Alitalia DC-8, but the aircraft was deprived of this distinction by a Qantas 707 carrying a load of VIPs. One year later the two southern domestic carriers also transferred their operations from the original facility where Ansett had been based since 1936 and Australian Airlines since 1946.

The location of the airport enables it to operate without restriction while weather problems rarely force any disruption to services. An attractive low-line three-storey building serves as the international terminal with a two-level concourse leading to the air-bridges. This section is flanked by the domestic structures each having a pier stretching over the apron. All three terminals are interconnected on the first floor to ensure speedy passenger handling.

Two runways were built roughly parallel to those at Essendon which simplifies the air traffic arrangements. The older airport is now an active general aviation centre specialising in freight, charter and commuter services operating in conjunction with Melbourne. Meanwhile the latter has been the subject of long-term planning studies to make provision for the expected needs well into the 21st century.

Situated at the centre of the Sydney-Adelaide-Hobart triangle which encloses 12 million people representing 70% of the entire Australian population, Melbourne's own catchment area embraces some 3 million inhabitants. Forecasts indicate that the annual passenger figures will increase from its present 8 million or so to eventually reach 37 million. To cater for such substantial growth, it is proposed to construct two additional parallel runways thereby doubling the airport's capacity. A major programme will also update the international terminal and increase the number of gates from 8 to 14. When this becomes insufficient, a new complex will be developed on a site south of the existing area. A freight centre is planned to combine both international and domestic cargo operations at one location.

Location and access: Situated 12 miles (19km) northwest of the city. The Skybus Express service from the city centre (Skybus stop, Franklin St) takes 30min for the journey. There is also Shuttle service 440 which originates at Elizabeth Street in the city centre. A major freeway links the airport with Melbourne.

Terminals: The three buildings incorporate all modern features to give maximum efficiency and comfort. With the exception of the duty-free shop, all concessions in both

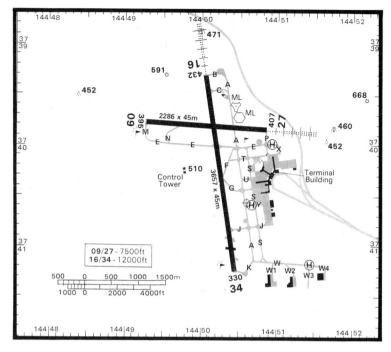

the international and two domestic terminals are open to the public.

Spectator facilities: There is an excellent observation deck overlooking the apron which affords plenty of scope for photography with the sun conveniently in the right place.

Operators: Scheduled services by Air Caledonie (Boeing 737), Air China (Boeing 747), Air Lanka (TriStar), Air Nauru (Boeing 737), Air New Zealand (Boeing 747/767), Air Pacific (Boeing 747/767), Air Vanuatu (Boeing 727), Alitalia (Boeing 747), Ansett (Boeing 737, Fokker 50, Fellowship), Ansett Express (Fokker 50, Fellowship), Australian Airlines (Airbus A300, Boeing 727/737), British Airways (Boeing 747), Compass (Airbus A300), Cathay Pacific (Boeing 747), Continental Airlines (Boeing 747), East-West Airlines (BAe 146, Fellowship), Eastern Australia (Dash Eight), Garuda (DC-10), Hazelton Airlines (Navajo), Japan Airlines (Boeing 747/767), Kendall Airlines (Metro, Saab SF340), KLM (Boeing 747), Lufthansa (Boeing 747), Malaysian Airline System (Boeing 747), O'Connor Airlines (Conquest), Olympic Airways (Boeing 747), Philippine Airlines (DC-10), Qantas (Boeing 747/767), Singapore International (Boeing 747), Sunstate (Short SD3-30/60), Thai International (Boeing 747), United Airlines (Boeing 747) and Yugoslav Airlines (DC-10). *Charter, IT and freight carriers:* Antonov Airlines (An-124), Britannia Airways (Boeing 767) and Polish Airlines (IL-62).

Movements (1990): Total 114,702. Total passengers 8,404,865. These compare with the 1989 figures of 106,079 and 7,325,666 respectively.

Runways: 16/34 (12,000ft/3,657), 09/27 (7,500ft/2,286m).

Radio frequencies: 120.5MHz (Tower), 118.9MHz, 129.4MHz (Departure), 121.7MHz, 121.2MHz (Ground).

Telephone: 339 1600.

Operated by: Federal Airports Corporation.

Miami, Fl USA

Aviation was introduced to the Florida city in 1911 when a flying machine was demonstrated for the entertainment of the local residents. There was little further involvement during the next few years, until in 1917 the US Navy installed a training school in the vicinity. Civil operations began in 1923 when Florida Airways was established to fulfil mail contracts and a short-lived passenger service between Jacksonville and Atlanta. Miami became the base of the fledgling Pan American Airways in March 1927, an airline originally intended to compete with Florida Airways on the Havana route. In the event the latter was absorbed by the newcomer which went on to create its own facility only a few miles from Miami. Known as Pan American Field, the site's first scheduled service was operated by a Sikorsky S-38 amphibian on 15 September 1928 when it carried mail and passengers to Key West.

During the 1930s, PAA was joined at Miami by Eastern Air Lines and National Airlines, all three being responsible for the steady growth of traffic into the Florida airport. It was not until the early postwar years that the local authorities decided that it was in their interest to acquire the complex from PAA, a step taken in 1949. A comprehensive programme of development began immediately, resulting in maintenance bases for the resident airlines plus a new terminal building. Passenger figures continued to climb throughout the 1950s elevating Miami International into one of the world's busiest airports. A further boost was given by National Airlines on 10 December 1958 when it flew the first US scheduled domestic jet service between the Florida city and New York, albeit by leasing a 707 from PAA.

Subsequently MIA has been steadily expanded, the terminal arrangements resulting in a semi-circular main building with seven piers arrayed around it. Over 100 aircraft stands were available when these were completed, but the ever-present need for more produced a series of plans for remote satellites. Nevertheless, even at Miami there is a limit to the amount of land available. A considerable area is used for the enormous

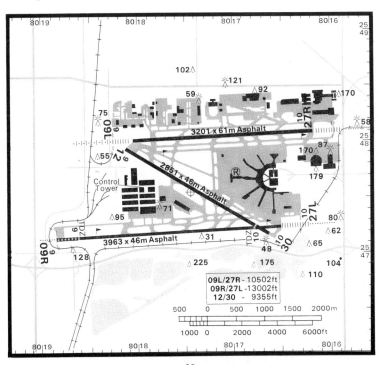

09L/27R - 10502ft
09R/27L - 13002ft
12/30 - 9355ft

Above:
Iberia's DC-10-30 EC-CBP landing on Runway 09R at Miami. *AJW*

Below:
Miami is guaranteed to produce interesting subjects for photographs. The Challenge Air Cargo 707 is N8402. *A. S. Wright*

quantities of cargo passing through the airport, particularly to and from South American countries. Much of this is located on the southwestern perimeter, but the entire length of the northern boundary has dealings with cargo or aircraft maintenance.

Location and access: Situated 7 miles (11km) northwest of Miami. Metrobus service 3 runs from the city centre (South East 1st Street and 3rd Avenue at Amerifirst Building) with a journey time of 38min. Service 20 manages to complete the trip from Northeast 1st Avenue and Northeast 1st Street in 37min, while route 34 takes 43min to travel to the airport from Miami Beach. These times are somewhat flexible since the congestion on the local roads is acute at peak times.

Terminals: The main building and its concourses are equipped with every service likely to be required by the most discerning and demanding travellers.

Spectator facilities: The Miami authorities enterprisingly built an observation deck on top of the international satellite which affords an excellent vantage point for viewing and photography. Access is no longer available to casual visitors, but is restricted to travellers with boarding cards. The prospects for a return to the previous arrangement seem doubtful. Fortunately there are ample alternative spots around the the perimeter, although a car is essential bearing in mind the heat and distance involved. The road along the southern boundary runs parallel with Runway 09R/27L and there are several parking areas at convenient intervals. At the western end, landing shots present no problems. Similarly the area adjacent to the thresholds of Runways 09L and 12 offer ample opportunities for both ground and airborne photographs, although a suitable object upon which to stand is helpful. With the constant building programmes, there are often piles of earth dumped at strategic points to make ideal, if unofficial, grandstands. The northern boundary has a number of access roads leading to maintenance and freight facilities, many of which provide good vantage points to acquire shots of the inmates. Frequently these are weary-looking types which are not to be found elsewhere.

Operators: Scheduled services by Aero Coach (Cessna 402), Aerolineas Argentinas (Boeing 747), AeroMexico (DC-9/10), Aero Peru (DC-8), Air Aruba (Boeing 757), Air Canada (Boeing 727/747/767, DC-9), Air France (Boeing 737/747), Air Jamaica (Airbus A300, Boeing 727), Airways International (Cessna 402), Alitalia (Boeing 747), ALM Antillean Airlines (DC-9), American Airlines (Airbus A300, Boeing 727/747/757/767, DC-10), American Eagle (Jetstream, Saab SF340), Avensa (Boeing 727), Avianca (Boeing 727/747/767), Bahamasair (Boeing 727/737), British Airways (Boeing 747), BWIA International (DC-9, TriStar), Carnival Airlines (Boeing 727), Cayman Airways (Boeing 737), Continental Airlines (Airbus A300, Boeing 727/737/747, DC-9/10), COPA Panama (Boeing 737), Delta Air Lines (Airbus A310, Boeing 727/757/767, TriStar), Dominicana de Aviacion (Boeing 727), Ecuatoriana (Boeing 707), El Al (Boeing 747), Faucett Peru (DC-8), Guyana Airways (Boeing 707), Haiti Trans Air (Boeing 727), Hispaniola Airways (DC-8), Iberia (Boeing 747, DC-10), LAB Airlines (Boeing 727), LACSA (Airbus A320, Boeing 727), Ladeco Airlines (Boeing 727), LAN Chile (Boeing 767), Lineas Aereas Paraguayas (DC-8), LTU (TriStar), Lufthansa (DC-10), Mexicana (Boeing 727), Northwest (Boeing 727/747/757, DC-9), Paradise Island Airlines (Dash Seven, Mallard), SAETA (Boeing 727), Surinam Airways (Boeing 747, DC-8), TACA (Boeing 767), TAN Transportes Aereos Nacionales (Boeing 737), Tower Air (Boeing 747), Trans Brazil (Boeing 767), Trans World (Boeing 727, DC-9), Trans World Express (Jetstream), United Airlines (Boeing 727/737/747/757, DC-10), USAir (Boeing 727/737/767, DC-9, Fellowship), Varig (Boeing 747/767, DC-10), Viasa (Airbus A300, DC-10) and Virgin Atlantic (Boeing 747).

Charter, IT and cargo operators: Amongst the numerous charter, IT and cargo carriers are Aerial Transit (DC-6), Aero Latinas (Boeing 727), Aerosur (Boeing 707), Agro Air (C-97), Airlift International (Friendship, DC-8), ARCA (DC-8), Caledonian Airways (TriStar), Challenge Air Cargo (Boeing 707/757), Florida West (Boeing 707), Haiti Air Freight (DC-6), LTU (TriStar), Million Air (Boeing 707), Monarch Airlines (Boeing 757), SAHSA (Boeing 737), Sterling Airways (Boeing 727), TAN Transportes Aereos Nacionales (Electra) and Zuliana de Aviacion (DC-8).

Movements (1990): Total air transport 394,300. Total passengers 25,837,000.

Runways: 09L/27R (10,502ft/3,201m), 09R/27L (13,002ft/3,963m), 12/30 (9,355ft/2,851m).

Radio frequencies: 118.3MHz, 123.9MHz (Tower), 119.45MHz, 125.5MHz (Departure), 121.8MHz (Ground north), 127.5MHz (Ground south).

Telephone: (305) 871-7000 (main switchboard), (305) 871-7515 (information).

Operated by: Aviation Department of Metropolitan Dade County.

Top:
A unusual livery is carried by the 707 CC-CAF operated by Fast Air and seen taxying at Miami. *A. S. Wright*

Centre:
Northwest's 747s are used on the airline's longhaul services from Miami, this example being N623US. *AJW*

Above:
While piston-engined types are becoming less common, it is still possible to find an example of the past at Miami, this subject being DC-6B operated at the time by APA International as N95BL. *A. S. Wright*

Milan (Linate)
Italy

Although associated with aviation from the early days of flying, the field now known as Linate was not developed as a civil airport until the 1930s, opening to traffic in 1936. Unlike Malpensa it was never intended for military use and since the Italians were keen to employ seaplanes, the new site was also provided with an artificial lake. In Europe only Berlin/Templehof is situated nearer to a city centre than Linate, the latter being only five miles from the heart of Milan. This highly convenient position was certainly one of the main factors for the postwar decision to develop it in preference to Malpensa. After a comprehensive modernisation programme which consumed two years, a DC-6B of Lebanon International Airways had the distinction of becoming the first movement at the rejuenened airport on 25 June 1960.

From September all European and domestic traffic was transferred from Malpensa, a move welcomed by travellers and airlines alike. Unfortunately this happy state of affairs was not to last. Traffic growth exceeded all expectations until Linate reached saturation point. Normally further development work would have kept pace with the growing numbers, but because of its prime location on the outskirts of the city the necessary land was just not available. Consequently capacity problems now exist at the airport which will not be resolved until at least the first phase of the Malpensa modernisation scheme is ready for service in the early 1990s. By 1991 a number of carriers had already transferred their operations, an example to be followed by all international services, leaving Linate to handle only domestic schedules and those to the Mediterranean islands.

Location and access: Situated 6 miles (10km) south of Milan which is linked to the airport by a City bus every 12min, the journey taking 20min to complete. Alternatively a bus from the central railway station takes 30min and runs every 20min. Ample car parking is provided for those

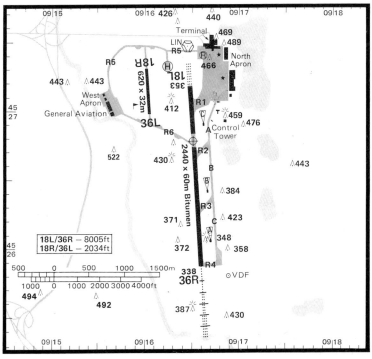

braving the Fiat infested streets.

Terminal: This two-storey building contains a restaurant, buffet, bars, shops and two banks. During the course of its modernisation the whole facility was greatly enlarged.

Spectator facilities: None specifically provided although a gallery exists in the departure area on the first floor. While there are good views through the tinted glass of movements on the apron and elsewhere, the vantage point is of little use for photography for much of the time due to the position of the sun. A more suitable location can be found around the perimeter road at a point where Runway 18L/36R is quite close.

Operators: Aer Lingus (Boeing 737), Air France (Boeing 727/737, Airbus A300/320, Fellowship, ATR-42, Saab SF340), Air Littoral (ATR-42), Air Portugal (Airbus A310, Boeing 737), Alitalia (Boeing 747, DC-9, Airbus A300), ATI (DC-9), Austrian Airlines (DC-9), Avianova (ATR-42), Birmingham European (One-Eleven), British Airways (One-Eleven, Boeing 737/757/767), Contact Air (Dash Eight), Hamburg Airlines (Dash Eight), Iberia (Airbus A300/320, Boeing 727, DC-9), KLM (Boeing 737, Airbus A310), Lufthansa (Airbus A310/320, Boeing 737), Lufthansa CityLine (Fokker 50), Meridiana (DC-9), NFD (Metro), Olympic Airways (Airbus A300, Boeing 727/737), Sabena (Boeing 737), SAS (DC-9) and Swissair (Airbus A310, DC-9, Fokker 100).

Movements (1990): Total 135,396. Total passengers 9,413,745.

Runway: 18L/36R (8,005ft/2,440m), 18R/36L (2,034ft/620m).

Radio frequencies: 118.1MHz, 119.25MHz (Tower), 126.75MHz (Approach), 132.7MHz (Departures), 121.8MHz (Ground).

Telephone: (02) 74851.

Operated by: Societa Esercizi Aeroportuali (SEA).

Milan (Malpensa)
Italy

On 27 May 1907, Giovanni Caproni took to the air from a field adjacent to the sheds in which his machine, a CA-1, was built. It was not long before the small unit housed the Caproni factory and the field an airstrip destined to become an international airport. A flying school was formed in 1911 which became responsible for the training of pilots taking part in the conflict between Italy and Turkey and also World War 1. One of those to pass through the establishment during this period were the future ace Francesco Baracca and poet Gabriele D'Annunzio. Apparently the latter found inspiration for his sonnets while machine-gunning the Austrian trenches. Maybe the targets preferred this to a bombardment of words.

When the nation's air arm was formally created in 1923, Malpensa took a leading role by becoming the main source of trained personnel for the new force. Nevertheless commercial flying also began at the airfield about this time, continuing until a new site was completed at Linate in 1936. During the occupation in 1943, the German army built a new runway capable of handling the increasing number of heavy transport movements required to support the ground forces. However, the creators of the strip were also responsible for its destruction at the end of April 1945, when strategically placed mines ended a short, but useful life.

Soon after the war the Societa Aeroporti di Busto assumed control although it was not long before this organisation was renamed Societa Esercizi Aeroportuali (SEA), the title it retains today. Malpensa was rebuilt in 1948 generally to take over the role of Milan's airport, the first revenue earning movement taking place on 21 November. For the next 12 years or so the airport coped with all the traffic, but in 1960 the completion of work at Linate brought relief. At this point most of the European and domestic flights were transferred to the new location leaving only intercontinental services at the older site.

Malpensa entered a new era in 1972 when the Italian Ministry of Transport approved a new plan to develop the airport to meet the long-term requirements towards the end of the century. Included in the project was a terminal with two satellites capable of handling 12 million passengers each year. Construction work has been carried out at a leisurely pace with phase one due for completion during the early 1990s when the capacity will reach 8 million travellers. In addition the newly built cargo facility will be capable of dealing with some 200,000 tons annually. In due course all international services will then operate from Malpensa, with the domestic traffic remaining at Linate. By 1991 a number of carriers had already transferred their operations as the first stage of the redevelopment was put into service.

Location and access: Situated 29 miles (46km) northwest of Milan in the Province of Varese off Autostrada A7. A regular bus links the airport with the city's Porta

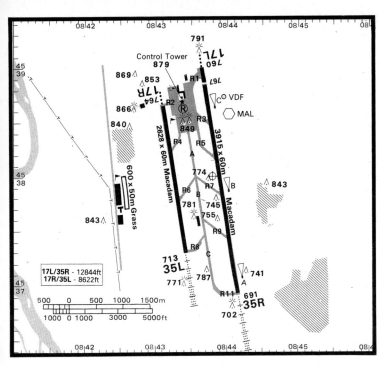

Garibaldi railway station, the journey time being 60min.

Terminal: Contains restaurant, bar and shops.

Spectator facilities: A first floor terrace along the side and front of the terminal offers excellent opportunities for photography and viewing of all movements on the aprons. Some years ago this facility was officially closed for the usual reasons, but recently it has been reopened occasionally. However no confirmation of this was forthcoming from the authorities. In any case there is unlikely to be any such area in the new building. As an alternative a spot near the end of runway 35R offers some consolation.

Operators: Scheduled services by Aeroflot (Tu-154, IL-86), Alitalia (Boeing 747, DC-9), ATI (ATR-42), Canadian Airlines (Boeing 767, DC-10), Czechoslovak Airlines (Tu-134), Malev (Boeing 737, Tu-134/154), Meridiana (DC-9), Olympic Airways (Boeing 727/737, Airbus A300), Royal Air Maroc (Boeing 757), Trans World (Boeing 747/767), Tunis Air (Boeing 727), Turkish Airlines (Boeing 727, DC-9), Varig (Boeing 747), Viasa (DC-10) and Yugoslav Airlines (Boeing 727/737, DC-9).

Charter and IT operators: ATI (DC-9), Britannia Airways (Boeing 737), Monarch (Boeing 737), Ryanair (One-Eleven), TEA Italy (Boeing 737) and various American carriers.

Movements (1990): Total 33,104. Total passengers 3,616,637.

Runways: 17L/35R (12,844ft/3,915m), 17R/35L (8,622ft/2,628m).

Radio frequencies: 119.0MHz, 128.35MHz (Tower), 126.75MHz (Approach), 132.7MHz (Departures), 121.9MHz (Ground).

Telephone: (02) 74851.

Operated by: Societa Esercizi Aeroportuali.

New York (John F. Kennedy), NY USA

Construction of New York's international airport began in April 1942, when the city authorities were contracted to fill the marshy tidelands on the site of Idlewild golf course. Originally known by this name, the complex was designed to become twice the size of LaGuardia and with the availability of seven runways, it was expected to handle 1,000 movements per day. After much delay, commercial flying began on 1 July 1948, followed 31 days later by the official opening. By this time the airport had adopted the title of New York International and was under the control of the Port Authority.

An eliptical centre area was allocated to the terminal buildings, although those erected in the early days were intended to be a temporary expedient to enable operations to begin. After hangars and a new 11-storey control tower had been completed in the early 1950s, attention turned to the provision of permanent structures for passenger handling. An international arrivals complex was created with two adjoining east and west wings, but the remainder of the individual terminals were allocated to specific airlines. The latter became responsible for the design of their own premises leading to a wide variation of styles.

Through the years the centre area has been expanded considerably despite having to cope with the demands for more space, but this is strictly limited due to the layout of the site. Inevitably some of the runways have been sacrificed leaving two pairs of parallel main strips plus a fifth for the use of general aviation amd commuter aircraft. With the southern perimeter bordered by Jamaica Bay, the only prospect for more expansion is to reclaim additional land from the sea.

Even by the mid-1960s, John F. Kennedy (as it was renamed in December 1963), was handling an enormous amount of air cargo. It already possessed the world's largest freight centre, but plans were made to increase significantly the area and give it the benefit of better road access.In the late 1980s a major redevelopment programme began at JFK, the first project involving a new control tower, which at 321ft, is the tallest in North America. Located on the ramp side of the international arrivals complex, it was due to become operational during 1991 and will allow the 1952-built tower to be demolished to make way for further moderisation of the central area. Studies have also begun into the feasibility of a rail link to connect the terminals with the Long Island Railroad and New York City subway system at Jamaica station in Queens. An extension of the track to LaGuardia is also being actively considered.

Location and access: Situated 14 miles (22km) southeast of mid-Manhattan. A JFK Express subway connects Manhattan and Brooklyn with Howard Beach station. An MTA shuttle bus links the latter with the airport taking 60min for the journey. Other bus services include the half-hourly Carey Airport Express from 125 Park Avenue near Grand Central terminal and Olympia Trails Express which runs from Brooklyn (Long Island Railroad station) and the World Trade Centre in Manhattan. All take 60min for the trip. Green Bus Line Q10 runs from Queens with connections to the subway. There are vast areas of car parks but needless to say these are expensive and frequently congested. There is a free 24hr shuttle bus linking all terminals.

Terminals: Nine buildings serve the numerous airlines with the main carriers responsible for their own facilities. All buildings are self-contained with the usual concessions and services.

Spectator facilities: None specifically provided nowadays, so alternative vantage points have to be found. Although restricted views though the windows can be obtained from several of the terminals, even these spots are not accessible to non-travellers following the tightening of security. The car park on the roof of the Pan Am Worldport is still popular, although the authorities have succeeded in creating more problems by adding slats to the existing fence. Fortunately gaps can be found so all is not lost. As an alternative there is a location near to the British Airways' terminal which is suitable as a base for photography. Elsewhere good vantage points exist near the threshold of Runway 13L and nearby taxiways, but it should be borne in mind that the US law enforcers are programmed to question the right of individuals to stand still. They certainly do not understand the needs of aviation enthusiasts. Nevertheless with due care some rewarding photographs can be obtained.

Operators: Scheduled services by Aerolineas Argentinas (Boeing 747), Aer Lingus (Boeing 747), Aeroflot (IL-62/86), AeroMexico (DC-10), Air Afrique (DC-10), Air China (Boeing 747), Air France (Airbus A310, Boeing 747, Concorde), Air India (Boeing 747), Air Jamaica (Airbus A300), Air Portugal (TriStar), Alitalia (Boeing 747), ALM Antillean Airlines (DC-9), America West (Boeing 747/757), American Airlines (Airbus A300, Boeing 727/767, DC-10),

New York's JFK gets rail link

DECADES OF delay came to an end last week with the award of the contract to build a light rail link to JFK airport in New York.

The £554M design and build contract was awarded to the Air Rail Transit Consortium, led by the American arm of Swedish contracting giant Skanska, along with Bombardier Transit Corporation and Perini Corporation.

In addition to the design and build contract, the consortium will operate and maintain the line for up to 15 years for client Port Authority of New York and New Jersey.

New York's transport planners have recognised the need for a rail link to the airport since the 1960s, but previous proposals were never taken up.

Skanska and Perini will carry out design and construction of the civil works, which include 13.5km of track. There will be a 3.2km loop to link all nine passenger terminals at the airport, a 5km long link to the Jamaica subway station and transportation hub, plus a 5.3km long link to Howard Beach subway station. Ten stations are also included in the design – six to serve the passenger terminals, one for rental car areas, two subway interchanges and a link to long term and employee car parks.

Construction work is expected to start in September. The project has a 53 month programme to opening in 2002.

Construction will be paid for by a combination of Port Authority funds and airport taxes – but once in operation, revenue is expected to exceed operating costs.

Helena Russell

s safety scare

using hydraulic scaffold towers to
[...] on the building facade and dam-
[...] repaired immediately. Inside the
[...] planks were placed on the upper
[...] engineers to examine beams.
[...] as highlighted the failings of the
[...] and reopened debate surround-
[...] he stadium – known as The Home
[...] ch celebrates its 75th anniversary
[...] w York mayor Rudolph Giuliani
[...] ner George Steinbrenner caused
[...] by suggesting that the traditional
[...] eft in favour of a new stadium in

arrangement will be to move to a
new senior management structure," he said.

Ford had been chairman since
1994 and was previously a main
board director at P&O. Non-exec-
utive vice chairman Brian Apple-
ton takes over until a permanent
appointment is made.
(See *Commentary*, page 12)

*UP ON THE ROOF: Tenders are
expected to go out in the next
two weeks for work to refurbish
Newcastle Station's historic
south barrel roof – part of a
£20M package of works by
Railtrack to modernise the
station. The roof was designed
by local architect John Dobson
between 1845 and 1850 but for
the last three years has been
propped by temporary
scaffolding after the steel truss
structure was damaged by fire.
The contract will include
substantial structural repairs
and strengthening, with work
expected to start in June, with
the whole station
refurbishment completed by
2000.*

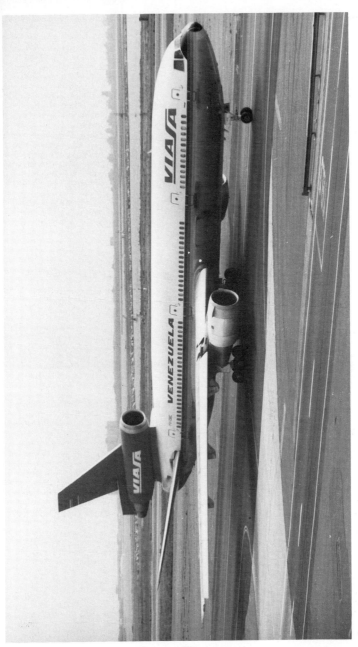

New York JFK offers plenty of subjects including the Viasa DC-10 YV-138C. *A. S. Wright*

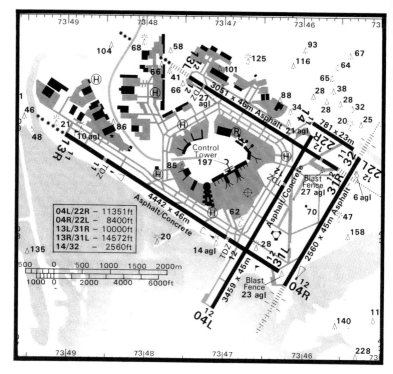

Runway	Length
04L/22R	11351ft
04R/22L	8400ft
13L/31R	10000ft
13R/31L	14572ft
14/32	2560ft

American Eagle (ATR-42, Metro, Short SD3-60), Austrian Airlines (Airbus A310), Avensa (Boeing 727), Avianca (Boeing 727/767), British Airways (Boeing 747, Concorde, TriStar), BWIA International (DC-9, TriStar), Carnival Airlines (Boeing 727), Cayman Airways (Boeing 737), China Airways (Boeing 747), Czechoslovak Airlines (IL-62), Delta Air Lines (Airbus A310, Boeing 727/757/767), Dominicana (Boeing 707), Ecuatoriana (DC-10), Egyptair (Boeing 747/767), Finnair (DC-10, MD-11), Gulf Air (Boeing 767, TriStar), Guyana Airways (Boeing 707), Iberia (Boeing 747, DC-10), Icelandair (Boeing 757), Japan Airlines (Boeing 747), KLM (Boeing 747), Korean Air (Boeing 747), Kuwait Airways (Boeing 747/767), Ladeco (Boeing 707), LAN Chile (Boeing 767), Lacsa Airlines (Boeing 727), LTU (TriStar), Lufthansa (Airbus A310, Boeing 747, DC-10), Malev (Airbus A310), Mexicana (Boeing 727), MGM Grand Air (DC-8), New York Helicopters (S-58), Nigeria Airways (DC-10), Northwest Airlines (Boeing 727/747/757, DC-10), Olympic Airways (Boeing 747), Pakistan International (Boeing 747), Philippine Airlines (Boeing 747), Polish Airlines (Boeing 767), Qantas (Boeing 747), Royal Air Maroc (Boeing 747), Royal Jordanian (TriStar), SAS (Boeing 767), Sabena (Airbus A310, Boeing 747), Saudia (Boeing 747), Surinam Airways (DC-8), Swissair (Boeing 747, DC-10), TACA International (Boeing 727), Tarom (Boeing 707), Tower Air (Boeing 747), Trans World (Boeing 727/747/767, DC-9, TriStar), Trans World Express (Beech 1900, Saab SF340, Dash Seven), Turkish Airlines (Airbus A310), USAir (Boeing 737, Dash Eight), United Airlines (Boeing 747/767, DC-10), Varig (Boeing 747), Viasa (Airbus A300), Virgin Atlantic (Boeing 747), Yugoslav Airlines (DC-10) and Zambia Airways (DC-10).

Movements (1990): Total air transport 293,000. Total passengers 29,787,000.
Runways: 04L/22R (11,351ft/3,460m), 04R/22L (8,400ft/2,560m), 13L/31R (10,000ft/3,048m), 13R/31L (14,572ft/4,442m), 14/32 (2,560ft/780m).
Radio frequencies: 119.1MHz, 123.9MHz

(Tower), 132.4MHz (Approach), 135.9MHz (Departure), 121.65MHz, 121.9MHz (Ground).

Telephone: (718) 656-4520.
Operated by: Port Authority of New York and New Jersey.

New York (LaGuardia), NY USA

During the 1920s some of the site now covered by the airport was the home of the Gala Amusement Park. Transformed in 1929 into a 105-acre private flying field, it originally adopted the name Glenn H. Curtiss, but this was later changed to the North Beach Airport, a more appropriate in view of its proximity to the water. In the mid-1930s New York's enthusiastic Mayor LaGuardia was mainly responsible for the facility's development as a businessmen's airport, a venture which was to prove highly-successful.

Under the new ownership, work commenced on enlarging the site by filling in 357 acres of waterfront along the east side.

Construction then went ahead as a joint exercise by the City of New York and the Federal Works Progress Administration, until on 15 October 1939 all was ready for the opening ceremonies followed by the first commercial services on 2 December. The mayor's contribution to the project was recognised in 1947 when his name was bestowed upon the airport, at the same time that control was transferred to the Port Authority.

The original building, known as the Overseas Terminal, was located on the west side adjacent to the bay; a convenient spot for handling both flying boats and landplanes. While the need for this dual function has long gone, the structure is still employed by commuter carriers and the Washington and Boston shuttles. It also provides the airport's base for the regular water ferries to downtown Manhattan.

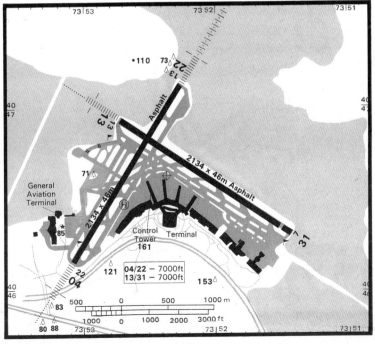

Above:
Business Express is to be found at LaGuardia where it uses Beech 1900s including N817BE.
A. S. Wright

Below:
An unusual departure from LaGuardia was made on this occasion by the Delta 727 N544DA.
A. S. Wright

The Central Terminal was opened in 1964 and serves most of the scheduled airlines. This impressive four-storey structure has four two-level piers projecting from it, in total offering 38 aircraft gates. Although there was sufficient capacity for many years, in March 1981 the new Shuttle Terminal was opened to the public. At the same time the commuter traffic was temporarily relocated in the adjacent, but suitably modified Hangar 8, until a further move was necessary when the latter was earmarked for redevelopment. Delta was another airline to construct its own facility at LaGuardia, the new complex entering service in June 1983 at the eastern end of the airport.

From the outset the amount of land available was strictly limited, so only two runways were laid. Although their length was adequate for the piston-engined types in service in the early days, the demands of the modern jets forced an expensive project to be completed in 1967 whereupon both strips were extended over the water to 7,000ft (2,134m). They were built on L-shaped piers wide enough to accommodate a taxiway and holding pad in each case, while a further extension provided the base for the approach lights and associated equipment.

A major problem manifested itself in the late 1970s when Eastern announced its intention to introduce the Airbus A300 on to its New York-Miami services. Although widebodies were already handled, it was feared that the new taxiways were not strong enough to withstand the different weight distribution of the European machine. Fortunately for the well-being of American/Franco relations, the airport authorities agreed to strengthen the pier sections at a cost of some $850,000. LaGuardia still handles a considerable proportion of New York's domestic traffic, its convenient position making it ideal for the purpose.

Location and access: Situated 8 miles (13km) from mid-Manhattan adjacent to the Grand Central Parkway between exits 5 and 7. A number of airport and public transport buses connect LaGuardia with Manhattan at frequent intervals. There is a water shuttle from the Marine Air Terminal to 34th Street Pier (midtown) and Pier 11 (Wall Street) in downtown Manhattan. A direct scheduled bus service links LaGuardia with Kennedy every 30min, while a similar journey to Newark involves a change of bus.

Terminals: A vast assortment of amenities are to be found on the second floor of the central building, but each finger also has its share of similar facilities. In addition, such services are to be found in the Marine Air, Trump Shuttle and Delta Terminals which are separate buildings to the east and west of the central complex. As a part of the Port Authority's master plan for decentralisation, work began in 1990 on the construction of a new terminal for the use of Continental. Due to open in early 1992, the new building is located on the east side and shares some of the Trump Shuttle facilities.

Spectator facilities: Sadly LaGuardia's excellent terrace has been closed for a long time with no official replacement. The American Airlines' pier is a reasonable substitute, its position at the western end of the apron ensuring that all movements can be seen and most photographed through the glass. Access involves passing the security check which may require the production of a boarding card, depending upon the current state of the nation's nerves. Other vantage points around the perimeter are to be found, although the chainlink fence can introduce photographic problems due to the close proximity of the subjects.

Operators: Schedules services by Air Canada (Boeing 727, DC-9), American Airlines (Boeing 727/757, DC-9/10), America West (Boeing 737), Business Express (Beech 1900, Saab SF340, SD3-30/60), CommutAir (Beech 1900, Dash Eight), Continental Airlines (Boeing 727/737, DC-9), Continental Express (ATR-42, Beech 99, Brasilia), Delta Air Lines (Boeing 727/757/767, TriStar), Henson Airlines (Dash Eight), Long Island Airlines (Twin Otter), Midway Airlines (DC-9), Midwest Express (DC-9), Mohawk (Beech 99/1900), Northwest Airlines (Airbus A320, Boeing 727/757), Precision (Dornier 228), Trump (USAir) Shuttle (Boeing 727), Trans World (Boeing 727/767, DC-9, TriStar), Trans World Express (Beech 1900, Dash Seven), United Airlines (Boeing 727/737/757) and USAir (Boeing 727/737, DC-9, Fokker 100).

Movements (1990): Total air transport 334,200. Total passengers 22,754,000.

Runways: 04/22 (7,000ft/2,134m), 13/31 (7,000ft/2,134m).

Radio frequencies: 118.7MHz (Tower), 120.8MHz (Approach), 120.4MHz (Departure), 121.7MHz (Ground).

Telephone: (212) 466-7503.

Operated by: The Port Authority of New York and New Jersey.

New York (Newark), NJ USA

Opened on 1 October 1928, Newark was built on 68 acres of swampland and quickly became the world's busiest airport. As the first to serve the New York/New Jersey area, it has always been in the forefront of developments, being equipped at an early stage with paved runways, a weather bureau, night lighting and an Air Traffic Control Centre. Newark witnessed many historic events during the pioneering years, including the inaugural coast-to-coast service in 1930 operated by a Ford Tri-Motor under the command of Charles Lindbergh.

During World War 2 the airport was acquired by the US Army Air Corps, but in 1948 control passed to the Port Authority of New York under a lease from the City of Newark. The new operator quickly added an instrument runway, a new terminal building and cargo centre, but traffic continued to grow relentlessly during the 1950s, so plans had to be made for a major reconstruction of the facilities. Almost immediately after the

details were announced in 1964, work commenced upon a new terminal complex, an additional runway and a vast expansion of the parking areas. Nevertheless, it was 1970 before the first of the improvements was ready for service followed by the remainder during the next two years or so. At this point in 1972, the airport officially became Newark International.

With the two terminal buildings A and B in use, the previous congestion was greatly reduced, but, after the airline deregulation in the late 1970s, a deluge of new carriers threatened to swamp the facilities. One of the newcomers was People Express which introduced a series of frequent, low-cost services from Newark. However, the company took over the original north terminal building for its exclusive use, the rental being much less than the accommodation in the central area. The authorities decided that it was time for some major expansion, so Terminal C was erected and duly opened in 1988. Once the latter was operational, attention was turned to bringing B up to international standard after a career devoted to domestic movements. The task was completed in 112

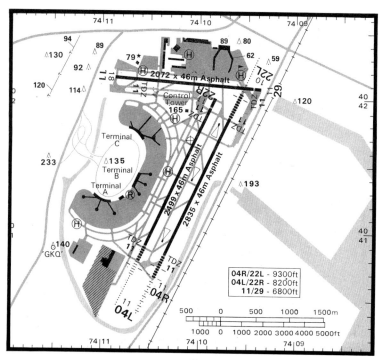

days and created a much better impression for arriving passengers than the old premises on the north side which was subsequently earmarked for conversion into a cargo and office complex.

Location and access: Situated 16 miles (26km) southwest of Manhatten, 2 miles (3.2km) south of Newark. It lies between the New Jersey Turnpike (Exits 13A and 14) and US Routes 1 and 9. There are a number of bus services linking the airport with New York, most visiting Grand Central station, Port Authority bus station and the World Trade Centre. Journey times vary, but are quoted as between 25min and 45min on average. This can probably be achieved in the middle of the night, but certainly during the day traffic conditions do not encourage fast runs.
Terminal: There are three buildings known as Terminals A, B and C. The first two branch out to three circular satellites, while the third has two concourses projecting from the main section. All terminals are self-sufficient and offer all the usual amenities.
Spectator facilities: None of the three buildings have allocated areas for viewing. Access to the various concourses and satellites is possible via a security check, but tinted glass is in widescale use. Photographs can be obtained, although afternoons are preferable because of the east-facing aspect. There are a number of small external landings at the ends of the terminals which are officially classed as emergency exits, so care has to be taken not to cause any obstruction. Nevertheless they provide good vantage points for shots of the aircraft, both on the stands and taxying.
Operators: Scheduled services by Air

Canada (DC-9), Air France (Boeing 747), Air Portugal (TriStar), America West (Boeing 757), American Airlines (Boeing 727/757/767, DC-9/10), British Airways (TriStar), Continental Airlines (Airbus A300, Boeing 727/737/747, DC-9/10), Continental Express (ATR-42, Beech 1900, Brasilia, Twin Otter, Dash Seven), Delta Air Lines (Boeing 727/757/767), Delta Connection (Beech 1900, Saab SF340), First Air (Boeing 727), Lufthansa (Airbus A310), Midwest Express (DC-9), Mohawk Airlines (Beech 99), Northwest Airlines (Boeing 727/757, DC-9/10), Northwest Airlink (Metro, Beech 1900, Dornier 228), Polish Airlines (Boeing 767), SAS (Boeing 767), Trans World (Boeing 727/747/767, TriStar, DC-9), Trans World Express (Beech 1900, Saab SF340), United Airlines (Boeing 727/737/747/757/767, DC-8/10), USAir (Boeing 727/737, DC-9, Fellowship, Fokker 100), USAir Express (Beech 1900, SD3-60) and Virgin Atlantic (Boeing 747).
Charter operators: Aerocancun (Airbus A310, DC-9), Air Europa (Boeing 757), American Trans Air (TriStar, Boeing 757), LTU (Boeing 767, TriStar), La Tur (DC-9), Martinair (Airbus A310, Boeing 747), DC-10 and Carnival Airlines (Boeing 727/737).
Movements (1990): Total air transport 359,300. Total passengers 22,255,000. Peak year was 1986 with 400,126 movements and 29,433,046 passengers.
Runways: 04L/22R (8,200ft/2,499m), 04R/22L (9,300/2,835m - used mainly for landings), 11/29 (6,800ft/2,072m).
Radio frequencies: 118.3MHz, 134,05MHz (Tower), 119.2MHz (Departure), 121.8MHz, 126.15MHz (Ground).
Telephone: (201) 961-2000.
Operated by: Port Authority of New York and New Jersey.

Nice (Côte d'Azur) France

Generally thought of as a holiday centre, Nice became the scene of some of the earliest flying to take place in Europe. As early as 1901 the French pioneer, Capitaine Louis Ferber, carried out the first tests with his machine which was suspended from the arm of a structure resembling a tower crane. The tethered creation was then able to propel itself in a circular movement in a similar manner to a roundabout at a fairground. Nine years later the town organised a series of large meetings for European aviators, offering attractive prizes for outstanding successes. These functions encouraged both

speed and altitude records to be established with machines such as the Antoinette.
By the early 1920s a site was earmarked for use as an aerodrome and a 700m grass runway was laid with its western end near to Nice race course. Most of the activity was devoted to sport flying between its opening and the early 1930s, but by 1936 the French carrier Potez Aéro-Service had introduced scheduled services between Nice, Toulouse, Bordeaux and Corsica using Potez 56 airliners. Noting the success of this enterprise, plans were drawn up for the development of the airport, but before any action could be taken on the proposals World War 2 tended to move it down the scale of priorities.

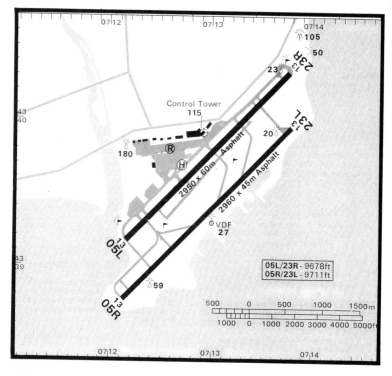

For much of the period there was no change at the site, but in 1944 the Allies invaded southern France. This led to the construction of a hard runway over 4,000ft (1,219m) in length principally for the use of the logistics base which had been set up in support of the Italian campaign. After the war the strip proved a useful asset, encouraging Air France to start scheduled services. Development was considered to be in the public interest so work started on strengthening the runway, which at the same time was also extended to 5,577ft (1,700m). By the end of the first year the airport was able to report that 34,267 passengers had used the facilities and that there had been 5,091 aircraft movements.

By 1949 not only was the French flag carrier operating from Nice, but both BEA and Swissair were in evidence. Routes to London and Geneva therefore resulted, while long-haul sectors were introduced to such unlikely places as Tehran, Brazzaville and Saigon. From 1946 the airport had taken the name of Nice-Le-Var, but in 1955 the present identity of Côte d'Azur was adopted. Now officially recognised as a regional centre, at the end of the next year over 500,000 passengers were recorded for the first time. Fortunately this growth had been anticipated several years earlier when work had begun on the development of a complex for the French Riviera capable of meeting the demands of the expanding holiday industry. On 2 December 1957 the new Nice airport was opened.

Although utilising the same site, the existing buildings had been replaced by a smart new terminal and freight centre. Adequate for the period, as the larger airliners began to appear so expansion became necessary once again, until by 1969 the terminal had been enlarged twice to enable it to cope with an annual capacity of 2.5 million. Naturally the runway also needed some more stretching if it was to handle the new types of aircraft, so by 1973 it had grown to 9,840ft (3,000m). Unfortunately the limits for any further increase in size had almost been reached due to the compactness of the area bordered by the sea to the south, the city of

Nice to the north and east plus the Var river in the west.

Studies were begun to find a solution to this difficult problem which culminated in the decision to build a second runway on land reclaimed from the sea. It was a bold step and one which took considerable governmental thought, but on 24 December 1974 approval was given for the scheme. For several years a constant stream of lorries shuttled between nearby Le Collet de Crémat quarry and the airport laden with the material needed for the in-fill until finally the enormous task was completed with the opening of the new south runway on 23 October 1983. The year also saw 4 million passengers for the first time which helped to provide the incentive to start the first stages of Terminal 2 in April 1985. Built to a modern design, when opened two years or so later it took over the handling of the domestic traffic, itself generating an annual total of well over 2 million passengers.

Once the new accommodation was on line, thoughts turned towards the next project which was duly begun in May 1990. This time it was the turn of the much-modified original building now known as Terminal 1. One of the first steps taken was to construct a new roof over the entire complex, thereby allowing the dismantling of the previous cover and a start to be made on the revised interior layout. To facilitate this activity and to allow the smooth running of the airport to continue, a temporary building was erected alongside the south side of Terminal 2. Known as Zone 3, the structure was built to the same standards as its permanent neighbours, but by using new techniques was ready for service in five months. It then took over most of the check-in activities, enabling work to proceed apace on the virtually new international Terminal 1 which is designed to have an annual capacity of 5 million passengers when operational in 1994.

At this point the workforce will not become unemployed because it is then intended to proceed with a second module for Terminal 2. In the meantime a new freight complex was created on the west side of the site. When opened in 1991, its capacity of 50,000 tonnes more than doubled the previous handling capacity of the airport.

Nice is now France's second airport and is preparing to cope with 10 million passengers by the turn of the century. This target is by no means impossible in view of the campaign already underway to promote the area as the southern European gateway. Intensive efforts are being made to attract American and Asian carriers to the the Côte d'Azur on the eve of the unified Common Market, although it is intended that business traffic will be diverted into the expanded Cannes following the extension of its runway.

Location and access: Situated 4 miles (7km) southwest of Nice alongside the main coast road and adjacent to RN7. There is a bus service from Nice (Avenue Felix Faure) with a journey time of 15min. Car parks are available but are invariably busy. A free shuttle bus links the terminals at a frequency depending on demand.

Terminals: Terminal 1 is located on the northern side of the apron and will handle international movements when fully operational at the end of 1994. On the western edge of the site, Terminal 2 has two levels with most of the services located on the upper departure floor. There are three fixed airbridges connecting the building with the aircraft.

Spectator facilities: A useful open-air terrace was provided on the upper floor of Terminal 1 for many years but its opening became irregular as the fear of terrorism had its effect. Although facing south, photography was possible from this pleasant spot which gave excellent views. In view of the reconstruction work in progress, not surprisingly it was closed during 1990 but somewhat unexpectedly it was announced that it would reopen when the builders had completed that particular area. Fortunately there are alternatives. To the east of the airport the taxiway passes very close to the Promenade des Anglais, but the most useful spot is located at the mouth of the River Var. It is actually a part of the large CAP3000 shopping complex, so there is adequate parking and refreshments are on hand when required. From this comfortable vantage point all movements can be seen and photography is well within the scope of a 200mm lens. Conducted tours of the airport and a retired Caravelle are organised upon requests made at least one week in advance. Normally parties total between 15 and 50 people. Information can be obtained by telephoning 93 21 30 09 between Monday and Friday.

Operators: Scheduled services by Air Afrique (DC-10), Air Algerie (Boeing 737), Air Canada (Boeing 767), Air France (Boeing 727/737/747, Airbus A300/310/320, Fellowship), Air Gabon (Boeing 747), Air Inter (Mercure, Caravelle, Airbus A300/320), Air Littoral (ATR-42, Brasilia, Fokker 100, Metro, Bandeirante), Air Portugal (Boeing 737), Air UK (BAe 146), Alitalia (DC-9), Austrian Airlines (DC-9), Brit Air (ATR-42, Saab SF340), British Airways (Boeing

737/757, One-Eleven), British Midland (DC-9), Corse Mediterranee (ATR-42), Crossair (Saab SF340, Fokker 50), Dan-Air (Boeing 737, One-Eleven), Heli Air Monaco (JetRanger, Ecureuil), Heli Transport (Ecureuil), Iberia (DC-9), KLM (Boeing 737), Lufthansa (Boeing 737), Lufthansa CityLine (Fokker 50), Luxair (Fokker 50, Brasilia), Meridiana (ATR-42, DC-9), Middle East Airlines (Boeing 707), Proteus (Beech 1900), Royal Air Maroc (Boeing 727/737), Sabena (Boeing 737), SAS (DC-9), Saudia (TriStar), Swissair (DC-9), TAT (ATR-42, Brasilia, Friendship, Fellowship), Tunis Air (Boeing 737) and Yugoslav Airlines (DC-9). *Charter flights:* These are operated into the

airport but the majority of visitors use the scheduled services or arrive in one of the many executive jets to be seen at Cannes.
Movements (1990): Total 145,741 (air transport 68,542, helicopters 57,252). Total passengers 5,882,690. These compare with the 1989 figures of 133,311 (66,229, 47,722) and 5,739,339 respectively.
Runways: 05L/23R (9,678ft/2,950m), 05R/23L (9,711ft/2,960m).
Radio frequencies: 118.7MHz (Tower), 120.25MHz, 120.85MHz, 120.2MHz (Approach), 121.7MHz (Ground).
Telephone: Nice 93 21 30 30.
Operated by: Groupe Chambre de Commerce et d'Industrie Nice Côte d'Azur.

Orlando International, Fl USA

Florida became involved in aviation as early as 1910, but it was 1928 before Herndon became Orlando's first municipal airport.

Two runways were provided for this comparatively modern facility which soon became a transit stop for a mail service between Jacksonville and Miami. When the US entered the war in December 1941, control passed to the US Army Air Corps, but the civil authorities promptly acquired another site

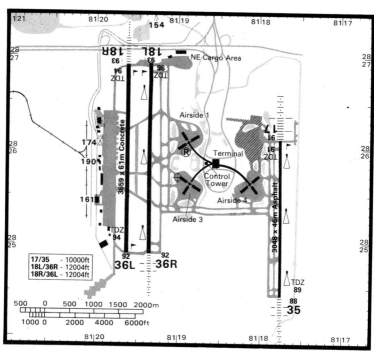

It is not difficult to photograph a United Parcels 727 at Orlando, this example being N210UP.   A. S. *Wright*

111

south of Orlando to create a second municipal flying field. It was not long before this was also leased to the military, whereupon it was expanded and given the title of Pinecastle before becoming the home for B-17s.

At the end of the war both airfields reverted to their civil owners, with Herndon once more handling Orlando's airline traffic. As agreed earlier, the temporary residents at Pinecastle restored the site to its original condition before leaving, although there was an understanding that in the event of another national emergency the air force could return. Such a reason was provided by the Korean War, so 1952 found the USAF restoring Pinecastle AFB to house a divisional headquarters for the Strategic Air Command.

This time the airfield remained under military command, although in 1957 the base was renamed McCoy in memory of a wing commander killed during a SAC bombing competition. Meanwhile, larger aircraft made the 5,500ft (1,676m) runways inadequate, so two new 12,000ft (3,658m) strips were laid. Subsequently, in 1962 permission was granted for the airlines to operate their jet flights from the east side of McCoy, a far more satisfactory arrangement for all concerned. As a long-term venture, the city authorities began to acquire land adjacent to the base, until by 1969 it possessed 3,657 acres, all of it east and south of the terminal. It was a wise investment, because in 1973, the Pentagon announced plans to close McCoy AFB, an act performed in April 1975. At this point the US Government formally transferred the title of the property to the City of Orlando to pave the way for the base to become a fully-fledged international airport in 1976.

The original terminal facilities were located on the northeast perimeter alongside the Bee Line Expressway, but in view of the restricted space available for expansion, design studies were undertaken during the 1970s on the presumption that the airport would be used by four major carriers. Deregulation forced a rapid revision of this forecast, but fortunately it was not too late to modify the arrangements to meet the demand.

A unique complex consisting of a main landside building linked by transit systems to two satellites was eventually chosen, a layout which would enable future development without the disruption of normal traffic at the airport. The effectiveness was demonstrated when a third unit was constructed in the late 1980s to take the number of gates available to 72. Sufficient space exists for a fourth to be added in due course, at which point 96 gates would be shared amongst the satellites. The latter buildings are identical and consist of a four-sided centre hub supporting a pier on three faces, with the fourth used for the entry of the transit track. A third runway became operational in 1989 which now allows simultaneous flight operations during most weather conditions.

This expansion became necessary because of the rapid increase in the traffic during the 1980s. Much of this was due to the popularity of Florida as a holiday area, especially with the close proximity of the Disney theme parks and other similar attractions. Already there are provisional plans for a completely new 100-gate facility to the south of the existing airport, but for the moment there is sufficient capacity to cope.

Location and access: Situated 10 miles (16km) southeast of Orlando adjacent to the Bee Line Expressway. Shuttle buses operate to the downtown area and the Disney parks. Self-drive is the main mode of transport with some 32,000 cars using the airport's extensive road network each day.
Terminals: The third floor of the landside terminal contains all the usual facilities, while the first and second levels deal with check-in and baggage reclaim. Each of the satellites has refreshment facilities but no shops.
Spectator facilities: None provided. Good views and photographs can be obtained through the satellite windows, but access to these buildings is restricted to those with a boarding pass. Some excellent vantage points exist around the perimeter, but of course a car is necessary due to the considerable distances involved. At the northern end, the service road parallel to the expressway leads to a car park alongside the runway threshold, but its westerly aspect can make photography difficult in the bright sun. On the eastern side of the old terminal building is a retired B-52 to commemorate the type's connections with McCoy AFB. In the opposite direction the road assumes the name Tradeport Drive once past the thresholds of the two runways. After travelling south to the distant end a good spot can be found for both viewing and photography if 36L is in use.
Operators: Scheduled services by American Airlines (Boeing 727/767, DC-9/10), American Trans Air (Boeing 727/757), Bahamasair (Boeing 737), British Airways (Boeing 747), ComAir (Brasilia, Bandeirante), Continental Airlines (Airbus A300, Boeing 727/737, DC-9), Delta Air Lines (Airbus A310, Boeing 727/757/767, DC-9, TriStar), Hensen (Dash Eight),

Icelandair (Boeing 757), KLM (DC-10), Linea Aeropostal Venzolana (DC-9), Mexicana (Boeing 727), Northwest (Boeing 727/757, DC-9), Trans Brasil (Boeing 767),Trans World (Boeing 727), Trump (Boeing 727), United Airlines (Boeing 727/737/747) and USAir (Boeing 727/737/767, DC-9, Fellowship).

Charter and IT flights: Aero Cancun (DC-9), Air Canada (Boeing 767), Air France (Boeing 747), Air Jamaica (Airbus A300), Air Nova (BAe 146), Air 2000 (Boeing 757), America West (Boeing 737), Britannia Airways (Boeing 767), Caledonian Airways (TriStar), Canada 3000 (Boeing 757), Canadian Airlines (Boeing 767), Carnival Airlines (Boeing 727/737), Emerald Airlines (DC-9), First Air (Boeing 727), Key Airlines (Boeing 727), Midwest Express (DC-9), Monarch (Boeing 757), Nationair (Boeing 747/757), Sun Country (Boeing 727), Tower Air (Boeing 747), Trans Florida Airlines (Cv240) and Virgin Atlantic (Boeing 747).

Cargo flights: Airlift International (Friendship), Burlington (DC-8), DHL (Boeing 727), Emery Worldwide (Boeing 727, DC-8), Evergreen (Boeing 727, DC-8/9), Federal Express (Boeing 727), Mountain Air Cargo (Beech 99, SD3-30), Southern Air Transport (Boeing 707, DC-8) and United Parcel Service (Boeing 727/757, DC-8).

Movements (1990): Total air transport 282,000. Total passengers 18,397,830.
Runways: 18L/36R (12,004ft/3,659m), 18R/36L (12,004ft/3,659m), 17/35 (10,000ft/3,048m).
Radio frequencies: 118.45MHz, 124.3MHz (Tower), 119.4MHz, 135.3MHz (Departures), 121.8MHz (Ground).
Telephone: (407) 825-2001, (407) 825-2055 (information).
Operated by: Greater Orlando Aviation Authority.

Oslo (Fornebu) Norway

Although chosen as the site for a future airport in September 1934, it was June 1939 before Fornebu was opened. During that first summer KLM, ABA and Lufthansa all started scheduled services, although the national carrier, DNL, continued to operate from the neighbouring seaplane base at Gressholmen. This situation was not to last. Only a very brief civilian life was enjoyed before the German forces arrived in the spring of the following year. Thereafter the facilities were used by the invaders for military purposes until the end of the war in 1945.

After a period of renovation, the airport resumed its civilian status in February 1946. Expansion was necessary through the ensuing years, culminating in the opening of a new passenger terminal in 1964. This proved adequate for the next decade or so, but by the early 1980s plans were being prepared to bring Fornebu up to modern standards. A new international building was subsequently constructed on the north side of the main complex for the use of departing international passengers, the latest addition (Pier C) being opened in May 1988. Two satellites (A and B) are connected to the main building by covered walkways, while another is due to be added to the west end of Pier C.

In the meantime the original terminal has also been extensively modernised to give much more space in the waiting area, together with a large shopping centre plus improved catering and bar facilities. In late 1991 the two resident handling agents, SAS and Braathens, were allocated their own domestic arrival/departure halls. At the same time arriving international passengers began to use a new facility, a development that was designed to ease the traffic flow through the airport still further.

Built on land bordered by the sea on three sides, Fornebu still has the useful ability to handle seaplane traffic in addition to that more usually found at airports. This geographical feature on the other hand has restricted the runway lengths, so all trans-Atlantic movements are handled at Gardemoen some 32 miles (51km) from the city. With the completion of the latest modernisation and expansion programme at Fornebu, there seems little likelihood of a new site taking over as Norway's major international gateway in the foreseeable future. However, since the 1960s there have been plans to construct a brand new airport, but it was not until 1988 that the government actually decided where it would be located assuming it ever materialises. There seems no great hurry because no action can be taken until the funds are forthcoming and that is likely to encourage renewed and prolonged debate. Opponents to the scheme were given fresh hope as traffic volume declined during 1989, but this was to be short-lived due to a reversal in the trend in the following year.

Location and access: Situated 5 miles (8km) southwest of Oslo via E18 (Drammen)

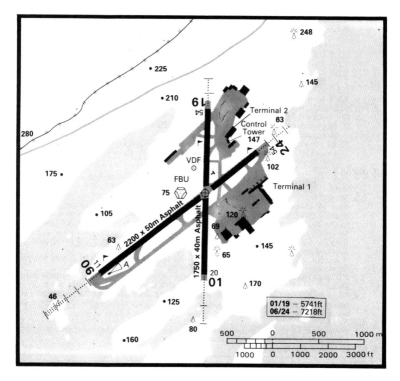

01/19 – 5741ft
06/24 – 7218ft

road. Bus route 31 runs every 20min between the Central railway station and the airport with a journey time of 25min.

Terminal: A four-storey building, the ground and first floors are devoted to arrivals and departures respectively with the second containing refreshment facilities and administration, the latter also taking the entire top floor.

Spectator facilities: None are provided although from the second floor buffet area a limited view is possible. On the other hand the car park offers excellent opportunities for photography of both arriving and departing aircraft, while the presence of float planes on the adjacent lake is an added attraction. Within easy walking distance is the general aviation area and the hangars used by Braathens and Fred Olsen. Fornebu is worth visiting if in the area, but the likely rewards do not really justify a special sortie

Operators: Scheduled services by Aeroflot (Tu-134/154), Air France (Boeing 727/737), Air Nordic (Jetstream), Alitalia (DC-9), Braathens (Boeing 737), British Airways

(Boeing 737/757), Coast Air (Twin Otter), Dan-Air (One-Eleven, BAe 146), Delta Air Transport (BAe 146), Finnair (DC-9), Fred Olsen (Electra), Icelandair (Boeing 737/757), KLM (Boeing 737), Lufthansa (Boeing 737), Muk Air (Bandeirante, SD3-30), Norway Airlines (Boeing 737, DC-9), SAS (Fokker 50, DC-9, Boeing 767), Trans World (TriStar), Turkish Airlines (Boeing 727) and Wideroe (Twin Otter, Dash Seven).

Charter and IT operators: Busy Bee (Friendship, Fokker 50, Boeing 737), Fred Olsen (Electra), Maersk Air (Boeing 737), Norway Airlines (Boeing 737), SAS (DC-9), Scanair (DC-9) and Sterling Airways (Caravelle, Boeing 727/757).

Movements (1990): Total 134,847 (air transport 104,478). Total passengers 6,622,464. Long-haul non-scheduled traffic accounted for most of the 850,746 passengers passing through Gardermoen during the course of 7,183 movements.

Runways: 06/24 (7,218ft/2,200m), 01/19 (5,741ft/1,750m).

Radio frequencies: 118.1MHz (Tower),

120.45MHz (Approach), 119.65MHz (Departure), 121.7MHz (Ground).

Telephone: (02) 59 33 40.
Operated by: Oslo Airport Authority.

Palma Mallorca

Before tourists descended upon the Island of Mallorca in their millions, the airfield at Son Bonet was quite capable of handling the modest flow of traffic despite possessing only two grass runways offering a maximum length of 4,900ft/1,493m. As tour operators began to sell ITs in ever-increasing numbers, so the Spanish authorities recognised the need for some development. With little scope for any major changes at the existing site, it was decided to utilise the military base to the east of Palma which had the benefit of being near to the coast with no obstructions to the south. In 1966 a scheduled service terminal was duly opened at Son San Juan to be followed in 1972 by another for the use of the charter flights. Subsequently the airport's apron areas have

been greatly extended to accommodate the ever-growing number of airliners, most of which have to park on stands away from the buildings. Usually one terminal is sufficient for the winter season when movements drop away dramatically. Despite the encouraging sounds made by the travel industry, Mallorca is not a haven for sun-seekers at that time of year, although it does enjoy higher temperatures than northern Europe.

For many years Palma managed with just one 10,500ft/3,200m runway, although in the 1970s a second was laid but never used. Instead it became a parking spot for the withdrawn airliners such as the Coronados and DC-8s of the defunct Spantax and TAE. However, in the early 1980s another attempt began to extend the airport, the result being that a brand new runway was ready for service by the end of 1987. Strangely enough during the period of construction little thought seems to have been

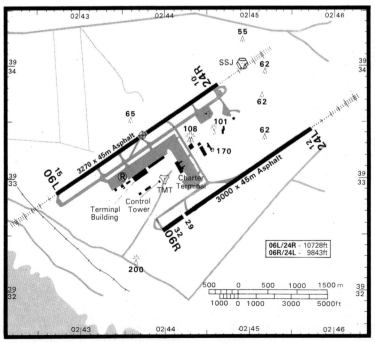

06L/24R - 10728ft
06R/24L - 9843ft

Above:
While the various vantage points around Palma are likely to be used mainly for photographs of airliners, it is possible to obtain an occasional shot of a Spanish military machine such as the P-3 coded 22-23. *AJW*

Below:
During the summer peak Palma often hosts some unusual specimens, the Aerolineas Argentinas 727 LV-MIM being one such subject when operating for Lineas Aereas Canarias in 1988. *G. W. Pennick*

given to the existence of the hotels and houses on the nearby coastal strip, many of which are directly under the flight path. Any objections went unheard until the new creation was ready for service whereupon pressure was brought to bear to restrict the runway's use to off-peak periods. This of course defeated the whole object of the exercise although it had already been accepted that it would only be used for northerly take-offs or southerly landings to reduce the noise nuisance. As a result there was little relief for the congestion suffered by the airport during the summer peaks.

In anticipation of the opening of the new runway, plans had also been made for the erection a more suitable control tower. Several years passed as the work leisurely proceeded, but when eventually completed in 1987 it gave the controllers a much improved view from their elevated position. This ability was long overdue because throughout the growth of the civilian facilities, the military presence has remained at the northern end of the runway. Spanish Air Force aircraft are therefore quite common ranging from fighters to search and rescue types, so the mix is carefully monitored.

Location and access: Situated 4.5 miles (7km) east of Palma to which it is linked by motorway. A bus service runs from the city to the airport. Otherwise the easiest method from elsewhere is by taxi or hire car.
Terminal: Both buildings are similar in layout and have the usual buffet facilities. These are generally inadequate to cope with the crowds of passengers waiting for their flights. Refreshments are also expensive. The charter terminal in particular can become very hot and crowded although there is a small external section to the buffet if there is a desire to seek fresher air.
Spectator facilities: Palma once had a terrace on the first floor which overlooked the apron used by the scheduled flights. This is no more, of course, neither is anything provided in the charter building, although its large glass panels do give departing passengers a limited view across the apron. Since a collection of multi-national finger marks decorate these panes, the chances of a reasonable photograph are poor. A narrow field of vision is just possible from the outdoor buffet area, but is hardly worth the effort. Better vantage points both for viewing and photography are to be found around the boundaries. When runway 06L is in use good landing shots can be obtained from the shore to the west of C'an Pastilla. Elsewhere, a track parallel to this runway offers excellent opportunities for take-off pictures in the afternoons which can be

reached by hired cycle after about 20min of leisurely pedalling. However, care should always be taken to avoid the unwanted attentions of those intent on depriving enthusiasts of their belongings. In the mornings a trip to the side of 06R/24L is worth the exercise, again with the prospect of some excellent landing or take-off shots, depending on the wind direction
Operators: Scheduled services by Air Algerie (Boeing 737), Air France (Boeing 727/737, Airbus A300/310), Aviaco (DC-9), Iberia (DC-9, Boeing 727, Airbus 320), KLM (Boeing 737), Lufthansa (Airbus A320, Boeing 737), Luxair (Boeing 737), Royal Air Maroc (Boeing 737), Swissair (DC-9) and Viva Air (Boeing 737).
Charter and IT operators: Adria Airways (DC-9, Airbus A320), Aer Lingus (Boeing 737), Aero Lloyd (DC-9, Caravelle), Air Belgium (Boeing 737), Air Berlin (Boeing 737), Air Charter International (Boeing 727/737, Airbus A300), Air Europa (Boeing 737/757), Air France (Airbus A300, Boeing 727), Air Inter (Airbus A300), Air Holland (Boeing 757), Airmust (DC-9), Air Toulouse (Caravelle), Airtours (DC-9), Air UK (BAe 146), Air UK Leisure (Boeing 737), Air 2000 (Boeing 757), Alitalia (DC-9), Austrian Airlines (DC-9), Aviaco (DC-9), Aviogenex (Boeing 727/737), Balair (DC-9/10), Braathens (Boeing 737), Britannia (Boeing 737/757/767), British Airways (Boeing 737/757), British Midland (DC-9), Busy Bee (Boeing 737), Caledonian Airways (Boeing 757, TriStar), Conair (Airbus A320), Condor (Boeing 737/757, Airbus A310, DC-10), CTA (DC-9), Dan-Air (Boeing 727/737, One-Eleven, BAe 146), Euro Belgian Airlines (Boeing 737), Finnair (DC-9/10), Germania (Boeing 737), Hapag Lloyd (Boeing 737, Airbus A310), Iberia (DC-9, Boeing 727, Airbus A300/320), Inter European (Boeing 737), Lufthansa (Airbus A300, Boeing 737), LTU (TriStar, Boeing 757/767), Luxair (Boeing 737), Maersk Air (Boeing 737), Martinair (DC-9/10, Airbus A310), Meridiana (DC-9), Monarch (Airbus A300, Boeing 737/757), Oasis (DC-9), SAS (DC-9), Scanair (DC-10), Sobelair (Boeing 737), Spanair (Boeing 767, DC-9), Sterling Airways (Boeing 727/757, Caravelle), Transavia (Boeing 737), Transwede (DC-9) and Viva Air (Boeing 737, DC-9).
Movements (1990): Total air transport 86,700. Total passengers 11,319,000.
Runways: 06L/24R (10,728ft/3,270m), 06R/24L (9,843ft/3,000m).
Radio frequencies: 118.3MHz (Tower), 119.4MHz, 119.15MHz (Approach), 121.7MHz (Ground).
Telephone: Palma 26 46 28.
Operated by: Spanish National Airports.

Paris (Charles de Gaulle) France

Research into a suitable spot for another Paris airport began in 1957 with the knowledge that Le Bourget could not be extended any further and its capacity was only 3 million passengers. Already Orly was being developed, but even there expansion possibilities were not unlimited. Once again the planners were very fortunate in finding a large area of land in a region known as the Plain of Old France, yet situated only 20km from the city. Just how sparsely populated the site was before construction work started in 1966 was confirmed when only one farm had to be demolished in the interests of progress. During the new airport's early days it took the local name of Roissy, but this was dropped at the time of opening in favour of Charles de Gaulle (CDG).

At the first stage in its development the new complex was centred around the terminal (CDG-1) and its seven out-lying satellite buildings, a cargo facility and maintenance areas belonging to UTA and Air France. When designing the passenger accommodation three particular requirements were borne in mind by the planners: walking distance between car or coach and the aircraft should be as short as possible; loading, unloading and servicing must be both simple and speedy; and, finally, the building had to be able to handle multiples of wide-bodied aircraft without congestion. A circular configuration was chosen to meet these demands while the satellites were wedge-shaped and capable of each dealing with four aircraft at one time. Passengers reach the gates via underground walkways equipped with travelators; a mode of transport used extensively within the main building where escalators also proliferate.

It resulted in an impressively futuristic layout, but in the light of experience not particularly beneficial for the operators. Originally it was planned that five of these conglomerations would be built as growth dictated, but as the airport capacity began to reach saturation point in the late 1970s, construction was started on the second unit (CDG-2) located in the southeast section of the site. When completed it was intended for the use of Air France, so the carrier collaborated with the design at an early stage. Learning from experience, this time the configuration was more conventional comprising of a pair of elliptical units inter-connected by a service road. Opened on 28 March 1982, the newcomer was considered an improvement on its predecessor which offered no

opportunities for expansion. For several years Terminals 2A and 2B were adequate, but in 1987 work began on the second pair in the series of identical buildings to be provided as traffic demanded. When completed in 1990, the first became 2D and was allocated for the use of the growing number of commuter aircraft feeding the airport. Previously these were forced to park on a distant apron from where buses took the passengers to the terminal. Generally this was no longer the case because stands were available adjacent to the building. Meanwhile work continued on unit 2C to meet the planned service date in 1993. Unlike its three companions it will have departures and arrivals on different levels allowing better security control.

Design and initial earth-moving work for the future CDG-3 complex was already underway in 1990. It marks a new phase in the architectural development of air terminals, yet retains the principle of the speedy throughput of passengers, while at the same time directly serving a larger number of apron stands. Each of the individual units will be considerably larger than those at CDG-2, being about 1,300ft (400m) long compared with 800ft (250m). There will also be a pier extending from each end allowing almost twice as many airbridges to be installed. The overall result will be a 25% increase in capacity, but for a similar amount of traffic, the new terminals will give a third more space for passengers.

Back in the 1960s it was anticipated that CDG would have a comprehensive system of runways; but after some years with a single strip, only then was a second constructed to become operational in 1982. A intricate network of taxiways exist however, which together with the fast turn-off points, are of considerable help in keeping the traffic moving smoothly.

Location and access: Situated 14.5 miles (23km) northeast of Paris with access from the A1 motorway (toll free from the city). A major new highway is due to link CDG with the future EuroDisney theme park, plus a four-lane road to the twin towns of Cergy-Pontoise by 1995. A rail service connects the airport with the centre of the city at Gare du Nord taking about 30min for the trip. Better interchanges between the suburban and the high-speed train networks will be possible when the new station is completed at CDG later in the 1990s. A point-to-point automatic transit system linking all terminals is also planned, plus an alternative travelator between CDG-2 and 3. Using the RATP bus route 350 or 351, the elapsed time to the airport is 40min from either Gare

Above:
Avianova's ATR-42 I-ATRL is serviced at Charles de Gaulle during its turnround. *AJW*

Below:
Reasonable photographs can be taken through the glass at Charles de Gaulle with plenty of scope for Air France subjects. *A. S. Wright*

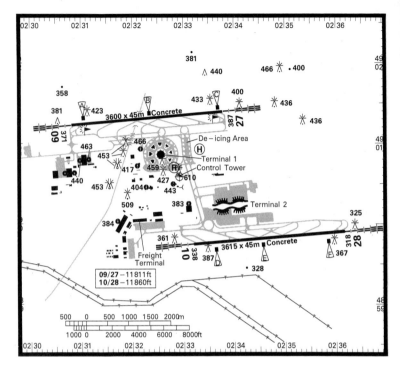

du Nord, Gare de l'Est or Nation. In addition Air France coaches travel between the city (Maillot) and CDG but are more expensive than the normal services. The airline's coaches also provide the facility for travel between Orly and CDG, a journey which takes 50min.

Terminals: Five floors of Terminal 1 are used by the public with one allocated to various amenities such as shops and buffets. Terminals 2A, 2B and 2D on the other hand are on one level which corresponds approximately to the height of an aircraft's cabin. Terminal 2C has reverted to the system for segregating arrivals and departures. The two complexes are about one mile apart but a frequent free shuttle bus links them. All airlines using CDG are to found at Terminal 1 with the exception of Air France (and carriers operating its flights), Air Inter and Sabena. These are handled at the second complex, with intercontinental services at 2A and those to European destinations at 2B.

Spectator facilities: In its early career Terminal 1 was blessed with a terrace, but like many others, it has been closed. From the road around the building somewhat restricted views can be obtained and even an occasional photograph, but attempting the latter usually arouses the interest of the prowling gendarmerie. Invariably this will quickly be confirmed by the piercing sound of a whistle, a device much favoured by the French when wishing to make a point. Around the Terminal 2 complex the service road also provides the basis for some shots providing discretion is used. As an alternative the car park at the Zone Technique has been employed successfully for some years and from this vantage point some good shots can be obtained of aircraft using Terminal 1. Probably because of its growing popularity with visitors, so the local law has taken a less tolerant attitude in recent times. Nevertheless despite all the problems it is still possible to photograph some interesting subjects at Charles de Gaulle.

Operators: Scheduled services by Aer Lingus (Boeing 737), Aeroflot (IL-62/86, Tu-134/154), Aero Lloyd (DC-9), Air Afrique (DC-10, Airbus A300), Air Canada (Boeing 747), Air China (Boeing 747), Air France

120

(Boeing 727/737/747/767, Airbus A300/310/320, Friendship, Fellowship, Concorde), Air Gabon (Boeing 747), Air India (Boeing 747), Air Inter (Airbus A300/320, Mercure, Caravelle), Air Lanka (TriStar), Air Madagascar (Boeing 747), Air Seychelles (Boeing 767), Air UK (BAe 146, Friendship), Alitalia (DC-9, Airbus A300), All Nippon Airways (Boeing 747), Austrian Airlines (Airbus A310, DC-9), Avianca (Boeing 747), British Airways (Boeing 737/757/767, One-Eleven), British Midland (Boeing 737, DC-9), Brymon Airways (Dash Seven/Eight), Canadian Airlines International (Boeing 747/767), Cathay Pacific (Boeing 747), Crossair (Saab SF340), Cyprus Airways (Airbus A310/320), Czechoslovak Airlines (Tu-134/154), Dan-Air (One-Eleven, BAe 146, Boeing 737), Finnair (DC-9), Garuda (Boeing 747), Gulf Air (Boeing 767, TriStar), Icelandair (Boeing 737), Japan Air Lines (Boeing 747), Jersey European (Friendship), KLM (Airbus A310, Boeing 737, Fokker 50, Saab SF340), Korean Air (Boeing 747), Kuwait Airways (Airbus A310, Boeing 767), Lufthansa

(Boeing 737, Airbus A310/320), Lufthansa CityLine (Fokker 50), Luxair (Fokker 50), Malaysian Airline System (Boeing 747, DC-10), Malev (Boeing 737), NFD (Metro, ATR-42), Northwest Airlines (DC-10), Polish Airlines (Tu-134/154), RFG (ATR-42), SAS (DC-9), Saudia (TriStar), Singapore International (Boeing 747), Swissair (Airbus A310, DC-9, Fokker 100), TAAG Angola (TriStar), TAT (ATR-42, Fellowship, Friendship), Thai International (Boeing 747), Trans World (TriStar, Boeing 747/767), Tyrolean Airways (Dash Eight), United Airlines (Boeing 727/767) and Varig (DC-10).

Movements (1990): Total 241,414. Total passengers 22,559,000.
Runways: 09/27 (11,811ft/3,600m), 10/28 (11,860ft/3,615m).
Radio frequencies: 119.25MHz, 120.65MHz, 125.325MHz (Tower), 121.15MHz, 119.85MHz (Approach), 124.35MHz, 133.375MHz (Departure), 121.6MHz (Ground).
Telephone: 1-8621914.
Operated by: Aéroports de Paris.

Paris (Orly)
France

Paris has always been considered an important city and as such has been well served by airports. From the start of commercial services in 1919, the grass field at Le Bourget was in use for both civil and military movements, but it soon became the airport for Paris. Taken over by the Germans in 1940, one distinct benefit derived from the occupation was that two concrete runways were laid, so when commercial flying recommenced in 1945 the airport could handle the heavier machines developed in the meantime. However, while Le Bourget was perfectly satisfactory for European traffic, the French needed another site for the use of intercontinental movements.

Prewar, a small area of grassland to the south of the capital had been employed by the French Navy as a training school. Known as Orly, it was developed by the Germans during their stay and again two hard runways were laid for the use of the Luftwaffe. At first the latter based bomber units at the airfield, but after a time aircraft production became the main occupation. It soon became apparent to the authorities that it was ideally suited for the international airport project, especially since it was also geographically well situated. No time was lost in using Orly for airline traffic after the

Liberation and in 1946 work began on a major scheme of expansion.

Due consideration was given to a tangential layout for the runways, but the system was not adopted. Instead an ambitious scheme for three parallel runways straddling the main Paris-Fontainebleau road was conceived. Nevertheless, by 1949 only a single additional strip had been constructed parallel to one of the pair left by the Germans. In common with many other airports developed in the immediate postwar years, Orly did not enjoy the luxury of permanent buildings, although in appearance and comfort they were far superior to the flimsy accommodation at Heathrow. With the financial state of France creating problems and the growth of air transport being slower than anticipated, Orly's completion became more of a very long-term project.

After a series of prolonged arguements, in 1957 work was at last started on the much delayed programme leading to the formal opening of Europe's newest terminal building by President de Gaulle on 24 February 1961. Intended to have a wing projecting from each end of the rectangular structure, only that to the west was operational at this stage although the second was completed during 1962 and like the first, was equipped with assembly lounges at each of the gates. The general design followed the Paris Airport Authority's precept that an air journey should begin and end at

A visit to Orly produced this photograph of the UTA DC-10-30 F-BTDC. A. S. *Wright*

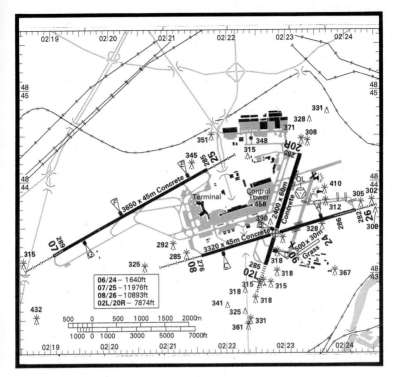

Runway	Length
06/24	1640ft
07/25	11976ft
08/26	10893ft
02L/20R	7874ft

the airport rather than at a city centre terminal. While such an establishment was retained at Les Invalides, it virtually became only a ticket and information office.

Some years later another phase of the expansion plan produced Orly Ouest, a much larger facility than the earlier building, itself now identified as Orly Sud. The newcomer was also equipped with two piers but these extended at right angles from the front of the main block, airbridges being a standard feature at the dozen or so stands. In the late 1980s there was a strong growth in passenger traffic which called for a substantial capacity increase. To meet partially this demand, the complete refurbishment of Hall 2 at Orly Ouest began so that it will be able to handle the larger wide-bodied types from mid-1990. Work also began on the construction of a new facility designed to accommodate four A330-size aircraft or a combination of six narrow-bodies after its scheduled opening in 1993. A five-level car park directly linked to the terminal is included in the project, while considerable benefit will be derived from the provision of a new tran-

sit system to link Orly Ouest and Sud on an elevated track before going underground for the runway crossing.

Location and access: Situated 9 miles (14km) south of Paris. Using Line C of the RER, the rail service from the city centre takes 35min to reach the airport. RATP bus route 215 from the city centre (Denfert-Rochereau) completes the trip in 25min.
Terminals: Both buildings have a full range of refreshment areas and shops with a useful supermarket in the basement of Orly Sud. The significance of this is apparent when comparing the prices elsewhere in the building.
Spectator facilities: Following the choice of Orly Sud for some terrorist activity some years ago, security was intensified and all facilities closed. There are reasonable spots within the building which can be used for viewing and photograhpy although care has to be taken through the glass. Outside, several other vantage points can be found particularly near to the VIP area. Here aircraft on their way to runway 25 pass very

close to the fence giving good opportunities for shots with different backgrounds. Whichever spot is chosen there is always the chance that the gendarmerie is opposed to the idea. While these officials generally tolerate the strange pursuits of English-speaking visitors, sometimes local happenings necessitate a tightening of security, especially when VIPs are due. At such times the number of official vehicles and their contents quickly multiply and it is wise to withdraw without delay. Even at the best of times discussion is normally a wasted effort due to the language barrier.

Operators: Scheduled services by Aerolineas Argentinas (Boeing 747), AeroMexico (DC-10), Air Algerie (Airbus A310, Boeing 727/737/767), Air Atlantique (Brasilia), Air Exel France (Brasilia), Air France (Boeing 727/737/747/767, Airbus A300/310/320), Air Inter (Airbus A300/320, Mercure, Caravelle), Air Littoral (Metro, Brasilia, ATR-42, Nord 262, Bandeirante, Fokker 100), Air Malta (Boeing 737), Air Mauritius (Boeing 747/767), Airmust (DC-9/10), Air Portugal (Airbus A310, Boeing 737, TriStar), Air Vendee (Beech 99), American Airlines (Boeing 767, DC-10), Austrian Airlines (DC-9), Balkan Air (Tu-134), Cameroon Airlines (Boeing 747), Cathay Pacific (Boeing 747), Continental Airlines (DC-10), Cubana (IL-62), Delta Air Lines (Boeing 767, TriStar), Egyptair (Airbus A300, Boeing 747), El Al (Boeing 757/767), Iberia (DC-9, Boeing 727, Airbus A300), Iran Air (Boeing 747), Iraqi Airways (Boeing 727), Kenya Airways (Airbus A310), Meridiana (BAe 146, DC-9), Middle East Airlines (Boeing 707), Olympic Airways (Airbus A300, Boeing 737), Pakistan International (Airbus A300, Boeing 747), Philippine Airlines (Boeing 747), Regional Airlines (Beech 99, Saab SF340), Royal Air Maroc (Boeing 727/737/757), Royal Jordanian (Airbus A310, TriStar), South African Airways (Boeing 747), Syrian Arab (Boeing 747), Tarom (One-Eleven, Tu-154), TAT (FH-227, Twin Otter, Fellowship, Fokker 100), Tunis Air (Airbus A300/310, Boeing 727/737), Turkish Airlines (Boeing 727737, Airbus A310), Viasa (DC-10), Viva Air (Boeing 737), Yemenia (Boeing 727) and Yugoslav Airlines (DC-9, Boeing 727/737). *Charter and IT operators:* Air Charter (Boeing 727/737, Airbus A300), Air Inter (Caravelle, Airbus A300), Airtours (DC-9), Airmust (DC-9/10), Corse Air (Boeing 737), Euralair (Boeing 737) and TAT (Fokker 100, Fellowship).

Movements (1990): Total air transport 191,400. Total passengers 24,330,000.

Runways: 07/25 (11,976ft/3,650m), 08/26 (10,893ft/3,320m), 02L/20R (7,874ft/2,400m), 06/24 (1,640ft/500m - grass).

Radio frequencies: 118.7MHz, 121.05MHz (Tower), 120.85MHz (Approach), 127.75MHz (Departure), 121.7MHz (Ground).

Telephone: 1-8843739.

Operated by: Aéroports de Paris.

Philadelphia, Pa USA

The City of Philadelphia officially became involved in air transport in 1925 when it provided 125 acres of land for training National Guard aviators. With commendable foresight, the authorities purchased the adjoining Hog Island in 1930, an area which had been derelict since World War 1. Unfortunately, it was destined to remain in a similar condition for another seven years before it was economically possible to start work on the site. Once the buildings and landing area had been completed, the airport was formally opened on 20 June 1940. Almost immediately it was added to the networks of American Airlines, Eastern Airlines, Trans World and United Airlines, all previously serving the city through nearby Camden, NJ.

During its first year of service, some 40,000 passengers were handled, most of them being carried in 21-seat DC-3s. In 1943 it was decreed that in order to maintain military security, it was necessary to close the airport for the duration of the war. Commercial services were reinstated on 26 June 1945, the year in which International was added to the airport's title following the inauguration of trans-Atlantic services by American Overseas Airlines.

By the 1950s air transport was showing healthy growth in the US, so the construction of a new terminal was begun with a completion target in December 1953. Yet more expansion became necessary towards the end of the next decade, resulting in the provision of an all-weather runway and high-speed taxiways. Some five months after these improvements were brought into service in December 1972, a modern international and charter terminal was completed. Modernisation of the domestic arrangements was the next project in the 1970s, which resulted in four separate units taking over from the single structure previously in use. A six year capital investment programme launched in 1988 included the renovation of the older buildings and the erection a new international facility known as the Richardson Dilworth Terminal A.

In the next few years an additional six to eight gates will be introduced, the precise number depending upon the needs of the airlines. A fifth unit terminal (F) is also planned for the area adjacent to terminal E, the newcomer increasing the total number of gates available by between 10 and 16. Airfield improvements included in the scheme should eventually produce a new runway for the use of commuter and general aviation aircraft plus the relocation of one of the existing parallel main strips.

Location and access: Situated 8 miles (13km) southwest of the city alongside Interstate 95. There is a Septa rail link between the city centre (Market East station) and the airport with a journey time of 26min. The trains run at half-hourly intervals and pause at Penn Centre and Amtrak 30th Street stations during the trip.

Terminals: Facilities are spread around the five terminals although the more important amenities such as refreshments are to found in greater profusion. On the other hand those requiring the services of a barber or beautician are obliged to visit Terminal C. Conveniently this concourse also houses the first aid arrangements.

Spectator facilities: None provided. Views are possible through the windows of the main building, but the individual pier terminals provide greater scope. These have to be reached via a security checkpoint, which may not be permitted for non-travellers.

Operators: Scheduled services by Air Jamaica (Airbus A300, Boeing 727), American Airlines (Airbus A300, Boeing 727/757, DC-9), American Eagle (SD3-30/60), British Airways (Boeing 747), Continental Airlines (Boeing 727/737, DC-9), Continental Express (ATR-42), Delta Air Lines (Boeing 727/767, DC-9, TriStar), Delta Connection (Beech 1900, Saab SF340), Lufthansa (Boeing 747, DC-10), Mexicana (Boeing 727), Midwest Express (DC-9),

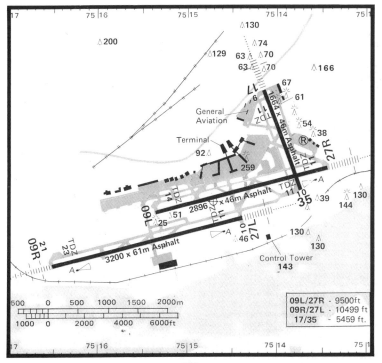

Mohawk Airlines (Beech 99/1900), Northwest (Boeing 727/747/757, DC-9/10), Northwest Airlink (Dornier 228), Swissair (Boeing 747, DC-10), Trans World (Boeing 727/767, DC-9, TriStar), Trans World Express (Beech 1900, Saab SF340), United Airlines (Boeing 727/737/757, DC-10), USAir (Boeing 737/767, DC-9, Fokker 100, Fellowship, Friendship), USAir Express (SD3-30/60, Dash Seven/Eight, Beech 1900, Jetstream) and Wings Airways (Twin Otter, Trislander). United Parcel Service has established a hub at the airport using Boeing 727/757/747 and DC-8s.

Movements (1990): Total 388,615. Total passengers 15,695,300. These compare with the 1989 figures 395,358 and 15,097,538 respectively.

Runways: 09L/27R (9,500ft/2,896m), 09R/27L (10,499ft/3,200m), 17/35 (5,459ft/1,664m).

Radio frequencies: 118.5MHz (Tower), 119.75MHz, 124.35MHz (Departure), 121.9MHz (Ground).

Telephone: (215) 492-3000.

Operated by: Philadelphia Department of Commerce, Division of Aviation.

Rome (Leonardo da Vinci/Fiumicino) Italy

Officially named Leonardo da Vinci, Rome's international airport opened for business on 16 January 1961 replacing Ciampino in the process. Designed by the Italian Ministry of Air Defence, the airport was actually built by the Ministry of Public Works on a large area of flat ground eminently suitable for future expansion when required. Unusually for the time, the national carrier, Alitalia, was invited to join in the planning stages of the new terminal block which therefore received the benefit of the airline's practical experience.

Initially the new airport covered about 250 acres to accommodate two runways, international and domestic terminals and a freight centre. In its first year of service some 2,246,000 passengers used the facility, a total which grew throughout the decade. Eventually in the mid-1970s it became necessary to lengthen the main runway and to construct a new building for the use of domestic operations.

Meanwhile as a result of an Act of Parliament which became law on the 10 November 1973, a new company had been set up to control the running of Leonardo ds Vinci and the civilian activities at Ciampino. Known as Aeroporti di Roma SpA, it formally took over the responsibility from the State on 1 July 1974. Under the agreement, almost all airport services that had previously been managed by a number of small contractors were transferred to the new organisation.

A third runway was brought into use in August 1973 and by the end of that year the number of passengers handled annually had risen to 9,705,000, a figure still within the capacity of the airport which was then the fourth busiest in Europe. To keep ahead of the steady growth, a master plan was produced by the authorities in the 1980s aimed at catering for up to 30 million by the year 2005. Once again Alitalia was actively involved because in 1983 it became a majority shareholder in Aeroporti di Roma.

This latest project, which was conceived with the assistance of an American airport and aeronautical engineering consultancy, will be carried out in stages to prevent any significant disruption of normal activities. In due course a massive new international and domestic terminal covering 300,000sq m is to be constructed, a considerable increase in size over the 90,000sq m area currently in use. In conjunction with this development 50 airbridges will be installed together with another 25 stands for the aircraft, most of them clustered around two additional piers. The first of the latter was earmarked for the use of domestic traffic when completed, in this case adding 14 airbridges to the total available. However, it will be the mid-1990s before the international section enters service together with another nine gates. In addition to this expansion, two satellites will eventually be built on the north side to be situated in the centre of the present aircraft parking area. Connected to the main buildings by both overhead and underground walkways, travelators will be necessary in view of the increased distances involved.

Until the late 1980s Aeroporti di Roma financed all of the improvement programmes with the dual purpose of both enhancing the appearance of the concourse and restaurant areas in the international terminal and at the same time ensuring that efficiency is maintained at a high level. With the enormous cost of the latest project, the company will in fact only be responsible for about one third of the initial phase.

Location and access: Situated 22 miles (35.4km) southwest of Rome. Ample car parks are provided, P1 being that devoted to

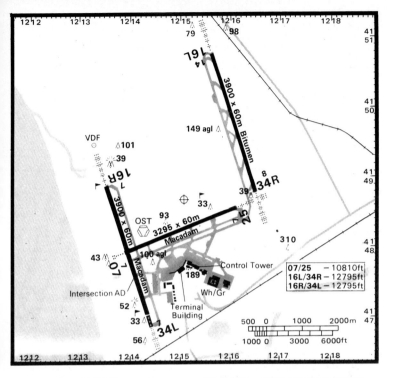

short-term stays. ACOTRAL runs a bus service from Rome to the airport every 15min from 07.00 to midnight. Outside these hours the frequency becomes hourly. In the city the terminus is located next to the main railway station. Eventually there will be a rail link between the two points which will be much faster if not cheaper.

Terminals: Both two-storey buildings contain the usual facilities such as restaurants, bars and shops.

Spectator facilities: When constructed, the terminals were provided with an excellent terrace which extended across the front of both buildings. Needless to say this has long been closed leaving no officially dedicated areas for visitors to observe the movements. From the restaurants a restricted view can be obtained, but the effort is hardly worthwhile. Outside vantage points are also almost non-existent and in any case the local law enforcers are stirred into action at the sight of a camera.

Operators: Scheduled services by Aer Lingus (Boeing 737), Aeroflot (IL-62/86), Aerolineas Argentinas (Boeing 747), Air Afrique (Airbus A300, DC-10), Air Algerie (Boeing 727/737), Air China (Boeing 747), Air France (Airbus A300/320, Fellowship), Air Gabon (Boeing 747), Air India (Boeing 747), Air Lanka (TriStar), Air Littoral (Brasilia), Air Malta (Airbus A320, Boeing 737), Air Mauritius (Boeing 767), Air Portugal (Airbus A310, Boeing 737), Air Seychelles (Boeing 767), Air Zaire (DC-10), Alitalia (Airbus A300, DC-9, Boeing 747), ATI (ATR-42, DC-9), Austrian Airlines (DC-9), Avianova (ATR-42), Balkan (Boeing 737, Tu-154), Bangladesh Biman (DC-10), British Airways (Airbus A320, Boeing 757/767, One-Eleven), Canadian Airlines (Boeing 767, DC-10), Cathay Pacific (Boeing 747), Contactair (Dash Eight), Crossair (Saab SF340), Czechoslovak Airlines (Tu-154), Egyptair (Airbus A300, Boeing 767), El Al (Boeing 737/757/767), Ethiopean Airlines (Boeing 767), Finnair (DC-9), Garuda International (Boeing 747), Ghana Airways (DC-10), Iberia (Airbus A300/320, Boeing 727, 737), Iran Air (Boeing 747), Iraqi Airways (Boeing 727), Japan Air Lines (Boeing 747), Kenya

Airways (Airbus A310, Boeing 757), KLM (Airbus A310, Boeing 737), Kuwait Airways (Airbus A310, Boeing 767), Libyan Arab (Boeing 727), Lufthansa (Airbus A310/320, Boeing 737), Lufthansa CityLine (Fokker 50), Luxair (Boeing 737), Malev (Boeing 737, Tu-134/154), Meridiana (ATR-42, BAe 146, DC-9), Middle East Airlines (Boeing 707), Nigeria Airways (Airbus A310, DC-10), Olympic Airways (Airbus A300, Boeing 727/737), Pakistan International (Airbus A300, Boeing 747), Philippine Airlines (Boeing 747), Polish Airlines (Tu-154), Qantas (Boeing 747), Royal Air Maroc (Boeing 727/737/757), Royal Jordanian (Airbus A310/320), Sabena (Boeing 737), SAS (DC-9), Saudia (TriStar), Singapore Airlines (Boeing 747), Somali Airlines (Airbus A310), South African Airways (Boeing 747), Sudan Airways (DC-9), Swissair (DC-9), Syrianair (Caravelle,

Tu-154), Tarom (IL-18, One-Eleven), Thai International (Boeing 747), Transavio (Friendship), Trans World (Boeing 747, TriStar), Tunis Air (Airbus A300, Boeing 727), Turkish Airlines (Boeing 727, DC-9), Uganda Airlines (Boeing 707), Viasa (DC-10), Yemenia (Boeing 727), Yugoslav Airlines (Boeing 727/737, DC-9), Zambia Airways (DC-8/10) and ZAS Airline of Egypt (DC-9). Charter traffic is not vast and is carried out by the usual carriers such as Britannia, Caledonian, Ryanair etc.
Movements (1990): Total 155,100. Total passengers 16,916,000.
Runways: 16L/34R (12,795ft/3,900m), 16R/34L (12,795ft/3,900m), 07/25 (10,810ft/3,295m).
Radio frequencies: 118.7MHz, 119.3MHz (Tower), 119.2MHz (Approach).
Telephone: 60121.
Operated by: Aeroporti di Roma SpA.

San Francisco International, Ca USA

On 7 May 1927, the city's mayor opened Mills Field Municipal Airport to serve the needs of San Francisco. At the end of its first full year the statistics revealed that 22,352 flight arrivals had carried 38,302 passengers, in the process generating $11,619 in revenue. Unfortunately this sum was more than swallowed by the expenditure of $287,325 over the same period, mainly due to construction and other costs. An advance warning was also included in the report to prepare its readers for the news that another $4 million would be needed to cover the future development of the airport.

In the pioneering days of the 1930s, San Francisco's (SFO) waterfront position enabled it to handle both flying boats and landplanes in equal numbers. Much of the land required for the runway pattern was in fact reclaimed from the Bay, a feature which has always caused problems when expansion is considered. A continuous programme of maintenance is also necessary because the material used for the infill sinks at various rates, causing a cracked, undulating surface unless checked regularly.

During the 1970s it was apparent that some major expansion was overdue if the airport was to retain its position of importance. A master plan was devised with the first phase involving the construction of the North Terminal for completion in 1979. Once this was operational, the 27-year-old central building was completely redesigned and

rebuilt before returning to service specifically to handle international traffic in 1983. The South Terminal was next for attention with the modernisation work being carried out in three distinct stages ending in June 1988. By this time the number of aircraft gates had risen to 80, 48 of which were capable of accommodating wide-bodied aircraft.

At the end of this 10 year programme SFO had grown considerably, but the authorities were already preparing for the future. Another master plan was drawn up in the early 1990s which calls for the construction of a new international terminal. The structure will possess 22 Boeing 747-400 gates plus four for the use of narrow-bodied aircraft, while within the building a much enlarged Customs facility will be able to process 5,000 passengers per hour. Once final approval has been received for this project, the work is expected to be completed by 1995.

One of the less desirable features of northern California, especially around the San Francisco area, is the risk of an earthquake. In an effort to counter this threat, the terminal walls are braced with reinforced steel columns so that they can withstand violent movement without serious damage. On 17 October 1989 the design was put to the test by nature when a severe earthquake struck the Bay area. Measuring 7.1 on the Richter scale, it caused extensive cosmetic damage to the North and International Terminals, but no major structural problems. Amazingly, although over 15,000 people were within the complex at the time, there was only one serious injury. Within 12 hours the airport was operational once again and in full service less than 36 hours after the disaster.

San Francisco is now the fifth busiest airport in the US and also handles passenger volumes in excess of all but two foreign centres, the exceptions being Heathrow and Tokyo. An impressive quantity of freight also passes through the facility which has prompted the construction of a new cargo complex.

Location and access: Situated 15 miles (24km) south of the city between Bayshore Freeway and San Francisco Bay. SFO Airporter bus service from downtown takes 30min for the journey between the terminal and the airport. There are Greyhound services to numerous other Californian cities, while Bay Area Bus Services link the airport with Oakland at regular intervals, the journey time being 45min. Full details with maps are contained in a booklet issued by Landside Operations, PO Box 8097, San Francisco, CA94128.

Terminals: There are currently three terminals each with two levels. Enclosed

passageways allow convenient transfers between buildings, but if walking is not a welcome form of exercise, a brown shuttle bus circles the upper roadway every 5min stopping in front of each terminal. If completely disorientated after a few circuits, there are electronic 'You Are Here' systems located throughout the complex. If all else fails there are conspicuous white courtesy telephones placed in strategic positions with operators only too willing to give advice. Naturally there is an abundance of all forms of shops, restaurants, snack bars and other services deemed necessary for the travellers' needs scattered throughout the buildings.

Spectator facilities: None provided nowadays. Viewing through the terminal windows is possible, but a better spot for photography exists at the threshold of Runway 01R. Elsewhere around the perimeter there are vantage points overlooking the executive apron.

Operators: Scheduled services by Air Canada (Boeing 767), Air China (Boeing 747), Air Portugal (TriStar), Alaska Airlines

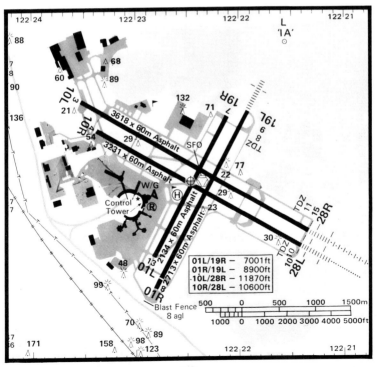

01L/19R	—	7001ft
01R/19L	—	8900ft
10L/28R	—	11870ft
10R/28L	—	10600ft

(Boeing 727, DC-9), America West (Boeing 737/757), American Airlines (BAe 146, Boeing 737/757/767, DC-9/10), American Eagle (Metro), American Trans Air (TriStar), British Airways (Boeing 747), Canadian Airlines (Boeing 737), China Airlines (Boeing 747), Continental Airlines (Boeing 727/737/747, DC-9/10), Delta Air Lines (Boeing 727/757/767, TriStar, Hawaiian Air (TriStar), Japan Airlines (Boeing 747), LTU (TriStar), Lufthansa (Boeing 747), Mexicana (Boeing 727, DC-10), Midwest Express (DC-9), Northwest (Airbus A320, Boeing 727/747/757, DC-10), Philippine Airlines (Boeing 747), Qantas (Boeing 747), Singapore Airlines (Boeing 747), Southwest Airlines (Boeing 737), TACA (Boeing 737),

Trans World (Boeing 747/767, TriStar, DC-9), United Airlines (BAe 146, Boeing 727/737/747/757, DC-10), United Express (Brasilia, Jetstream, SD3-60) and USAir (BAe 146, Boeing 737/767).

Movements (1990): Total air transport 397,500. Total passengers 34,427,000.
Runways: 10R/28L (10,600ft/3,231m), 10L/28R (11,870ft/3,618m), 01L/19R (7,001ft/2,134m), 01R/19L (8,900ft/2,713m).
Radio frequencies: 120.5MHz (Tower), 120.9MHz, 135.1MHz (Departure), 121.8MHz (Ground).
Telephone: (415) 761-0800.
Operated by: San Francisco Airports Commission.

Seattle (Tacoma International), Wa USA

This US West Coast city has been associated with aviation since William Boeing established his business during World War 1, with Boeing Field thereafter for many years supporting most of the aviation activity. However, in the late 1930s, a pair of enterprising men named Dean Spencer and George Wolffwere tried to find a reasonable location for a light aviation strip within reasonable distance of the city. Eventually their search produced two possibilities, but the choice rested with a 70-acre piece of land where the fog seemed to dissipate slightly faster than elsewhere. Many months of work were then necessary, much of which was spent in blasting tree stumps up to nine feet in diameter. Finally the rough strip was completed towards the end of 1940, allowing a Taylorcraft to make the first landing at the infant Bow Lake Airport.

Following the attack on Pearl Harbor on 7 December 1941, all private flying was banned within 150 miles of the Pacific coast. This effectively closed down the airfield, but in any case its two owners became military pilots for the duration of the war. Meanwhile, during 1942 the Port of Seattle authorities decided to build a new airport to supplement Boeing Field, so once again a survey was undertaken to find a suitable spot for the project. As had been the case a few years earlier, two sites were short-listed. One was west of Lake Sammamish and had only seven existing buildings to demolish, although in order to level the terrain some two million cubic yards of earth needed to be rearranged. The alternative was the area

around Bow Lake airstrip, but here 55 buildings were already present and there was at least twice as much earth to move.

Despite the attraction of the time and money savings, the authorities opted for the latter, no doubt influenced to some degree by the fact that both United and Northwest Airlines were strongly in favour. Both considered Bow Lake would be far more convenient for the growing community south of Puget Sound and would therefore generate new traffic. Furthermore the approach path to the Sammamish site was partially blocked by Sqak Mountain, an undesirable landscape feature by any standards. The two airlines backed their opinions by offering to advance up to $25,000 in annual rent until the airport was completed. With such financial support, the Port of Seattle readily agreed to acquire the necessary land from 260 individual owners at a cost of some $660,000 for 906 acres.

Although construction began in 1943 with the first official landing carried out by United Airlines in 1944, it was another three years before airline operations commenced with 10 daily flights shared by the two pioneering carriers. By this time the airport was known as Seattle-Tacoma, a name quickly abbreviated to Sea-Tac for convenience. Traffic growth continued at a fairly steady pace after handling 130,549 passengers in the first year, so when Alaska Airlines began operations in 1951, it helped to take the annual total to 643,509. Sea-Tac's passenger count passed the million mark in 1954 for the first time, but it was 1959 before a foreign carrier included the airport in its route network. Japan Airlines had this distinction during a year when Pan American inaugurated a scheduled jet service to the West Coast city.

Mount Rainier provides the backdrop for a United 727 as it takes off from Seattle-Tacoma.   *Port of Seattle*

Throughout the 1960s and 1970s the airport was expanded to keep pace with the traffic. In 1968 work commenced on the provision of a second parallel runway, while at the same time a major $90 million programme involved the terminal facilities. On completion in 1973 the building occupied two sides of a triangle with two piers protruding from it. Nearby were two remote satellites each having the capability of handling eight aircraft. Both terminals can be reached by underground passageways from the main building, but Sea-Tac also possesses a transit system to speed up the movement of passengers. When commissioned in 1972, it was one of the first such devices in the world to be provided for inter-terminal transfers. Consisting of over 9,000ft of track, the underground railway has two separate loops linking the main building with each satellite plus a connection between the two beneath the terminal. While no longer unique, Sea-Tac's transit is still considered to be one of the most efficient in the US with a 99% reliability factor.

There was further expansion in the 1980s when the south satellite received a new lounge area, duty-free shop and four international gates in 1983. Four years later it was the turn of the main structure to be given more space for administration, baggage handling, public waiting areas and shops. A total of 15,241,072 passengers passed through Sea-Tac in 1989, so a committee was formed to determine the future requirements beyond 2000. This led to the upgrade of the 30-year-old Concourses B and C plus lengthening D in order to accommodate six new gates. All the interiors were redesigned and finished in light and bright neutral colours to instil a sense of welcome into visitors to the northwest. This latest project was planned to be completed before the start of the 1992 summer programme.

Unfortunately for Tacoma, fog still remains as much of a threat to the airport's smooth operations as it did in the early airstrip days of the late 1930s. Known as warm fog, it covers areas that are above freezing point and is more stubborn than the cold variety. Needless to say both reduce visibility to unacceptable levels so a programme of seeding is necessary to disperse the unwelcome coverage. This usually has

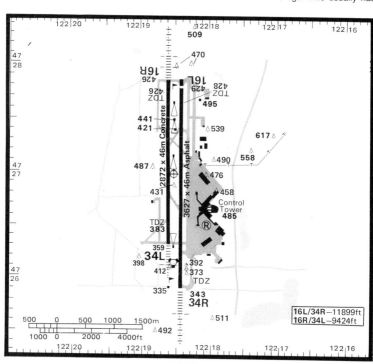

the desired effect and allows the airport to remain operational for far longer periods without interruption. In fact in 1990 Sea-Tac became the first US airport to be approved by the FAA for take-offs with visibility at 400ft.

Even with this handicap, Seattle-Tacoma is among the top 22 US centres in terms of passenger traffic volume and 14th when comparing air cargo results. Geographically it is the closest to Pacific Asia of any major continental US airport, being 350 and 650 miles nearer to Tokyo than San Francisco and Los Angeles respectively. In addition by using the trans-polar routing, flight times to Europe rival those of New York.

For many years Sea-Tac has served as a transit centre for military personnel. Normally the 25-year-old United Services lounge handles about 10,000 people each month, but the 1991 Gulf crisis increased this figure considerably. There were a number of side effects, one being the continued high level of security in evidence.

Location and access: Situated 13 miles (21km) south of downtown Seattle off US Highway 99 between South 136th and South 210th Streets. Greyhound bus takes 50min between the city coach station and the airport. Metro bus services are also available (Enquiries (206) 447-4800).
Terminal: Consists of main building with four concourses plus north and south satellites. There are 69 gates, 65 of which are equipped with airbridges. The south satellite is designed for international passengers with adequate signs in a variety of languages. In addition 20 interpreters are available speaking more than 20 different languages, so there is every chance that most travellers will be able to understand something. A barber's shop is one of the numerous shops provided which could be useful in the event of extended delays. There are hotels and banks adjacent to the airport.
Spectator facilities: None provided but most activity can be observed from within the buildings. Since there are few subjects that cannot be seen and photographed more easily elsewhere, any time in the area would be more profitably spent around the nearby seaplane bases.
Operators: Air BC/Air Canada (Dash Seven, Dash Eight, Twin Otter), Alaska Airlines (Boeing 727/737, DC-9), Alaska Airlines Commuter (Metro, Dash Eight, Fellowship), America West (Boeing 737), American Airlines (Boeing 727/737, DC-9/10), British Airways (Boeing 747), Canadian Airlines (Dash Seven/Eight), Continental Airlines (Boeing 737/747, Airbus A300, DC-9), Delta Air Lines (Boeing 727/757/767, TriStar), Great American Airways (DC-9), Harbor Airlines (Navajo), Hawaiian Airlines (TriStar), Horizon Airlines (Metro, Dash Eight, Fellowship), Japan Airlines (Boeing 747), Kenmore Air (Beaver), Lake Union (Beaver), Martinair (Metro, Dornier 228), Mexicana (Boeing 727), Northwest Airlines (Boeing 727/747/757, Airbus A320, DC-10), SAS (Boeing 767), Sun Country Airlines (Boeing 727), Thai Airways (Boeing 747, DC-10), Trans World (Boeing 747, DC-9, TriStar), USAir (Boeing 737), United Airlines (Boeing 727/737/747/767) and United Express (BAe 146, Jetstream, Brasilia).
Freight services: Airborne Express (DC-9), Burlington Express (DC-8), Cargolux (Boeing 747), DHL Worldwide (Boeing 727), Emery Worldwide (Boeing 727, DC-8), Federal Express (Boeing 727/747, DC-10) and Martinair (Caravan).
Movements (1990): Total air transport 343,900. Total passengers 16,240,309. These compare with the 1989 figures of 334,924 and 15,241,258 respectively.
Runways: 16L/34R (11,900ft/3,627m), 16R/34L (9,424ft/2,872m).
Radio frequencies: 119.9MHz (Tower), 119.2MHz, 119.5MHz, 120.4MHz, 123.9MHz (Approach), 121.7MHz (Ground).
Telephone: 433-5388 (Admin), (800) 544-1965 (Skyline information).
Operated by: Port of Seattle.

Singapore (Changi) Singapore

Singapore's introduction to aviation came in 1911 when an early device was demonstrated by the British and Colonial Aeroplane Co. Movements thereafter were somewhat sparse because eight years passed before the next flight was recorded, this time by a Vimy calling during its pioneering trip from England to Australia. Commercial flying began in 1930 when the government authorised the use of Seletar military field, although it was 1933 before Singapore was served by an airline. In this year the city became a stop on KLM's Amsterdam-Jakarta route, while at the end of 1934 Imperial Airways inaugurated a link with Brisbane. Another service to Australia began shortly after, this time a joint venture by the British carrier and Qantas.

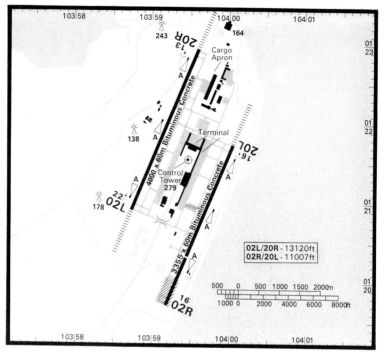

It was soon apparent that Seletar was inadequate to handle the increasing civilian traffic, so it was decided to build a brand new airport at the Kallang Basin. Although a swamp, the site was close to the city and offered the choice of sea or landplane operations. When opened on 12 June 1937 the facilities were claimed to be the finest in the British Empire. Almost immediately Malaya's first domestic service was launched to link Singapore with towns in the Malayan Peninsula. Operated by Wearne's Air Service, eight-seat Rapides were used for the thrice-weekly sorties, a frequency which soon became a daily event.

The development of civil aviation in Singapore was abruptly interrupted in 1942 following the uninvited arrival of the Japanese. For three years the country suffered from this occupation, but at least there were two benefits derived from the unpleasant experience. Construction of a hard runway at Kallang was very useful, while similar improvements at Changi were equally valuable in the longer term. Postwar brought the reintroduction of internal scheduled services, this time by Malaysian Airways which

as a stop-gap measure operated five-seat Consuls before the first DC-3 was acquired in late 1947. Two years later Kallang Airport had regained its earlier importance.

By the 1950s larger airliners were in service with the major carriers and were staging through Singapore on their trips between Europe and the Far East. Soon regular visits were being made by the early Comets, but it rapidly became clear that despite its modern facilites, Kallang would have to be replaced. The search for an alternative site culminated in the choice of an area of marshland at Paya Lebar, some seven miles from the city. Officially opened on 20 August 1955, Singapore's latest airport soon justified its existence as traffic figures soared in the late 1950s. By the end of the next decade some 2 million passengers were using the complex with the annual aircraft movements reaching 51,000. To cope with this mounting pressure, the runway was lengthened several times, until at 13,200ft it had become one of the longest in the world.

Unfortunately this development was still unable to keep pace with the growth, so once again the authorities began the now

If in the right spot within Singapore's enormous terminal, it is possible to acquire shots through the glass, the subject being JA8551, a DC-10 of Japan Air System. *Peter Weber*

familiar task of surveying possible sites for another airport. Bearing in mind that Singapore island is only 26 miles long and 14 miles wide, space is at a premium. During the war the Japanese had made use of an air base at Changi, later developed into an important RAF station. It was decided that this would become the new civil facility, although a considerable proportion of the land required was to be reclaimed from the sea. When Singapore Changi Airport was opened on 1 July 1981, it was considered one of the finest and most modern in the region with a 78m-high tower, impressive passenger terminal and the largest column-free hangar in the world for Singapore Airlines.

In its first year of operational life Changi handled 63,100 movements, in so doing contributing 8.1 million passengers and almost 200,000 tonnes of freight to the airport's statistics. Subsequently the number of travellers has shown a steady annual growth of about 7%, to reach a total of over 15 million in 1990. This was countered by the opening of second terminal building on 22 November 1990, the latest addition boosting the airport's capacity to some 24 million passengers per year. Plans to meet the forecast rise to 36 million are already well advanced, the solution being the construction of a third terminal. Air freight has not been overlooked by the authorities because there are long-term plans to establish Singapore as the premier international cargo centre for the Asia-Pacific region.

Location and access: Situated at the eastern end of Singapore, 12.4 miles (20km) from the city to which it is linked by the East Coast Parkway. Singapore Bus Services operate four routes (24, 57, 149 and 390) between the airport and various interchanges throughout the island.
Terminals: The two three-storey buildings share an enormous number of shops, restaurants and other services. There is an inter-terminal transfer system known as Skytrain, each vehicle accommodating 100 passengers for the 1min journey.
Spectator facilites: Both buildings offer extensive third floor viewing malls giving excellent views of the various stands. Such is the length of the deck that it takes up to 5min to walk from one end to the other, but by consulting the TV screens, the amount of exercise can be restricted to trips to the

indicated gate. Although the glass has a slight tint, colour photography is perfectly satisfactory. While a standard lens is adequate for most of the parked subjects, taxying aircraft require something approaching 200mm, while for runway shots a 300mm zoom covers all eventualities.
Operators: Scheduled services by Aeroflot (IL-62/86), Air Canada (Boeing 747), Air China (Boeing 767), Air India (Airbus A310, Boeing 747), Air Lanka (TriStar), Air Mauritius (Boeing 747), Air New Zealand (Boeing 767), Air Niugini (Airbus A310), Air Seychelles (Boeing 767), All Nippon Airways (Boeing 767), Bangladesh Biman (DC-10), British Airways (Boeing 747), Cargolux (Boeing 747), Cathay Pacific (Boeing 747, TriStar), China Airlines (Airbus A300, Boeing 747), Czechoslovak Airlines (IL-62), Emirates (Airbus A310), Federal Express (Boeing 747), Finnair (DC-10), Garuda (Airbus A300, Boeing 747, Fellowship), Gulf Air (Boeing 767), Indian Airlines (Airbus A300), Japan Airlines (DC-10), Japan Air System (DC-10), KLM (Boeing 747), Korean Air (Airbus A300), Lauda Air (Boeing 767), Lufthansa (Boeing 747), Malaysian Airlines System (Airbus A300, Boeing 737), Myanma Airways (Fellowship), Nippon Cargo Airlines (Boeing 747), Northwest Airlines (Boeing 747), Olympic Airways (Boeing 747), Pakistan International (Airbus A300, Boeing 747), Philippine Airlines (Airbus A300), Polish Airlines (IL-62), Qantas (Boeing 747/767), Royal Brunei Airlines (Boeing 757/767), Royal Jordanian (TriStar), Royal Nepal Airlines (Boeing 757), Sabena (DC-10), SAS (Boeing 767), Singapore Airlines (Airbus A310, Boeing 747), Swissair (DC-10), Tarom (Boeing 707, IL-62), Thai Airways (Airbus A300/310, Boeing 737), Tradewinds (Boeing 737, DC-9), Trans Mediterranean (Boeing 707), Turkish Airlines (Airbus A310), United Airlines (Boeing 747) and Yugoslav Airlines (DC-10).
Movements (1990): Total air transport 97,675. Total passengers 14,403,000.
Runways: 02L/20R (13,120ft/4,000m), 02R/20L (11,007ft/3,355m).
Radio frequencies: 118.6MHz (Tower), 121.65MHz, 121.85MHz (Approach), 124.3MHz (Ground).
Telephone: 5421122.
Operated by: Civil Aviation Authority of Singapore.

Stockholm (Arlanda) Sweden

Prior to the opening of Arlanda the Swedish capital had been served by the conveniently situated Bromma airport only five miles from the city. However as early as 1946 it had been recognised by the government that something larger would be required for the anticipated rapid growth in air transport. After due consideration it was decided to build a major new facility at Halmsjon, some 25 miles from Stockholm and initially intended to take over the international traffic. Clearance work was quickly started on the site which was located in an area covered by a vast forest in the Uppland countryside, but after a relatively short time the project was suspended in 1948. Traffic had not reached the proportions forecast by the authorities, therefore it was concluded that Bromma would be able to cope for many years to come.

After a four year break, construction was restarted in 1952, but this time the scheme was intended to proceed in stages at a more leisurely pace with the first step being the provision of a concrete runway. Costs had escalated in the intervening period, a factor which resulted in the contractors severely over-spending on the budget. In an attempt to rectify this problem, it was decided to reduce the quality of the runway to the absolute minimum, but of course this solution was hardly sensible. It meant that when completed in 1954 the strip was so bad that not surprisingly pilots refused to land on it. With the financial limits imposed little attempt had been made to level the ground, so the undulating runway rose and fell some 9m along its length. In addition, at the eastern end of the 60m wide expanse of concrete there was a difference of 0.9m in height between the two sides. Scarcely a good start for an international airport.

Nevertheless, despite the high level of criticism the government decided to continue with the Halmsjon site, although not until after alternatives at Malaroarna and Jordbro had been investigated. Another three years had passed when the go-ahead was given in October 1957, hopefully to bring completion of the first phase in 1960 to allow at least some of the traffic to transfer from Bromma where noise problems were becoming intolerable. Well before this event it was apparent that the name 'Halmsjon' was not particularly suitable because only Swedes would be able to pronounce it correctly. Something that international travellers could handle was therefore desirable so a contest was held to find a candidate. Half a dozen proposals were awarded prizes, but it was the place-name Commission which had the task of making the final short-list. After exhaustive discussions both Lunda and Arlanda were proposed and on 9 May 1958 the King-in-Council decreed that the latter would be used in future.

With phase one completed as planned, it was possible to commence commercial operations at the new airport in 1960. On 26 June a short ceremony was held to mark the departure of the inaugural flight to New York by a SAS DC-8, but it was to be another two years before Arlanda was officially opened by His Majesty The King. By now it handled all scheduled international movements to which were added charters in 1968 and domestic jet-powered aircraft a year later. With this influx the original single terminal quickly became inadequate so plans were made to provide a separate building for domestic passengers with temporary relief given by the erection of tented accommodation. Charter flights were also rapidly increasing in number, so another terminal was opened in 1972 to handle this business. That same year authorisation was given for a brand new structure capable of absorbing all international traffic both scheduled and charter, a role it assumed in 1976.

Next it was the turn of the domestic operators to acquire new premises, an event which took place on 1 October 1983 thereby allowing the removal of the earlier building. Such a fate did not await the charter terminal when it ceased to be used for its intended purpose. Instead this was converted into a freight centre in 1985 for the growing number of cargo aircraft using Arlanda. As an interim measure, the building had enterprisingly been used to house an exhibition of historic and vintage aircraft which have all now been rehoused in a Space and Aviation Museum within the airport. During its first 25 years Arlanda has been steadily expanded, the latest development including a third runway and the domestic terminal which opened in 1989. It is also envisaged that another pier will be necessary for international use by the turn of the century and at some time in the future a fourth runway will be laid. Access roads to the airport are to be improved in view of the volume of passengers attempting the journey from Stockholm and a rail link with the city is receiving active consideration, a development first mooted as long ago as 1963.

Location and access: Situated 25 miles (40km) northwest of Stockholm. There is a frequent SL City Line bus service from the

Central railway station which takes 45min for the journey. SL West surburban line runs from the city centre via a number of points connecting with the underground system. This trip takes 50min.

Terminal: Separate buildings for international and domestic use with two and one piers respectively. Airbridge loading is carried out on all three. All the necessary refreshment facilities are contained in both terminals with a fine array of shops located in A pier of the international building. Arlanda Centre is a new complex located between the two terminals and is intended to improve the service to passengers by providing yet more shops and other facilities.

Spectator facilities: A charge is made for entry to the terrace, but for viewing and photography a window seat in the cafe produces greater rewards. Movements on the apron can be seen from spots at either end of the terminal building.

Operators: Scheduled services by Aeroflot (IL-62, Tu-134/154), Air France (Airbus A300/320, Boeing 737), Air Hudik (Dornier 228, Short SD3-60), Airborne of Sweden

(Titan), Alitalia (DC-9), American Airlines (Boeing 767), Austrian Airlines (DC-9), Avia (Short SD3-30/60), Balkan (Boeing 737, Tu-154), Birmingham European (One-Eleven), British Airways (Airbus A320, Boeing 737/757, One-Eleven), Czechoslovak Airlines (Tu-134/154), Delta Air Transport (BAe 146), El Al (Boeing 737/757), Finnair (ATR-42, DC-9), Golden Air Commuter (Metro, Saab SF340), Holmstrom Air (Dornier 228), Iberia (DC-9), Icelandair (Boeing 737/757), KLM (Boeing 737), KLM CityHopper (Fellowship), Lufthansa (Airbus A310/320, Boeing 737), Linjeflyg (Boeing 737, Fellowship), Maersk (Fokker 50), Malev (Boeing 737), Northwest Airlines (Boeing 747), Polish Airlines (Tu-134/154), Sabena (Boeing 737), Salair (Metro, Saab SF340, BAe 146), SAS (Boeing 767, DC-9, Fokker 50), Swedair (Saab SF340), Swissair (Airbus A310), Thai International (Boeing 747, DC-10), Tower Air (Boeing 747), Transwede (DC-9), Trans World (TriStar), Turkish Airlines (Airbus A310, Boeing 727) and Yugoslav Airlines (Boeing 727/737, DC-9).

Charter and IT operators: Conair (Airbus

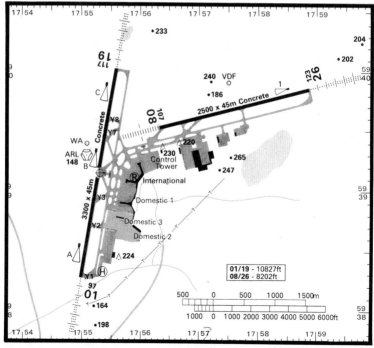

A320), Linjeflyg (Boeing 737, Fellowship), SAS (DC-9), Scanair (DC-10), Sterling (Caravelle, Boeing 727/757) and Transwede (DC-9).

Movements (1990): Total air transport 254,600. Total passengers 14,947,000.
Runways: 01L/19R (10,827ft/3,300m), 08/26 (8,202ft/2,500m). A new 10,000ft

runway will become 01R/19L in the mid-1990s, while a fourth strip is part of the long term strategy.
Radio frequencies: 118.5MHz, 125.0MHz, (Tower), 120.5MHz, 123.3MHz (Approach).
Telephone: (08) 797 6000.
Operated by: Board of Civil Aviation.

Sydney (Kingsford Smith) Australia

In 1921 a grass area in the Sydney suburb of Mascot was chosen as the site for a flying field, which for many years proved large enough to handle the limited number of movements. Inevitably this satisfactory state of affairs could not last indefinitely. As business gradually increased, so the boundaries were moved and new features added, until by 1945 the airport possessed three hard runways arranged in the traditional triangular formation. Although aware of the need to

expand the facilities to meet the anticipated postwar demand, the authorities were faced with a sizeable problem. On the western perimeter the Cooks River meandered its way into Botany Bay, in the past providing an effective natural barrier. Now it was a major inconvenience which had to be removed. In 1946 a massive reconstruction programme began, the first stage involving the diversion of the waterway along a mile-long course. Once it was happily flowing along its new channel, the original track was filled in to provide the base for two new runways and associated taxiways.

While both strips were initially adequate

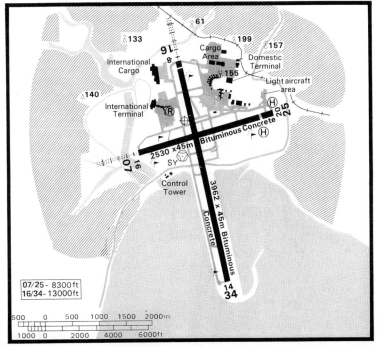

Above:
Needless to say, Sydney provides plenty of opportunities for photographs of the Qantas fleet, the 747SP VH-EAB being one such subject. *Peter Weber*

Below:
Air Caledonie International has one 737 registered F-ODGX which is used for regular visits to Sydney. *Peter Weber*

to cater for the airliners of the day, when the jets began to enter service it was apparent that both needed extending. Once again the task was not straightforward because at the southern end of Runway 16/34 the Bay remained an obstacle. Undeterred, the authorities embarked upon some land reclamation, culminating in the extension of the runway in 1968. Subsequently, another section was added in 1975 to take the length to an impressive 13,000ft, half of which used the land projecting into the sea. Construction of an international terminal designed to handle such types as the Boeing 707 and DC-8 began in May 1970, but several upgrades have subsequently proved necessary to accommodate the passenger loads of the 747 and other wide-bodies. Two other buildings deal with domestic traffic, while both general aviation and cargo aircraft have their own facilities.

Unusually, the forecasts responsible for the last major development in the early 1970s proved to be accurate, but by the late 1980s there were signs that the present day conditions were creating increasing congestion. To rectify this undesirable feature, work began in 1990 on a new international terminal complex adjacent to the existing building with completion due towards the end of 1992. New taxiways and enlarged aprons have also been provided which will help to give Kingsford Smith sufficient capacity until 2010. However, this will very much depend upon the result of studies set up by the government in March 1989. These were to intended to investigate the various options for enlarging the airport, but in particular the advantages of providing a new parallel north-south runway protruding into Botany Bay. There are considerable benefits to be derived from this ambitious scheme, a popular improvement being a marked decrease in noise levels, since most take-offs will be made over the sea. Ground access will be improved, while the parallel runways will bring greater efficiency and safety, because use of the shorter east-west strip would be restricted to occasions of adverse weather conditions. Assuming an early go-ahead, the new project could be completed by the mid-1990s.

Location and access: Situated on the north shore of Botany Bay 5 miles (8km) from the centre of Sydney. An Airport Express 300 bus service runs every 20min to the city, while the 350 travels to Kings Cross every 30min. Both operate daily. The Kingsford Smith Bus Service is slightly cheaper and provides an alternative every half hour. Buses also connect the Woolongong and Central Coast areas with the airport. The nearest rail station is located 1.9 miles (3km) from the airport at Tempe with Sydenham at 2.5 miles (4km) offering more city connections. There are several car parks both multi-storey and surface with charges dependent on the location and duration of stay.

Terminals: The international terminal has three levels and is connected to the parking bays by three concourses each equipped with airbridges. All of the usual shops and services are readily available. There are also two separate domestic terminals, operated by Ansett and Australian Airlines.

Spectator facilities: Small observation decks are provided in both the domestic and international terminals, the latter also offering views through its windows. It is a considerable distance by road between the two complexes, so it is not advisable to change vantage points too frequently. Elsewhere there is a spot at the western end of the main runway which offers reasonable possibilities.

Operators: Scheduled services by Aerolineas Argentinas (Boeing 747), Aeropelican (Twin Otter), Air Lanka (TriStar), Air Nauru (Boeing 737), Air New South Wales (Fokker 50, Fellowship), Air New Zealand (Boeing 747/767), Air Nuigni (Airbus A300), Air Pacific (Boeing 747), Air Caledonia (Boeing 737), Air Vanuatu (Boeing 727), Air Zimbabwe (Boeing 747 — operated by Qantas), Alitalia (Boeing 747, DC-10), All Nippon Airways (Boeing 747), American Airlines (DC-10), Ansett (Airbus A320, Boeing 727/737/767), Australian Airlines (Airbus A300, Boeing 727/737), British Airways (Boeing 747), Air China (Boeing 747), Canadian Airlines (Boeing 747), Cathay Pacific (Boeing 747), Compass (Airbus A300), Continental Airlines (Boeing 747, DC-10), Cook Island International (Boeing 767), Eastern Australia Airlines (Dash Eight, Jetstream, Titan), Eastwest Airlines (BAe 146, Fellowship), Garuda (Airbus A300, DC-10), Gulf Air (Boeing 767), Hawaiian Airlines (DC-8), Hazelton Air Services (Bandeirante, Beech 1900, Short SD3-60, Saab SF340), Japan Airlines (Boeing 747), KLM (Boeing 747), Korean Airlines (DC-10), Lauda Air (Boeing 767), Lufthansa (Boeing 747), Malaysian Airlines System (Boeing 747), Olympic Airlines (Boeing 747), Phillipine Airlines (DC-10), Polynesian Airlines (Boeing 747), Qantas (Boeing 747/767), Singapore Airlines (Boeing 747), Thai International (Boeing 747), United Airlines (Boeing 747, DC-10) and Yugoslav Airlines (DC-10). *Cargo services:* Air Hong Kong (Boeing 707), Evergreen International (Boeing 747), Federal Express (Boeing 747), Japan

Much of Sydney's runway was constructed on reclaimed land. *Federal Airports Corporation*

Airlines (Boeing 707) and Qantas (Boeing 747).

Movements (1990): Total air transport 194,100. Total passengers 12,223,000.
Runways: 16R/34L (13,000ft/3,962m), 16L/34R (7,874ft/2,400m-proposed), 07/25 (8,300ft/2,530m).
Radio frequencies: 120.5MHz (Tower), 123.0MHz (Departure north), 125.3MHz (Departure south), 122.3MHz (Ground).
Telephone: (02) 667 9841.
Operated by: Federal Airports Corporation.

Tokyo International (Narita) Japan

In the mid-1960s, the Japanese government decided to investigate a number of sites likely to be suitable for a new major airport to serve Tokyo. A growing state of urgency surrounded the project because it was already widely recognised that the city's existing facility at Haneda was rapidly becoming saturated. After carefully considering some 20 different areas, the authorities finally selected Narita for development. It is inevitable that proposals to provide or expand any airport will always attract the attention of objectors, but never on the scale experienced in Japan. Although construction was started in 1970, it was accompanied by continuous opposition from a variety of groups. Some of these were genuinely concerned about the effects on the environment, but for many it was an excuse to endulge in some extreme political agitation. Their obstructive tactics delayed the completion of the airport for almost four years beyond the planned opening in 1974, so Tokyo travellers had to endure the overcrowding at Haneda until 1978.

When Narita was designed, it was envisaged that in its first phase it would be able to handle up to some 16 million passengers annually. A central terminal building with north and south wings was provided, to which a total of four circular satellites were connected by short piers. A comprehensive

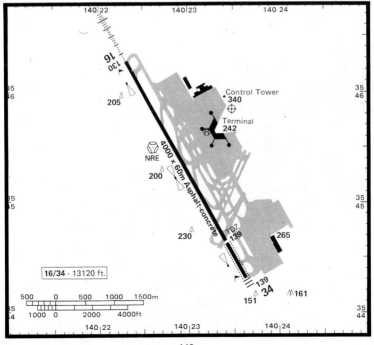

16/34 - 13120 ft.

network of taxiways gave access to the single runway, while a large area of concrete created the considerable apron space for passenger and cargo movements alike. Throughout the 1980s traffic steadily increased until by 1990 the time arrived for phase two to be implemented. Unusually this had been conceived at the outset, so with all the necessary land already available, it was possible for construction to begin at once.

The main work concerned the provision of two new runways, one parallel to the existing strip, with the second angled to give greater safety in crosswind conditions. Construction of a second terminal is also well underway and initially will consist of a main six-storey building linked to a four-storey parallel satellite. When Phase 2 of the project is implemented in due course, a pier will extend from each side of the main structure to increase the number of gates available. The whole new complex will be equipped with its own transit system plus a series of people-movers for the convenience of passengers.

One of Narita's less attractive features is its distance from Tokyo. Surface transportation was therefore high on the list of priorities, with a rail link strongly favoured. For many years two separate lines have linked the city with its airport, but a bus shuttle is necessary for the final stage of the trip. In the late 1980s the decision was taken to extend the lines into the airport station, thereby reducing the journey time to about one hour when services began in 1991.

In addition to its importance for passenger traffic, Narita also handles a considerable volume of freight. This has elevated the airport into the world's largest in terms of tonnage passing through the facility.

Location and access: Situated 41 miles (65km) east of Tokyo. The East Japan Railway (JR line) offers services from Toyko to Narita taking about 100min for the trip, while Sky Liner trains are operated by the alternative Keisei line and take about 70min from Keisei Ueno station. Both journey times should reduce to about 60min after the extension of the tracks. There is a choice of using the limousine bus routes either from the Hakozakicho City Air Terminal or other points in the city. A journey time of 60min is possible, but much depends upon traffic conditions. Needless to say this mode of transport is expensive.

Terminals: The original building consists of a main building and two angled wings. Floors one and three are generally allocated to arrivals and departures respectively, with the fourth containing all the various shops

and services. A similar arrangement will be used in Terminal 2 when completed.

Spectator facilities: Observation decks are provided between the north and south wings. There is no charge and the facility is open from 08.00 to 20.00 daily. Enterprisingly, holes have been officially cut in the fence to assist photographers, a welcome change from most other airports. There are also ample windows elsewhere in the building through which most of the movements can be seen and many photographed with few problems. Due to the unpopularity of the airport with the local residents, the security force is very much in evidence complete with defensive weapons.

Operators: Scheduled services by Aeroflot (IL-62), Air China (Boeing 747/767), Air France (Boeing 747), Air India (Boeing 747), Air Lanka (TriStar), Air New Zealand (Boeing 747), Air Pacific (Boeing 747), Alitalia (Boeing 747), All Nippon Airways (Boeing 747/767, TriStar), American Airlines (Boeing 747), Asiana Airlines (Boeing 737), Austrian Airlines (Airbus A310), Bangladesh Biman (DC-10), British Airways (Boeing 747), Canadian Airlines International (DC-10), Cathay Pacific (Boeing 747, TriStar), China Eastern Airlines (Airbus A300/310), Continental Airlines (Boeing 747, DC-10), Delta Air Lines (TriStar), EgyptAir (Boeing 747), Finnair (DC-10), Garuda (Boeing 747), Iberia (Boeing 747), Iraq Airways (Boeing 747), Iranair (Boeing 747), Japan Airlines (Boeing 747/767, DC-10), Japan Air System (Airbus A300, DC-9), Japan Asia Airways (DC-10), KLM (Boeing 747), Korean Air (Airbus A300, Boeing 747, DC-9), Lufthansa (Boeing 747), Malaysian Airline System (Boeing 747, DC-10), Northwest Airlines (Boeing 747), Olympic Airways (Boeing 747), Pakistan Airlines (Boeing 747), Philippine Airlines (Airbus A300, Boeing 747), Qantas (Boeing 747/767), Sabena (Boeing 747, DC-10), SAS (Boeing 767), Singapore Airlines (Boeing 747), Swissair (DC-10), Thai Airways International (Airbus A300, Boeing 747, DC-10), THY Turkish Airlines (Airbus A310), United Airlines (Boeing 747, DC-10), Varig (Boeing 747) and Virgin Atlantic (Boeing 747).
Cargo flights: Federal Express (Boeing 747, DC-10), Nippon Cargo Airlines (Boeing 747), Northwest Cargo (Boeing 747), Trans Mediterranean (Boeing 707) and United Parcel Service (DC-8)

Movements (1990): Total air transport 121,000. Total passengers 21,672,000.
Runways: 16R/34L (13,120ft/4,000m). Both 16L/34R (8,200ft/2,500m) and 03/21 (10,500ft/3,200m) under construction in 1991.

Radio frequencies: 118.2MHz, 122.7MHz, 126.2MHz (Tower), 121.6MHz (Apron control), 121.9MHz (Approach).

Telephone: 0476-32-2012.
Operated by: New Tokyo International Airport Authority.

Toronto (Lester B. Pearson) Canada

Prior to the development of the present site located in the village of Malton, the city of Toronto and its environs were served by five small grass airfields. While these were adequate in the 1930s, when Trans Canada Airlines was formed in April 1937 its modern equipment meant that larger facilities were urgently needed. Fortunately, one year earlier the authorities had begun the necessary planning work for Toronto's new airport, so by 1939 it was ready for business. At the time, the location of Malton provoked much criticism, because it was thought that 17 miles was too far from the city centre. Nowadays it is almost surrounded by Metropolitan Toronto and local communities.

The first make-shift terminal and administration building was a converted farmhouse, but during 1939 a wood-framed structure of standard design was placed in service. It was employed until a more substantial brick-built replacement with an annual capacity of 400,000 passengers was introduced in 1949. Later, two extensions were incorporated, in 1954 and 1959, to assist the building with its battle to contain the ever-growing traffic, a duty it performed for some 15 years. However, even during the mid-1950s passengers were beginning to suffer from the effects of over-crowding, so planning began for a brand new terminal in late 1957.

Construction began in 1959, but it was 1964 before the highly original building was officially opened. The designers produced a completely circular structure which was devoted entirely to the needs of the travellers, instead of sharing part of the accommodation with the administrative staff. It was an island set in the middle of the apron and was reached by a series of tunnels. The intention was to minimise walking distances, provide speed of service and a reduction in noise levels, while a seven-storey car park was included in the centre of the complex. Known as the Aeroquay, the new facility initially succeeded in its aims, but it was not long before the limitations of such a layout were all too obvious.

Its design capacity was 3.2 million passengers per annum, but this rapidly proved insufficient. Consequently the Aeroquay was modified several times to increase the figure to over 6 million, not an easy task when

confined to the island concept. There was no alternative but to produce a second terminal, but this time the designers reverted to the traditional rectangular layout which at least gave plenty of scope for later expansion. Stage one was opened in 1972, but by the end of the decade two more extensions to Terminal 2 had been built. Basically the terminal is now a combination of three modules, each handling its own particular traffic. A tunnel links the building with the Aeroquay, now renamed Terminal 1, but its use is restricted to passengers transferring flights. In 1988, the domestic wing was enlarged, while a similar extension in the international area was completed at the end of 1990. The latter took the number of gates available to 31 and the terminal's annual capacity to 12.5 million travellers.

In addition to these developments, work also started on Terminal 3 in May 1988, which is located to the northwest of Terminal 1. Opened in early 1991, the latest building was the first in Canada to be owned and operated by private interests. Its design resembles the 19th century architecture to be found in the opulent railway stations of the era. In fact, the themes of Toronto's Union and New York's Grand Central station were applied to Terminal 3 to provide a 14m high, sky-lit departure hall free from supporting columns.

During its lifetime, the airport has undergone several changes of identity. For the first 25 years or so it was known as Malton, but on 18 October 1960 it adopted the grander title of Malton International, a name it carried for less than five weeks due to objections raised by the mayor. In accordance with his wishes the airport then became Toronto International for the next 23 years, until on 1 January 1984 it was christened Lester B. Pearson International. Whatever the name, it is Canada's busiest airport and still serves the City of Toronto.

Location and access: Situated 17 miles (27km) northwest of Toronto. Highways 409 and 427 to 400 and 401 serve the airport, with ample parking available at all terminals. To find the point of ground transportation services a series of numbered pylons are scattered aound the site and are used as bus stops. It is therefore necessary to refer to a map of the complex to ascertain the appropriate spot. Gray Coaches run a

Above:
The differing styles of Terminal 1 and 2 can be clearly seen in this view of Toronto with the circular building able to handle a relatively few aircraft before alll stands are full. *Toronto Airport*

Below:
Photography from the Terminal 1 carpark at Toronto produces almost aerial views as shown by the Nationair DC-8 C-GMXY. *A. S. Wright*

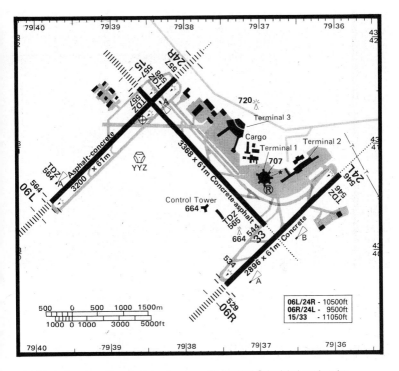

06L/24R	- 10500ft
06R/24L	- 9500ft
15/33	- 11050ft

schedule to downtown Toronto at regular intervals while other routes link neighbouring towns with the airport. Inter-terminal shuttle buses run every 15min.

Terminals: Terminal 1 is reached via a tunnel and is completely isolated from all other buildings. By comparison Terminal 2 is a traditional design extending along the edge of the extensive apron, while the more compact Terminal 3 is separated from the other pair by the cargo facility. All are self-contained with their own concessions.

Spectator facilities: None provided. Not surprisingly the multi-storey car park on top of Terminal 1 affords good views of most of the movements while photography is also possible from this lofty, seventh-storey perch. None of the terminals have any interior vantage points, but the perimeter fence near Terminal 3 provides close-up views of the aircraft on the stands. Elsewhere an access road passes the threshold of Runway 24L which is useful. At the distant end of the airport a similar spot can be found alongside Runway 24R and conveniently close to 15, 10 and the general aviation area.

Operators: Scheduled services by Aerolineas Argentinas (Boeing 747), Air Atlantic (BAe 146, Dash Eight), Air Canada (Airbus A320, Boeing 727/747/767, DC-9, TriStar), Air China (Boeing 747), Air France (Boeing 747), Air Jamaica (Airbus A300), Air Ontario (Dash Eight), Air Portugal (Airbus A310, TriStar), Air Toronto (Jetstream, Metro), Alitalia (Boeing 747), American Airlines (Boeing 727/767, DC-10), British Airways (Boeing 747), Business Express (Beech 1900, Saab SF340), BWIA International (TriStar), Canadian Airlines (Boeing 737/767, DC-10), Comair (Brasilia, Metro, Saab SF340), El Al (Boeing 747), Finnair (DC-10), First Air (BAe 747), Intair (Fokker 100), Japan Airlines (DC-10), KLM (Boeing 747), Korean Air (Boeing 747), Lufthansa (Boeing 747), Northwest Airlines (Boeing 727/757, DC-10), Olympic Airlines (Boeing 747), Ontario Express (ATR-42, Brasilia, Jetstream), Pakistan International (Boeing 747), Pemair (Navajo), SAS (Boeing 767), Sabena (DC-10), Swissair (Airbus A310, DC-10), Thai International (Boeing 747, DC-10), United Airlines (Boeing 727/757), USAir (Boeing 737, DC-9,

Fokker 100), Varig (Boeing 767), Viasa (Airbus A300, DC-10), Voyageur (King Air) and Yugoslav Airlines (DC-10).
Charter and IT carriers: Aeroflot (IL-62), Air Transat (TriStar), American Trans Air (Boeing 757, TriStar), Caledonian Airways (TriStar, Boeing 757), Canada 3000 (Boeing 757), Cubana (IL-62), Emerald Air (DC-9), First Air (Boeing 727), Guyana Air (Boeing 707), Hapag Lloyd (Airbus A310), LTU (TriStar), Martinair (DC-10), Nationair (Boeing 747/757), Polish Airlines (IL-62) and Sterling Airways (Boeing 727/757).
Movements (1990): Total air transport

309,100. Total passengers 21,525,000.
Runways: 06L/24R (10,500ft/3,200m), 06R/24L (9,500ft/2,896m), 15/33 (11,050ft/3,368m), 10/28 (3,400ft/1,036m - limited use by general aviation traffic, used as a taxiway).
Radio frequencies: 118.35MHz, 118.7MHz (Tower), 127.575MHz, 128.8MHz (Departure), 121.9MHz (Ground).
Telephone: (416) 676-3506 (Information services).
Operated by: Federal Department of Transport.

Vancouver International Canada

The airport officially celebrated its 60th anniversary in 1991, although there had been a limited amount of flying from as early as 1911. As interest in aviation increased in the 1920s, an effort was made to obtain a suitable site for commercial operations. Eventually Sea Island was chosen because of its flat terrain and absence of obstructions along the approaches. There was also ample land available for future expansion, although in 1931 no one could have envisaged how important this feature was to prove.

Three years after the opening, United Airlines introduced the airport's first major scheduled service on a trial basis. The sector linking Vancouver with Seattle proved extremely popular thereby justifying the carrier's experiment. Canadian travellers had the advantage of connecting with United's considerable route network, so as the years past, the frequency was steadily increased to meet the demand. Earlier the airport's development had been assisted by Federal financial backing which enabled two hard runways to be laid in 1937. The year also saw the creation of the national carrier, Trans Canada Airlines (now Air Canada), which began operations by introducing a Seattle service in competiton with the US company. Yukon Southern Air Transport also became active at this point by offering regular flights to a number of isolated locations in the country.

During the war a large factory was built by Boeing for aircraft production purposes, while other buildings housed engine overhaul facilities. This additional activity necessitated the construction of two new runways and a general enlargement of the terminal and administrative accommodation. When peace was restored the airport was returned

to its former civil owners, at the same time changing its name from Sea Island Airport to Vancouver International.

It was a period of rapid expansion for the air transport industry with Canadian Pacific introducing scheduled long-haul flights to Hawaii, Australia, Hong Kong and Tokyo in 1949. Meanwhile TCA was concentrating its efforts eastwards by establishing trans-Atlantic links with various European cities. This pattern continued throughout the next two decades until the end of the 1970s brought the need for some form of master plan. This was duly published in 1981 and attempted to forecast the requirements for the next 20 years. One of the primary recommendations was the expansion of the 1968-built terminal building which even at the outset was handling almost 2 million passengers per annum. Subsequently there has been progressive redevelopment of the facilities, but the new extension to the north-east has yet to be built. It is now proposed to undertake the work in three phases with the first stage involving the provision of a commuter terminal to the southeast of the existing premises. Once this is completed, a start will then be made on the northeast project, followed in the more distant future by a further extension as the need for greater capacity manifests itself. Also included in the 1981 Master Plan was the provision of a third runway to the north of the complex. This has also yet to materialise, but after full public hearings on the economic, social and environmental impact of the parallel strip, a decision was due during 1991. If approved it should be operational by 1994/1995.

Vancouver is one of the few major airports in the world which also handles floatplanes in some numbers. These operate from the river to the south of the island and shared a total of 44,000 recorded movements with helicopters in 1989.

Location and access: Situated 8 miles

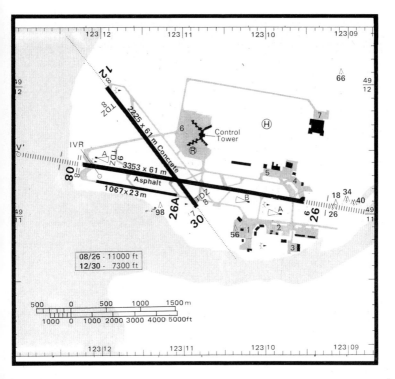

(13km) southwest of Vancouver and 23 miles (37km) north of the Canada/US border. Buses to and from the city take 45min for the journey while the average time for a car is 30min. Short term car parks are charged on an hourly sliding scale basis while a daily rate applies in the long term areas.

Terminals: The main terminal building has two piers angled from it, each with 10 stands for aircraft parking. There are six cafeterias and numerous shops spread around the three floors of the building. Buses leave from Level 2 for the south terminal which is used by the commuter airlines. Nearby are the seaplane jetties used by those operating from the Fraser River.

Spectator facilities: None specifically provided. Unfortunately, a boarding card is necessary to enter the piers so much of the traffic remains inaccessible. It is possible to view the apron through the glass, but if the near stand is in use the scope is somewhat restricted. The south side of the airport offers the most interest since the bizjet and

commuter terminal aprons are busy throughout the day and can be seen from a number of vantage points.

Operators: Scheduled services by Air Alliance (Dash Eight), Air BC (BAe 146, Dash Seven/Eight, Twin Otter), Air Canada (Airbus A320, Boeing 727/767, DC-9, TriStar), Air China (Boeing 747), Air New Zealand (Boeing 747), American Airlines (DC-9), Baxter Aviation (Beaver), British Airways (Boeing 747), Canadian Airlines (Airbus A320, Boeing 737/747/767, DC-10), Cathay Pacific (Boeing 747), Continental Airlines (Boeing 727/737, DC-9/10), Delta Air Lines (Boeing 727), Horizon (Dash Eight), Japan Airlines (Boeing 747), KLM (DC-10), Korean Air (Boeing 747), Lufthansa (DC-10), Pacific Coastal Airline (King Air), Qantas (Boeing 747), Singapore Airlines (Boeing 747), Time Air (Short SD3-60, Dash Eight), Tyee Airways (Beaver), United Airlines (Boeing 727/737), Wagair (Beech 99, Navajo) and Wilderness Airline (Super King Air).
Charter and IT carriers: Canada 3000 (Boeing 757), Canadian Airlines (DC-10)

and Nationair (Boeing 747/757, DC-8). Parcels carrierss Northwest Territorial (Electra) and Federal Express (Boeing 727).
Movements (1990): Total air transport 205,300. Total passengers 9,912,000.
Runways: 08R/26L (11,000ft/3,353m), 12/30 (7,300ft/2,225m), 26A

(3,501ft/1,067m), 08L/26R (9,940ft/3,030m - proposed for the mid-1990s).
Radio frequencies: 118.7MHz (Tower), 120.5MHz (Departure), 121.7MHz (Ground).
Telephone: (604) 276-6101.
Operated by: The Government of Canada Department of Transport, Airports Group.

Vienna (Schwechat) Austria

Austria was one of the first European countries to sustain regular air transport services, but it was just a year or so before the start of World War 2 that construction began on the site of Vienna's new airport located between the villages of Fischamend and Schwechat. By this time Germany had taken control of the country's affairs including the merging of the national carrier with Lufthansa. Very little civil flying continued during the war especially since the short-lived airport came under the control of the Heinkel organisation. Thereafter the base was used for flight testing many of the advanced prototypes conceived by the company, necessitating the laying of a 4,921ft (1,500m) hard runway. This later attracted the attention of the Allied air forces on a number of occasions resulting in serious damage being inflicted. With Germany defeated, the airport underwent a period of essential repair work before it could be used by the occupying forces.

Civil traffic was permitted to restart in 1946 on a small scale, but it was not until 1953 that much growth was apparent, growth coincidental with the formation of the Vienna Airport Authority. One of the latter's first decisions was to increase the length of the runway, followed by the design and construction of a new terminal. Even in the late-1950s the somewhat basic temporary arrangements were still in use for handling the passengers. A fairly orthodox design was adopted for the building although in the light of experience and airline requirements this now incorporates an eight-gate pier at its eastern end. When completed in 1988 it introduced the airport to airbridge loading, superseding to some extent the use of the traditional bus from terminal to aircraft. Some years earlier the single runway was deemed incapable of handling the traffic, so approval was sought to construct another strip. This was duly received and eventually 16/34 came into use on 6 October 1977.

Cargo work has also increased considerably at Vienna in recent years, which encouraged the provision of a new freight

centre in 1986. Several airlines now operate freight-only flights with 747s while others employ combi versions on their normal passenger routes.

Austria is, of course, well known for its abundance of snow. Whereas this pleases those wishing to slide down hills, its presence on the airport is not so welcome. Coupled with the high winds often experienced locally, the ground services are fully occupied in keeping Schwechat open during the winter months, but least the arrival of the white precipitation does not come as a surprise to the well trained staff operating the fleet of snow ploughs and blowers.

Location and access: Situated 11 miles (18km) southeast of Vienna. A motorway passes nearby from which there is an access spur. An hourly OBB rail service links the city centre stations (Wien Nord and Wien Mitte) directly with the airport, taking 30min for the journey. By OBB bus from the centre (Hilton Hotel) or from Wien South station, the trip takes 20min, while from Wien West another 15min has to be added.
Terminal: The large multi-storey building has acquired an impressive new arrivals hall. Although the usual restaurants, bars and shops exist within the main block, the new pier contains eight holding lounges each with its own security facility. Not a particularly new idea, nevertheless it was adopted by the Vienna authorities in accord with the airlines' wishes to speed the movement of passengers with greater security.
Spectator facilities: A roof terrace exists but is likely to be closed. As an alternative, on the first floor, there are windows giving good views of happenings on both the apron and runways. Outside, to the right of the terminal and beyond the cargo facility, lies the general aviation area. This is very close to the taxiway and from the vicinity of the office some good shots of passing traffic can be obtained. However, the availability of such spots may change from time to time depending upon increased security being imposed during times of political unrest.
Operators: Scheduled services by Aeroflot (Tu-134/154), Air Algerie (Boeing 737), Air Canada (Boeing 767, TriStar), Air France

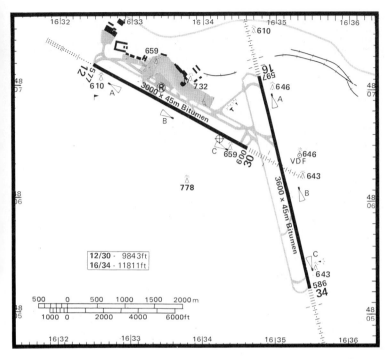

(Airbus A320, Boeing 737, ATR-42), Air Portugal (Boeing 737), Alitalia (DC-9), Austrian Airlines (Airbus A310, DC-9), Austrian Air Services (Metro, Fokker 50), Avianova (ATR-42), Balkan (Boeing 737, Tu-134/154), British Airways (Airbus A320, Boeing 737), Cyprus Airways (Airbus A320), Dan-Air (BAe 146, Boeing 737, One-Eleven), EgyptAir (Boeing 737), El Al (Boeing 737/757/767), EVA Air (Boeing 767), Finnair (DC-9), Garuda (Boeing 747), Iberia (DC-9), Iranair (Boeing 707), Iraqi Air (Boeing 727/737), KLM (Airbus A310, Boeing 737/747), Korean Air (Boeing 747), Lauda Air (Boeing 737/767), Libyan Arab (Boeing 727), Lufthansa (Airbus A300/310/320, Boeing 737), Lufthansa CityLine (Fokker 50), Malaysian Airlines System (Boeing 747, DC-10), Malev (Tu-134), NFD (ATR-42, Metro), Olympic Airways (Boeing 737), Polish Airlines (Tu-134/154), Rheintalflug (Dash Eight), Royal Air Maroc (Boeing 737), Royal Jordanian (Airbus A320), Sabena (Boeing 737), SAS (DC-9), Singapore International (Boeing 747), South African Airways (Boeing 747), Swissair (Airbus A310, DC-9, Fokker 100), Tarom (Boeing 707, One-Eleven, Tu-154), Thai International (DC-10), Trans World (Boeing 747), Tunis Air (Boeing 727/737), Turkish Airlines (Airbus A310, Boeing 727, DC-9), Tyrolean (Dash Seven/Eight) and Yugoslav Airlines (Boeing 727/737, DC-9, ATR-42). Charter and IT operators are not particularly active, but Lauda Air operates from the airport with Boeing 737s and 767s, while Tyrolean flies ITs to the Mediterranean with its Dash Sevens and Eights.

Movements (1990): Total air transport 79,900. Total passengers 5,715,000.
Runways: 16/34 (11,811ft/3,600m), 12/30 (9,843ft/3,000m).
Radio frequencies: 118.45MHz, 121.2MHz (Tower), 119.8MHz, 124.55MHz, 128.2MHz (Radar), 121.6MHz (Ground).
Telephone: 0222-77700.
Operated by: Vienna Airport Authority.

Washington (Dulles International) USA

Prior to the opening of Washington National in June 1941, the city had not enjoyed the services of an airport befitting the capital. When studies were conducted in the 1930s, President Roosevelt favoured the idea of two separate facilities for the area, but in the event no action was taken until the early 1950s. At this point National was already in some distress from over-crowding, so once again thoughts were turned seriously towards the prospect of a second major airport for Washington.

Originally a site at Camp Springs had been earmarked for the location of a future civil airfield, but during the war the military acquired it for its own use. This became known as Andrews AFB, but as National's plight became more acute, the CAA considered taking over the base by forcing the USAF to build a new complex further from Washington. Fortunately for the occupants this proposal was dropped in 1950, when Congress finally sanctioned the construction of a completely new airport some 27 miles west of the city. Nevertheless, it took another six years or so before, in 1957, the necessary funds were forthcoming, therefore emulating the problems affecting National's progress years earlier.

Work on the project actually commenced in September 1958, and continued until November 1962 when Dulles International was formally declared open before 50,000 spectators. The area chosen had been covered by acres of forest land, most of which had to be cleared before building could commence. When contracting the Finnish architect, Eero Saarinen, to design the terminal, the authorities must have realised that the result would be different. They were not disappointed. The main concourse was 600ft long and 200ft wide rising to 60ft high on both land and airside. In between there were no columns; instead a striking effect was achieved by the roof being supported by cables similar to those used for suspension bridges. Dulles also boasted an equally unusual control tower, which at 193ft high, was for many years, the tallest in the world.

From the beginning, the airport was intended primarily for international traffic, leaving National to handle the considerable domestic movements. After the convenience of the close proximity of the latter to the centre of the city, the much greater distance to Dulles has probably had an adverse effect upon its growth rate, which really has been very gradual compared with similar airports elsewhere. However, in more recent times there has been a greater willingness for carriers to relocate and to introduce connecting services for the long-haul flights.

While the terminal at Dulles was designed with the standard separate levels for arrivals and departures, moving the passengers to and from the aircraft was decidedly different. Travellers left the holding lounge to pass directly into a comfortably appointed coach capable of carrying up to 150 passengers. At the aircraft the whole superstructure was elevated until level with the airliner's floor, thereby allowing direct entry into the cabin with no inconvenient steps or rain-swept apron to cross. The reverse procedure was adopted by those arriving.

Towards the end of the 1970s it was found necessary to widen the main building for the greater comfort of departing passengers, followed by a series of improvements throughout the 1980s. A more ambitious undertaking began at the end of the decade with the construction of an international arrivals hall just west of the existing terminal. Opened early in 1991, the new facility greatly improved the efficiency of the processing arrangements for incoming passengers, something long overdue at all US gateway airports.

A contract was also awarded for the expansion of the main terminal in keeping with the original architecture of the late Eero Saarinen. The structure will be lengthened to 1,240ft (378m) in two stages by adding 320ft (97m) to each end, the west section becoming the first to be completed at the beginning of 1993. In the meantime several separate satellites have been erected on the apron as a temporary measure, although it is likely to be some years before they are replaced.

In the long term even the expanded main complex will be insufficient to handle the expected growth, so the solution involves the provision of six individual midfield terminals, each with 24 gates. The new blocks will be provided gradually, with the first pair scheduled to enter service in the mid-1990s. An underground transit system will convey passengers to and from the central area, eventually replacing the mobile lounges still employed.

Three runways have so far proved adequate to cope with Dulles's traffic, but in late 1991 work began on a 500ft (152m) extension of the cross-wind Runway 12/30. Since the authority already possesses the necessary land, a parallel strip can be provided when required, but it is more likely that a third north-south runway will preceed it,

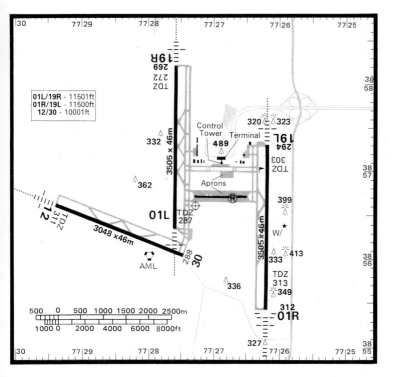

01L/19R - 11501ft
01R/19L - 11500ft
12/30 - 10001ft

19R
269
272
TDZ

320 △323
Control
Tower
332
Terminal
489
19L
294
303
TDZ

362
Aprons

399

01L TDZ
287
413
333

30
288
AML

336
TDZ
313
349

312
01R

327

3505 x 46m
3048 x46m
3505 x46m
311
TDZ
12

W/

500 0 500 1000 1500 2000 2500m
1000 0 2000 4000 6000 8000ft

assuming negotiations with the local landowners are successful. Fortunately there is no urgency so such an addition could be made anytime within the next 20 years.

Location and access: Situated 26 miles (43km) west of the city. Washington Flyer bus services run frequently to Dulles from the Downtown Airport Terminal taking 50min for the journey. A bus provides a direct link between the Metrorail station at West Falls Church and the airport every 30min. A direct access highway and a 14-mile expressway connects the city with the airport.

Terminals: An impressive single terminal building contains all the necessary amenities, but these are all located on the airside so are not accessible unless travelling. The future midfield terminals will be self-contained but the same restrictions will apply.

Spectator facilities: There is a small observation deck in front of the terminal, but it is not the best of spots for photography, especially for the long-haul types which tend

to park some distance from the building. On the other hand reasonable shots of the commuter traffic can be obtained from this vantage point, assuming it is open. Visiting Dulles is therefore hardly worth the effort and expense when National provides far more movements of note.

Operators: Aeroflot (IL-62), Air France (Airbus A310, Boeing 747), All Nippon Airways (Boeing 747), American Airlines (Boeing 727/767), British Airways (Boeing 737), British Airways (Boeing 747/767, Concorde), Business Express (Beech 1900, Saab SF340, SD3-60), Continental Airlines (Boeing 737, DC-9), Continental Express (ATR-42), Delta Air Lines (Boeing 737/757, DC-9), Lufthansa (DC-10), Mohawk Airlines (Metro), Northwest Airlines (DC-9), Saudia (Boeing 747), TACA International (Boeing 737), Trans World (Boeing 727/767, DC-9, TriStar), Trans World Express (Beech 1900, Saab SF340), USAir (Fellowship, Jetstream, Dash Eight, SD3-30/60, DC-9), United Airlines (BAe 146, Boeing 727/737/747/757/767, DC-10), United Express (Jetstream, Brasilia, Friendship)

and Wings Airways (Twin Otter).
Movements (1990): Total 242,209. Total passengers 10.4million.
Runways: 01L/19R (11,500ft/3,505m), 01R/19L (11,500ft/3,505m),12/30 (10,500ft/3,200m). A second 12/30 and third 01/19 in prospect.

Radio frequencies: 120.1MHz (Tower), 125.05MHz, 126.65MHz (Departure), 121.9MHz (Ground).
Telephone: (703) 739-8600.
Operated by: Metropolitan Washington Airports Authority.

Washington (National), Va USA

One of the first problems to confront the new Civil Aeronautics Authority when it became operational in August 1938, was the development of a modern airport to serve the US capital. Considering the importance of the city, the air transport facilities available at Washington were inadequate to say the least. The first major terminal in the area was Hoover Field, a privately-owned site opened in 1926 on the land now occupied by the Pentagon. After one year in business it found itself in competition with a second field located nearby which took the name of Washington Airport. For a time both operated as individual units, but with the advent of the Depression, the two were merged in 1930 to form Washington-Hoover Airport.

Unfortunately, when the planners selected the site in the 1920s it would appear that either a blindfolded official prodded a map with a pin, or the team lacked any imagination. The location chosen was remarkable for the number of undesirable features in the immediate vicinity including overhead electric cables, a high chimney on one approach and a dump which produced a never-ending supply of smoke. As if this was not enough, a main road bisected the single runway, so guards had to stop the surface traffic for every aircraft movement. Despite these hazards, Hoover had an excellent safety record during its career, but this was a somewhat misleading statistic because whenever there was a slight breeze, pilots refused to land.

Throughout the 1930s various government committees investigated possible sites for a new airport. By 1937 the long list had been reduced to three, one of which was that existing at Hoover. This option, however, was quickly vetoed by President Roosevelt, but with the recommendation that both Gravelly Point and Camp Springs should be developed. Naturally the merits of the projects provoked a great deal of political debate, but eventually the responsibility for making the decision was entrusted to the

CAA. The agency opted for Gravelly Point, primarily because of its close proximity to downtown Washington, a mere 10min by road. There was a snag of course; the area was largely under water, but at least most of it was already owned by the government. Finally official approval was formally bestowed on the 750-acre Washington National plan on 27 September 1938.

Work started almost immediately on building a dyke around the area followed by a massive dredging operation to ensure that the runways were laid upon the firm gravel base that existed 11ft below the surface. Even with all the subsequent infilling, the airfield still resembled a lagoon because the water was intentionally retained to allow the finer sand to settle before the draining process was undertaken in the spring of 1940. At last the airport appeared on dry land for the final phase of its construction to begin. Four runways were laid, the longest being the north-south 6,855ft (2,089m) strip. Elsewhere, the curved terminal building was designed in the southern colonial style to resemble Mount Vernon, the home of George Washington. It aimed to give the impression of spaciousness and tended to favour visitors rather than passengers, but within 10 years the accommodation was seriously congested.

Washington National opened for business on 16 June 1941 to become an immediate success. In its first year of service, it was ranked second busiest in the country when handling 79,164 aircraft movements and 636,729 passengers. Such was the interest generated locally that over 4 million non-flying persons also passed through the doors. Ironically, by the end of the 1940s National's success was beginning to have a detrimental effect upon its ability to survive. There were already suggestions that Washington needed a second airport, thereby reviving Roosevelt's original 1930s plan to develop Camp Springs. Unfortunately this option was no longer available because some years earlier the Army Air Force had established a base for its own purposes. While the field was perfectly satisfactory, in the 1940s Transport Command was given permission to operate into National for the

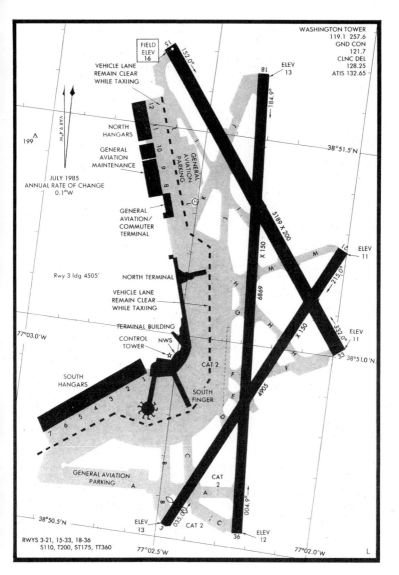

WASHINGTON TOWER
119.1 257.6
GND CON
121.7
CLNC DEL
128.25
ATIS 132.65

FIELD
ELEV
16

VEHICLE LANE
REMAIN CLEAR
WHILE TAXIING

152.0°

ELEV
13

NORTH
HANGARS

GENERAL
AVIATION
PARKING

184.9°

38°51.5'N

199

VAR 9.4°W

GENERAL
AVIATION
MAINTENANCE

JULY 1985
ANNUAL RATE OF CHANGE
0.1°W

GENERAL
AVIATION/
COMMUTER
TERMINAL

5189 X 200

Rwy 3 ldg 4505'

NORTH TERMINAL

VEHICLE LANE
REMAIN CLEAR
WHILE TAXIING

ELEV
11

X 150

6869

215.0°

77°03.0'W

TERMINAL BUILDING

CONTROL
TOWER

NWS

322.0°

ELEV
11

X 150

38°51.0'N.

CAT 2

SOUTH
HANGARS

SOUTH
FINGER

4905

CAT
2

GENERAL AVIATION
PARKING

CAT 2

004.9°

38°50.5'N

ELEV
13

035.0°

CAT 2

ELEV
12

RWYS 3-21, 15-33, 18-36
S110, T200, ST175, TT360

77°02.5'W

77°02.0'W

duration of the war. Once installed there was inevitably a marked reluctance to leave the much more convenient facilities without a struggle. The extra traffic certainly did not help the situation at the airport, which by 1950 had almost reached crisis proportions. At last the seriousness was recognised by Congress, so authorisation was given for a second civil airport to be built and the Military Air Transport Service was instructed to return to what had become known as Andrews AFB.

When finally opened in 1962, Dulles gave some welcome relief to its older neighbour, although the latter continued to cope with a vast number of domestic movements. Through the years various extensions were carried out to National's original terminal, including the addition of two piers to produce more aircraft stands. Eventually the authorities embarked upon a more comprehensive expansion programme in the 1980s so that Washington's busiest airport could retain its efficiency and usefulness. The largest item amongst the proposals was a new terminal building to be equipped with 35 airline gates when completed in 1994. There will also be direct access to the adjacent Metrorail station via a covered bridge equipped with travelators. To create the necessary space, all buildings north of the original terminal were earmarked for demolition, including the 1958-built north terminal, general aviation centre and Hangar 10.

Such drastic measures were bound to cause a certain amount of disruption, but this was kept to a minimum by providing adequate alternative airline facilities during the various phases of the redevelopment. For instance, Hangar 11 at the north end of the airport was converted into an interim terminal while the general aviation centre was recreated within the old Hangar 7. In conjunction with these improvements, the landside access and car parks were upgraded, while a new two-level structure has been provided for taxis to eliminate the congestion previously caused by these waiting vehicles. When all the construction work has been completed, work is due to start on a major refurbishment of the 1940s terminal to make it compatible both internally and externally with the modern buildings. Once back in service, the number of gates will be reduced to 12 and the rejuvinated structure will be used by the airport's commuter carriers.

Location and access: Situated 3 miles (5km) south of the city, east of the George Washington Memorial Parkway. The Washington Flyer bus links the airport with the city and Dulles, the trip between National and downtown taking 35min. A public Metrobus is available to areas not served by Metrorail, the latter being a part of the regions's subway system. The station

will eventually be linked to the terminal but until 1994 is accessible on foot or shuttle bus.

Terminals: Extensive building works will produce the main terminal alongside the original structure which will then handle the commuter traffic. Until 1994 the interim terminal will be used by all USAir flights including those of its commuter subsidiaries. Concessions within the original terminal are limited to essentials with none in the temporary accommodation.

Spectator facilities: None specifically provided. Limited views and photographs are possible from within the terminal, but with so much construction work in progress vantage points will change frequently for the next few years. Outside there were a number of spots to the south of the complex, but no doubt these will also be at risk. The vicinity of the new general aviation terminal (originally Hangar 7) could produce a good spot.

Operators: Scheduled services by American Airlines (Boeing 727/757, DC-9), American Eagle (SD3-60, ATR-42), America West (Boeing 737), Business Express/Delta Connection (Saab SF340, Beech 1900), Continental Airlines (Boeing 737, DC-9), Delta Air Lines (Boeing 727/757, DC-9), Midwest Express (DC-9), Mohawk Airlines (Metro), Northwest Airlines (Airbus A320, Boeing 757, DC-9), Trans World (Boeing 727, DC-9), Trans World Express (Beech 1900, Saab SF340), Trump (USAir) Shuttle (Boeing 727), United Airlines (Boeing 727/737/757), United Express (Jetstream, Brasilia), USAir (Boeing 737, DC-9, Fokker 100), USAir Express (SD3-30/60, Jetstream, Dash Seven/Eight). No wide-bodied aircraft operate into National and originating non-stop flights are limited to 1,250 miles range.

Movements (1990): 313,740. Total passengers 15,800,000.
Runways: 03/21 (4,905ft/1,495m), 15/33 (5,189ft/1,582m), 18/36 (6,869ft/2,094m).
Radio frequencies: 119.1MHz (Tower), 124.7MHz (Approach), 121.7MHz (Ground).
Telephone: (703) 739-8600, (703) 685-8000 (National Airport Information).
Operated by: Metropolitan Washington Airports Authority.

Zurich (Kloten) Switzerland

Surprisingly Zurich's international airport at Kloten handles over 12 million passengers annually, a total about 12 times greater than

the entire population of the city plus its environs. Of course its important business community generates a good proportion of the traffic, but its role as a gateway for much of Switzerland plus the southern areas of both Germany and Austria has swollen the numbers considerably. It is also actively marketed as a hub for intercontinental services which has resulted in travellers being ferried in for their long-haul flights from many other airports in Europe.

Of postwar construction, work on Kloten began in the summer of 1946 leading to the completion of the first runway in June 1948, followed by the main instrument landing strip in November of the same year. At this stage it was possible to transfer all commercial traffic from its previous base at the nearby military airfield of Dubendorf. Nevertheless it was not until mid-1953 that the new airport was completed and ready for its official opening on 29 August.

This event was also a turning point in Swiss aviation generally which quickly indicated to the authorities that their newly created facility was already inadequate. Plans were drawn up for a comprehensive expansion programme including the lengthening of the runways and the provision of more parking stands for the aircraft. Unfortunately the scheme was rejected following a referendum held for the citizens by the Canton of Zurich. They had already financed the origi-

nal project and were unwilling to invest yet more millions into the latest proposal. A revised plan of more modest proportions was submitted for approval in the following year which this time received the go-ahead. Runway extension was still included, but they were not taken to the lengths originally specified. Other building work carried out involved various administrative accommodation and the erection of a large hangar capable of housing 747s.

Even before the completion of this second phase, further expansion gained approval without delay. This time the principle improvement was the provision of a third runway for instrument approaches. A greatly increased area of apron was laid to help ease congestion on the ground, but probably the most important feature was the construction of Terminal B complete with pier and loading bridges. Subsequently Terminal A received the same facilities enabling it to handle between 13 and 18 airliners depending on type. After its reopening it was devoted exclusively to all European flights plus those of Pan Am and TWA. All inter-

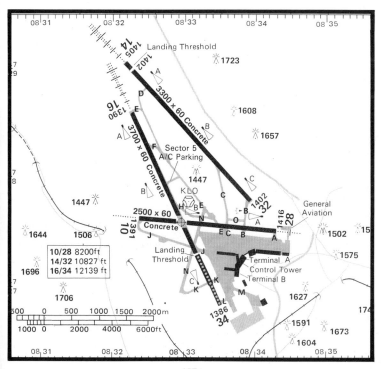

continental and charter operations thereafter became the responsibility of Terminal B. A planned third terminal is intended to accommodate the growing number of wide-bodied aircraft. With traffic well within the capacity of the existing runway system, it is very unlikely that a fourth will be laid. This is fortunate because any suggestion of such a development would be decidedly unpopular with the local population.

Access was greatly improved in 1980 when the Swiss Federal Railways connected the airport with its extensive and efficient network by integrating it into the main east-west line. Five trains per hour run to and from the city to play a major part in making this mode of transport increasingly popular with passengers and visitors. During its first year of operation the trains carried 3.9 million people, a total that continues to show a healthy annual increase. Located two floors below street level, the station is connected to both terminals either by bridge or tunnel. Passengers using this mode of transport now have the opportunity to check-in luggage at any of 100 Swiss rail stations plus some of the postal coach points. The bags are then conveyed to the final destination to await pickup.

Kloten's impact on the district's economy is considerable, providing employment for some 16,000 people, of whom 10,000 are with Swissair. A large number of important companies depend on the fast import and export of their goods to survive. Air freight movements have therefore increased steadily because it is a method of transportation favoured by those concerned with watches, clocks and delicate scientific instruments. Zurich serves about 60% of the total Swiss territory, with most of the remainder dependent on Geneva.

Location and access: Situated 7.5 miles (12km) north of Zurich. Direct motorway link with the city and other routes. When parking the signs indicating 'Zuschauer' should be followed. Regular SBB trains take 11min for the journey between the main railway station and the airport. The latter is also reached directly from a number of other locations. Bus route 68 (coloured blue) commutes between the airport and the city every 9min in rush hours, otherwise the frequency is between 15 and 30min. A red bus operates to and from Winterthur, while a PTT vehicle painted yellow links Kloten with Embrach, Bülach and Seebach.

Spectator facilites: An excellent observation deck is provided on the roof of Terminal B's pier, entry to which can be made on payment of a small amount. A strict security check is imposed with lockers provided for the safe-keeping of unacceptable items. Refreshment facilities of a high standard are available on the deck, which, although expensive, are extremely welcome on hot days. The area provides a fine vantage point for photography especially of the long-haul types. If Runway 16 is in use for take-offs, then it is possible to obtain some good action shots. However, since the reconstruction of Terminal A, it is more difficult to follow the movements on the far side of the building, but this can be overcome by moving to multi-storey car park A. As a bonus the airport offers regular tours by bus starting from the observation deck. Well worth the cost, during the course of the journey it is possible to secure photographs that would be impossible from other spots. Towards the end of the trip the bus visits a small fenced enclosure near to the intersection of runways 10/28 and 16/34. While luck plays a part, several movements will usually occur while out of the vehicle. For those with transport there are numerous locations around the perimeter which provide a change of scene, those particularly useful being near the thresholds of runway 10, 14 and 28. There is a car park complete with a coffee bar at the end of 14.

Operators: Scheduled services by Aer Lingus (Boeing 737), Aeroflot (Tu-154), Aerolineas Argentinas (Boeing 747), Air Algerie (Boeing 737), Air Canada (Boeing 767), Air China (Boeing 747), Air Engiadina (Jetstream), Air France (Airbus A320, Boeing 737, ATR-42), Air Lanka (TriStar), Air Madagascar (Boeing 747), Air Malta (Boeing 737), Air Mauritius (Boeing 747), Air Portugal (Airbus A310, Boeing 727/737), Alitalia (DC-9), American Airlines (Boeing 767), ATI (DC-9), Austrian Airlines (DC-9), Avianova (ATR-42), Balkan (Boeing 737, Tu-134/154), British Airways (Airbus A320, Boeing 737/757, One-Eleven), BWIA International (TriStar), Cathay Pacific (Boeing 747), Crossair (BAe 146, Fokker 50, Saab SF340), Cyprus Airways (Airbus A310), Czechoslovak Airlines (Tu-134/154, IL-62), Dan-Air (BAe 146, One-Eleven), Delta Air (Metro, Dornier 228, Saab SF340), Delta Air Lines (Boeing 767), Delta Air Transport (Fellowship), EgyptAir (Airbus A300), El Al (Boeing 737/757/767), Finnair (DC-9), Garuda (Boeing 747), Iberia (Boeing 727, DC-9), Japan Airlines (Boeing 747), KLM (Airbus A310, Boeing 737), Kenya Airways (Airbus A310), Korean Airlines (Boeing 747), Libyan Arab (Boeing 727), Lufthansa (Airbus A310/320, Boeing 737), Lufthansa CityLine (Fokker 50), Malev (Boeing 737, Tu-154), Malaysian Airlines (Boeing 747, DC-10), Meridiana (DC-9), Middle East Airlines (Boeing 707), Olympic

Airways (Boeing 727/737), Polish Airlines (Tu-134/154), Royal Air Maroc (Boeing 727/737), Sabena (Boeing 737), SAS (DC-9), Singapore International (Boeing 747), South African Airways (Boeing 747), Swissair (Airbus A310, Boeing 747, DC-9/10, MD-11, Fokker 100), Tarom (IL-62, One-Eleven), Thai International (Boeing 747, DC-10), Trans World (Boeing 747/767), Tunis Air (Airbus A320, Boeing 727/737), Turkish Airlines (Airbus A310, Boeing 727, DC-9), Tyrolean (Dash Seven/Eight), United Airlines (Boeing 727), Varig (DC-10), Viasa (DC-10) and Yugoslav Airlines (Boeing 737, DC-9).

Charter and IT operators: CTA (DC-9), Balair (Airbus A310, DC-9/10) and TEA Basle (Boeing 737) although various non-Swiss companies make occasional appearances.

Movements (1990): Total air transport 173,100. Total passengers 12,695,000.
Runways: 16/34 (12,139ft/3,700m), 14/32 (10,827ft/3,300m), 10/28 (8,202ft/2,500m).
Radio frequencies: 118.1MHz, 127.75MHz (Tower), 121.8MHz (Approach), 125.95MHz (Departure), 121.9MHz, 119.7MHz (Ground).
Telephone: (01) 816 2211.
Operated by: Zurich Airport Authority.

Above:
A Fokker 50 OE-LFC of Austrain Air Services at Zurich. *Leo Marriott*

Index